A Continuing
Journey

Also by Archibald MacLeish

POEMS

Collected Poems, 1917-1952
Songs for Eve

PLAYS IN VERSE

Panic
The Fall of the City
Air Raid
The Trojan Horse
This Music Crept by Me upon the Waters
J.B.
Herakles

PROSE

The Irresponsibles
The American Cause
A Time to Speak
A Time to Act
American Opinion and the War
Poetry and Opinion
Freedom Is the Right to Choose
Poetry and Experience
The Eleanor Roosevelt Story

A Continuing Journey

by
Archibald
MacLeish

Boston
Houghton Mifflin Company
1968

Grateful acknowledgment is due the following authors and publishers for permission to quote selections from the works cited:

Alfred A. Knopf, Inc.: *Translations from the Chinese* by Arthur Waley.
Atlantic-Little Brown and Company: *Cántico: A Selection*, by Jorge Guillén, edited by Norman Thomas di Giovanni, copyright © 1954, 1957, 1959, 1960, 1965, by Jorge Guillén and Norman Thomas di Giovanni.
Bollingen Foundation: *Chronique* by St.-John Perse, translated by Robert Fitzgerald. Bollingen Series LXIX. Copyright © 1961 by Bollingen Foundation, New York. Distributed by Princeton University Press; *Exile and Other Poems* by St.-John Perse, translated by Denis Devlin. Bollingen Series XV. Copyright 1949 by Bollingen Foundation, New York. Distributed by Princeton University Press; *The Limits of Art*, collected and edited by Huntington Cairns. Bollingen Series XII. Copyright 1948 by Bollingen Foundation, New York. Distributed by Princeton University Press.
Harcourt, Brace & World, Inc.: *Oedipus at Colonus*, translated by Robert Fitzgerald.
Harvard University Press: *Lyra Graeca*, Sappho, Vol. I, translated by J. M. Edmonds, Loeb Classical Library.
Holt, Rinehart and Winston, Inc.: "Come In" from *Complete Poems of Robert Frost*, copyright 1942 by Robert Frost.
The Macmillan Company: *Collected Poems* by William Butler Yeats. "An Acre of Grass," and "Lapis Lazuli": copyright 1940 by Georgie Yeats. "The Magi": copyright 1916 by The Macmillan Company, renewed 1944 by Bertha Georgie Yeats. "Leda and the Swan" and "Two Songs from a Play": copyright 1928 by The Macmillan Company, renewed 1956 by Georgie Yeats. "Vacillation," "His Confidence," and "Swift's Epitaph": copyright 1933 by The Macmillan Company, renewed 1961 by Bertha Georgie Yeats. "The Second Coming": copyright 1924 by The Macmillan Company, renewed 1952 by Bertha Georgie Yeats.
New Directions Publishing Corporation: *The Cantos of Ezra Pound*, copyright 1934, 1937, 1940, 1948 by Ezra Pound.
Oxford University Press: *Collected Poems* by Edwin Muir. Copyright © 1960 by Willa Muir. Reprinted by permission of Oxford University Press, Inc.
Peter Pauper Press: *The Songs of Sappho*, translated by David Moore Robinson.
William Morrow and Company, Inc.: *An Autobiography* by Edwin Muir, copyright 1954 by Edwin Muir.

FIRST PRINTING   C

Foreword

ANY WRITER who keeps up a running quarrel with his time — which means any writer — leaves a kind of unintended private history behind him like a dog's track on a beach. You can tell by the meanderings and sorties and retreats where the enormous wave almost engulfed him, where the dead crab stank beneath the heaped Sargossa, where the rubber boot enticed for other purposes behind the dune. If you follow far enough you can even learn where the expedition ended at the surf's edge in the obliterating sea.

This book is a private history in that sense. It was written piece by piece over a period of twenty years from the middle Forties to the middle Sixties for periodicals as diverse as *The Nation* and the New York *Times*, *Life* and the *Atlantic*, but because the scene throughout was the political and intellectual and literary foreshore of those uneasy years the parts compose a kind of whole, a continuing journey.

A journey, that is to say, continuous in its direction. In retrospect the Fifties and the years before and after take on a certain sad coherence. We can see now, with Vietnam to teach us, what our foreign policy in that period really was — what

"Containment" meant. We can understand with the help of the Goldwater campaign and the spokesmen of the New Right what "Anti-Communism" actually signified. We are even beginning to guess, with the "literature of extreme situations," where the Existentialist fad of the post-war years was headed. But at the time, in the Forties and Fifties themselves, patterns had not yet appeared. All one had was one's sense that something had gone wrong, even tragically wrong: that somehow, somewhere, the country — perhaps the age itself — had lost its bearings.

This was not, of course, a private, an isolated, feeling. It was shared by President Eisenhower at least to the point of establishing a Commission on the National Purpose which held hearings and published a report. It was shared too by magazine editors who ran articles on the same subject (see p. 77). And there were other examinations and inquests and interrogations. Literature was largely given over to critics inquiring into the ills of literature. Senators cross-examined citizens on their loyalty. Books were written about the inadequacies of the young. Religion was investigated and morals and education.

But to the man who merely lived in the time — the dog on the beach — this particular dog in any case — none of these various inquiries seemed to touch the problem. Whatever was wrong was obviously really wrong: wrong not only with a diplomacy dedicated to Anti-Russianism and a politics dedicated to Anti-Communism but with a literature dedicated to Anti-heroism or more precisely to victimism; wrong, that is to say, at the heart, at the human heart, at the point of man's conception of himself as man.

The various pieces which compose this book approach that question in one way or another from several points of view:

politics, poetry, teaching. They also examine it in its relation to certain figures on the scene, friends for the most part; some of them, like Mark Van Doren and Felix Frankfurter and Adlai Stevenson, close friends. The idea of man, the conception of man, is never a philosophical formula. It constructs itself, like all the rest of our notions of the world, out of instances, examples. One goes back, in a difficult time like this, to the actual men and women one has known: measures the current notions of the human creature against particular lives. Even when the lives change (the Hemingway of *In Our Time* against the Hemingway of *A Moveable Feast*) the moments of reality bear witness.

ARCHIBALD MACLEISH

Conway,
Massachusetts

Contents

I

The Idea
of Man

Who Precisely Do You Think
You Are?

1965

A YEAR AGO my friend, Mark Van Doren, was lunching with a table full of Amherst boys who astonished him by asking what they should do with their lives. "Whatever you want," said Van Doren, "just so long as you don't miss the main thing." "And what," they said, "is the main thing?" "Your lives," said Van Doren.

He was right, of course. A man can easily miss his life if he doesn't know who's living it — if he thinks a lawyer is living it or a professor of biochemistry or the head of a dry-cleaning plant or a mechanical engineer. He can wake up in his forty-fifth year and realize that it isn't he in his bed but the treasurer of the Second National Bank. And the same thing is true, even more true, of a woman — she can come to herself, as the phrase goes, only to discover that she has no self to come to: there is no one there but the children's nurse or the chauffeur of the family station wagon, or the fourth chair in a bridge game that has been going on and on, every other Monday night, for twenty years.

So that the question does present itself. To all of us. Or to all of us now, at least, in this questioning century. In simpler generations a woman could say, as Ophelia did, "We know what we are but we know not what we may become." It was only the grave that puzzled them then: the dark on the other side. With us it's the contrary: we know or think we know what we may become — it's what we are that haunts us.

Mankind? Certainly . . . but what is a man? We find it difficult to say. We know what a man was once because we have the record before us: what is literature but just that record? To Sophocles he was the wonder of the world. "Wonders are many on the earth," says the Chorus in the *Antigone*, "and of these man is the greatest." To Shakespeare he was like a god: "What a piece of work is a man! how noble in reason! how infinite in faculty! in form, in moving, how express and admirable! in action how like an angel! in apprehension how like a god! the beauty of the world! the paragon of animals!"

But what is man to us? Suppose you look at the folk art of the age, the graffiti of the advertising pages, the popular ballads from that world between the television programs where never is heard a discouraging word and the skies are unclouded all day. What is he there? A figure like a god? A wonder? Not precisely: a creature of rather different dimensions, a being whose dominant desire seems to be to smell sweet, to weigh less, to own the automobile everyone else will envy, and to go on smoking cigarettes even if they kill him — which they doubtless will. He has headaches, yes, sleeps badly, suffers or makes others suffer from tobacco breath, but none of this is tragic: he can always doctor himself with lozenges and pills, travel to Miami, buy a new detergent, and find at the end of it all, where Heaven used to be, a Lincoln Continental.

A satiric figure? Not in intention certainly: who would spend millions of dollars to subsidize the inanities of television merely to satirize the human race? No, the purpose is not satiric: merely the assumptions, the presuppositions. And they are not so much satiric as contemptuous. A creature presented as seeing himself solely in terms of his smell, his pills, his excitants, his soporifics and the neighbors' opinion of his possessions is a creature imagined by Jonathan Swift — a Jonathan Swift without talent, granted, but a Jonathan Swift notwithstanding.

And if you turn to literature, the literature of the time, the literature characteristic of the time and most specifically dedicated to it, the same opinion of humanity presents itself. "One of the primary features of literature (as of much activity in all the other arts) in our times," says Susan Sontag, one of the most perceptive critics of the generation, "is a chronic attachment to materials belonging to the realm of extreme situations — madness, crime, taboo sexual longings, drug addiction, emotional degradation, violent death. The motive or justification for this loyalty to extreme situations is obscure. It is felt that such situations are somehow 'more true' than others; that an art immersed in such situations is 'more serious' than other art; and finally, that only art that embraces the irrational and repellent, the violent and the outrageous, can make a valuable impact on the sluggish consciousness of the audience."

This, of course, is something more than a description of the writing of some of Miss Sontag's contemporaries: it is an account also of the beliefs about mankind on which their writing is founded. To say that the literature of "extreme situations" — of "madness, crime, taboo sexual longings, drug addiction, emotional degradation, violent death" — is felt by its authors to be "more true" means of course "more true" to man, more true to that human truth which is the measure of all literary truth. To say that an art immersed in "extreme situations" is felt to be "more serious" means more humanly serious, more worthy of serious human attention, because more *like* humanity.

Whether Miss Sontag's contemporaries would accept so blunt an interpretation of their views is questionable, but certainly the best of them would find it difficult to dissent. Man, to Samuel Beckett, is explicitly and dramatically something up to its neck in sand which would have hanged itself long ago except that the sand keeps rising. And most of the rest would agree in one form of metaphor or another. If the mirror held up by the advertising agencies is contemptuous, the mirror held up by art—by the art we call contemporary, "modern" — is derisory. The "absurdity" of human life, which the fashionable philosophers have taught us to see, has rubbed off on the human creature who lives it, and though we may call him Sisyphus and weep for him, we weep in pity — or self-pity: never as we weep for Oedipus or Lear.

And yet — and this, of course, is the heart of the matter — it is we who have produced these images: we or our surrogates, our writers, artists. And the pertinent question thus becomes the question, Why? Why have we produced them? Why has our conception of our human nature so changed in this particular time, this generation, this century? Why has the grandeur gone, the greatness, above all the wonder, so that no contemporary character on our stage could say without a snicker of self-consciousness what Hamlet said: "How infinite in faculty! in form, in moving, how express and admirable! in action how like an angel! in apprehension how like a god!"?

Is it because ours is a time without grandeur? — a time without event? On the contrary it is a great and tragic time which is also heroic as few ages have been heroic — an age which has produced, here and elsewhere, some of the most remarkable figures — remarkable both for good and for evil — the world has ever seen. It is a time of two world wars within a generation of each other with a space of hope and misery between — a time as memorable for courageous and unnoticed actions as it is for wholesale slaughters and unspeakable miseries. It is also, and at the same time, the epoch in which man has gone farther out toward the unknown, even the unknowable, than he had gone in all the centuries and millennia before. Prophecy is a fatuous and ungrateful business, but it hardly requires prophecy to foresee that men in future generations, if there are to be future generations, will look back on these few years as among the most terrible and splendid in the annals of the race.

Why then have we peopled them with pettiness and squalor? Why do we see mankind in the images we have created? Is it perhaps because we know something, in our newfound scientific knowledge, which those who lived before us did not know? Is it because we have discovered a truth about mankind which Sophocles never guessed and Shakespeare could not utter?

There are some who seem to think so. A British scientist lecturing recently at the Museum of Natural History in New York announced that "the explosive charge which, in this century, has split open the self-assurance of western man" is contained in what he called "the bland proposition" that "man is a part of nature." If it is true, he said, as it seems to be true, that "living matter is not different in kind from dead matter" then "man as a species will be shown to be no more than a machinery of atoms," and if man is no more than a machinery of atoms he cannot be a "person." It is "the nagging fear," Dr. Bronowski concluded, that we are not persons — that we are nothing but machines — which has produced the "crisis of confidence" in which we live.

But is it? That "nagging fear," if it is one, has been around for a long time. Dr. Bronowski's "bland proposition" was talked of in antiquity and stated in so many words by one of the greatest of scientific philosophers more than three hundred years ago: to Descartes all bodies, human as well as animal, were completely mechanistic in structure and behavior. The announcement produced no "crisis of confidence" in the seventeenth century even in France — least of all in France where Jean-Jacques Rousseau was shortly to appear together with the most unquestioning confidence in man the world had ever seen or has seen since.

But is the difference, perhaps, that now we *know* what Descartes could only assert? *Do* we know? Dr. René Dubos of the Rockefeller Institute, a man who is entitled to an opinion if anybody is, apparently doubts it. "From one end of the spectrum," he says, "man appears as an ordinary physiochemical machine, complex, of course, but nevertheless reacting with environmental forces according to the same laws that govern inanimate nature. From the other end man is seen as a creature that is rarely a passive component in the reacting system; the most characteristic aspect of his behavior is the fact that he responds actively and often creatively. . . . Man is the more human the better he is able to convert passive reactions into creative responses." What is human in man, in other words, is precisely that which is not mechanical and the mechanical definition, therefore, misses its point. Dr. Dubos suggests another: "Man — the creature who can choose, eliminate, assemble, decide and thereby create."

It is not for us — not for me certainly — to decide the rights and wrongs of this debate founded in the discoveries of biology and psychology. But even those who have no competence in science can speak for themselves when their own emotions are called into question, and I, for one, would seriously doubt that the "nagging fear" modern humanity is alleged to feel is really fear at all, or that our "crisis of confidence," if that is the proper term for our characteristic state of mind, can be attributed to the scientific discovery that we are made of atoms like everything else.

There may be men who have thought of mankind as composed of a special human material despite the famous admonition, "Dust thou art . . ." and such men may conceivably feel themselves betrayed by the demonstration that they are mere Meccano sets put together out of the common building blocks of the universe, as though a cross section of quartz had come to consciousness. If so they may think of Beckett's characters as appropriate symbols of their state — poor potted plants to whom nothing human is possible but an occasional erotic *frisson* faintly reminiscent of a biologic role no longer feasible under the circumstances. But that most of us feel and think in terms like these I simply do not believe.

I myself have never met a man or woman, even among college students where you can meet almost anything, who was actually frightened by the thought that he might be an atomic combination rather than the cousin-german of an angel. Quite the contrary. To men of our generation a machine that can think is, if anything, more attractive than an angel and certainly more wonderful.

But if I am right, if our faith in our humanity has not been shaken by the advances of science, what has shaken it? If it is not because we know something about ourselves which our ancestors did not know, why is it that we think of our humanity as so diminished? Could it conceivably be for the opposite reason? — not because we know something about ourselves earlier human beings did not know, but because we have forgotten something about ourselves earlier men once knew?

Consider that famous Chorus in the *Antigone* — consider what the old men of Thebes are saying about mankind. Man, they say, is the wonder of the world. He is the master of the ageless earth, bending that mother of the gods to his will by his continuing toil. He is the master also of all living things, birds, beasts — hunting them, teaching them. He learns the use of language, of the wind-swift mind: the laws of living together in great cities built against the winter and the rain. There is nothing beyond his power — nothing but one thing. He overcomes all chances, all the dangers, finds the remedy for every ill — every ill but one. Death he cannot overcome.

What Sophocles' Chorus is saying, in other words, is what men throughout those centuies were always saying, that man is the wonder of the world because, although he dies, although he has no remedy for destiny or death, he masters nevertheless the ageless earth, tames beasts, builds cities, races with the wind-swift mind. Heroism was never triumph to the Greeks of the great age: heroism was Prometheus with the eagle at his liver, Herakles among his murdered sons. And man was never anything but man, the mortal figure dignified by its mortality, like those magnificent forms of Leonard Baskin's, heavy with grandeur and with death.

And what has happened to that knowledge now? Nothing except that we have lost it. Nothing except that we have turned it inside out as those philosophers do who tell our generation that our world, *because we die*, is an absurdity: that Sisyphus is our symbol and our sign.

There is no proof one way or the other, I suppose. Sophocles' nobly tragic world may be a dream and ours the meaningless reality. There is no proof — but there is this to think of: that whenever in the history of our kind men have thought of man as Sophocles thought of him, art has flourished and the mind come clear. "What's the meaning of all song?" asks Yeats in that curious poem in *Vacillation*. "Let all things pass away." It is a hard saying but the truth is in it: it is when the human heart faces its destiny and notwithstanding sings — sings of itself, its life, its death — that poetry is possible.

And there is something else to think of: nothing in human life is more contemptible than self-pity. Pride may be delusion but, even if it is, self-pity is far worse. When it comes to that peremptory, that always haunting question, pride is the nobler fault. Who, precisely, do you think you are? A man. A woman.

Yeats and
the Belief in Life

1958

THERE IS a contemporary paradox which seems to me to be interesting, as paradoxes often are, not because it reveals the folly of our race but because it provides a clue to our wisdom — or what would be our wisdom if we were aware that we possessed it. I refer to the hunger for belief, for "affirmation," which characterizes, if not our time, at least the new generation which our time has produced, the generation of the young. On the face of it, a hunger for something to believe in, in a century such as ours, is a good bit like an appetite for coals in Newcastle. Our century is deafened by things to believe in. Indeed the principal danger which threatens the world and our lives is precisely the danger, as we all know, that the rival claims of competing dogmas may start a fire of words in some oil-soaked corner of the earth which will destroy the planet in a horror of diastrous flame. But the shouting of dogmas, though it has deafened the statesmen of the world and silenced the philosophers, has not satisfied the hunger of the young. Very few of them seem to be content with the existing ultimates.

Why this is so — why this hunger should have developed in the midst of surfeit — why students in American colleges

should be crowding into courses in existentialism and the new
theology when the air outside is full of final answers — I do not
know. It might be argued, I suppose, that one reason is a curious
kind of intellectual or spiritual accident which has befallen final
answers in our time. It can be illustrated by the changed behavior of the physicists. Once, we all recall, the physicists used
to talk about the Laws of Physics, meaning the Laws which govern the Universe. Nowadays if you find yourself at lunch, at the
faculty club of any institution of higher learning, beside a brilliant young physicist, you will do well to avoid mention of
the Laws of Physics. Physicists, you will be told, do not now
go searching the universe for laws. They do not even go searching the universe. Rather, they invent models of that part of the
universe which is not themselves — models which may or may
not correspond to the original and which are expected to be
judged, not as works of science used to be judged, by their
truth, but as works of art are sometimes judged, by their coherence and their elegance. I exaggerate of course. But it is true
nevertheless that even Lord Samuel once complained that the
physicist's formula no longer seems to stand clearly for events
in the "real physical world," and that Einstein, in reply, not only
agreed that the formal conveniences of theoretical physics do
not correspond to whirling atoms and orbits but went so far as to
assert that this failure of correspondence is the characteristic
of modern physics.

When science replaces laws with "conveniences" and the study
of the universe with the invention of possible "models," it is
obvious that the whole conception of ultimate certainty has
been diminished and that the power of laws, of certainties —
in brief, of dogmas — to satisfy the human mind has been dimin-

ished with it. It is not, as we "free thinkers" (nostalgic word) would have said in my time, that dogmas are the stones given those who ask for bread. It is rather that dogmas of all sorts have now ceased even to be stones and that their availability in the contemporary world, far from filling the belly of the eternal human hunger, merely aggravates it as shadows always do. The more the dogmas insist upon themselves and upon their conflicts with each other, the more obvious it becomes that they *are* dogmas: that they do not communicate certainty but merely declare it.

But the decline of the prestige of dogma in the modern world does not alone explain the hunger for belief. Hunger is not merely the consequence of a lack of food. It is a consequence also of the process of living. What we need to understand, as much as the depreciation of the ultimate formulations of belief, is the enhancement of the passion for believing in the modern mind. Is it a passion bred of fear: the fear of not believing — and is it enhanced because fear is enhanced? Is it a passion bred of loneliness: the shadow of that lunar cold — and have we grown lonelier? Do we wish more passionately to believe because we know in some inexplicable way that there is something more ultimately believable to be found if we could only find it? Do we wish to believe with increasing fervor because we are under some compulsion to make sense of our lives and because our lives are increasingly senseless? One can put the question in many ways but there is no way one can put it which will provide an automatic answer. It is only, I think, by observing this hunger for belief in a man of our own time — which means in a poet of our own time, for it is only in the writer of poems that anything so hidden, so secret, is revealed — that we may guess at the nature of the need which drives us all.

And the poet to choose is, of course, William Butler Yeats, for Yeats is not only the greatest but, in a very relevant sense, the most modern of modern poets — modern not in the false sense of style or manner but modern in the true sense of mind; for it is the dominant characteristic of the modern mind to wish to know, and to believe that knowledge is possible, and Yeats, from the beginning of his life to the end, wished to *know*. He wished to know, as the modern mind does, by every possible means including not only the intuitive means of poetry but the scaffolds of system. What he wished to know was what the modern mind wishes to know, the meaning of experience. "To know," in Yeats's vocabulary, meant to attain with certainty to those conclusions which earlier generations had reached only by faith — conclusions as to the "burden of the mystery" itself, to borrow a phrase Shakespeare begot upon Wordsworth.

You will find it all spelled out in a poem written very near the end of his life:

An Acre of Grass

Picture and book remain,
An acre of green grass
For air and exercise,
Now strength of body goes;
Midnight, an old house
Where nothing stirs but a mouse.

My temptation is quiet.
Here at life's end
Neither loose imagination
Nor the mill of the mind
Consuming its rag and bone,
Can make the truth known.

Grant me an old man's frenzy,
Myself must I remake
Till I am Timon and Lear
Or that William Blake
Who beat upon the wall
Till Truth obeyed his call;

A mind Michael Angelo knew
That can pierce the clouds,
Or inspired by frenzy
Shake the dead in their shrouds;
Forgotten else by mankind,
An old man's eagle mind.

You will see here the end and the means. The end is to make truth known; the second time he uses the word Yeats capitalizes it. And the means are "Neither loose imagination / Nor the mill of the mind" but "an old man's frenzy" which will remake him until he becomes Timon and Lear "Or that William Blake / Who beat upon the wall / Till Truth obeyed his call." And yet these means, though they exclude "the mill of mind / Consuming its rag and bone" do not exclude *mind*. On the contrary the last stanza relates the whole search to mind at its highest, mind inspired by frenzy, such a mind as Michael Angelo knew, "An old man's eagle mind." The end, in other words, is to know Truth itself, ultimate Truth, the Truth beyond the clouds, the Truth the dead know. The means are mind in its highest and most impassioned intensity. And the assertion of the poem is an assertion that by these means this end is possible.

It would have been difficult for men in earlier times to have grasped this assertion — to have understood that it is literally as well as proudly as well as humbly meant. But for us it is not difficult. We understand very well that a man might speak in this way because we ourselves, within our narrower limits, think in this way. We are the children, whether we have read it or not, of Rimbaud's *Saison en Enfner* which ends: "Il me sera loisible de posseder la verité dans une ame et un corps": "it will be lawful for me to possess truth in one body and one soul." We set no limits as men to the knowledge of truth we would possess if we could, and none to the knowledge of truth we think it possible for us to possess. And we therefore listen, as to a more gifted elder brother, to this man who cries out, near the time of his death, that he will beat upon the wall till *Truth* obey his call. We have seen men of science beating upon something harder than a wall and we have heard something answering which, whether it is Truth or not, has proven true.

But what we understand in "An Acre of Grass," you will notice — what we recognize in that poem — is a limitless need to *know* which we also share: *not* a need to believe. Indeed every accent of the poem makes it obvious that knowledge here is put in place of belief and above belief. It would be relatively easy, perhaps, to *believe* in that Truth behind the wall, that answer beyond the clouds. What is asserted here is the possibility of knowing it — of piercing the clouds with human mind, compelling Truth to answer by human passion.

That this distinction is indeed intended, an earlier and much more familiar poem makes obvious. Those of us who know Yeats at all know "The Magi":

> *Now as at all times I can see in the mind's eye,*
> *In their stiff, painted clothes, the pale unsatisfied ones*
> *Appear and disappear in the blue depth of the sky*

With all their ancient faces like rain-beaten stones,
And all their helms of silver hovering side by side,
And all their eyes still fixed, hoping to find once more,
Being by Calvary's turbulence unsatisfied,
The uncontrollable mystery on the bestial floor.

"The Magi" here are, of course, the three wise men of the Christmas carols: members of the Persian priestly caste and therefore skilled in the dark learnings of the East. In Yeats's poem, however, the Magi are placed not two thousand years ago in Bethlehem but "now as at all times" in "the blue depth of the sky." And they look not at all as we are accustomed to see them in Renaissance paintings of the Nativity in which they kneel in an ineffable blessedness with their fortunate star above them. Here they hover anxiously over the earth in their stiff painted clothes and their silver helms "pale and unsatisfied." "Unsatisfied" is surely the last word we Christians would think of in connection with those three who had followed the strange star down out of the high plateau of Persia and across the two rivers and on beyond the Arabian desert to find the Immortal revealed in mortality, the mystery communicated to the world of sense. The Magi of the old myth had seen what they had come so far to find. They had seen what men had never seen before. And yet, in Yeats's poem, they are "unsatisfied." Why? Because they had followed the star to Bethlehem for Knowledge, for Revelation, for the ultimate immeasurable answer: God made flesh. But Calvary had turned all this revelation, all this knowledge into something else. Calvary had turned it into promise of salvation, into reason for *belief:* no longer the purity of ultimate wisdom but the turbulence of suffering and love on which a faith is founded.

The Old Man of the "Acre of Grass" is, in possibility at least, a triumphant knower. The three old men of "The Magi" are defeated knowers. But in both these poems the power of knowledge is unquestioned and its limitless possibilities are assumed as the modern mind assumes them. There is, however, a third poem, more famous than either, in which the power is doubted, and it is that poem which brings Yeats closest to our generation, for we also, though we believe as he did in the power of mankind to know, question in our souls the sufficiency of that power. The third poem is "Leda and the Swan":

> *A sudden blow: the great wings beating still*
> *Above the staggering girl, her thighs caressed*
> *By the dark webs, her nape caught in his bill*
> *He holds her helpless breast upon his breast.*
>
> *How can those terrified vague fingers push*
> *The feathered glory from her loosening thighs?*
> *And how can body, laid in that white rush,*
> *But feel the strange heart beating where it lies?*
>
> *A shudder in the loins engenders there*
> *The broken wall, the burning roof and tower*
> *And Agamemnon dead.*
>
> 　　　　　　　　　　*Being so caught up,*
> *So mastered by the brute blood of the air*
> *Did she put on his knowledge with his power*
> *Before the indifferent beak could let her drop?*

Life in that passionate instant put on the power of the skies because it took the form of fate: human terror and helplessness bore the weight not only of the swan, brute blood of the air, but of the god himself, and in the joining of that impossible, that inexplicable, contradiction the destiny of mankind was determined. This much is obvious. But of what *knowledge* is there question here? I should assume that the knowledge is knowledge of the events which the power imposes: foreknowledge — foreknowledge of the breaching of the walls of Troy, of the fall of the city for Helen's sake, of the murder of Agamemnon by Clytemnestra on his return to Argos: such foreknowledge as Heaven, which can will these things, must have. What is being asked, then, is this: Did Leda *know* the events which she, as mortal flesh, now contained? Or rather, reading these images as the symbols they so evidently are, can humanity, touched by the necessity of God, *know* that necessity? Is it *possible* for us to *know* in this ultimate sense? Is it possible for us, even at the moment when we receive the impress of our human destiny from God, to *know* that destiny? We can know many things. There is nothing, indeed, we think we cannot know. But can we know the most important of all things: can we know the pattern of life, the purpose of life, the meaning?

There is no answer here. The question ends the poem. But as so often happens with this persistently reflective man, there is an answer somewhere else. Just before he died Yeats wrote to a friend in words which only this poem could have shaped: "It seems to me that I have found what I wanted. When I try to put it all into a phrase I say 'Man can embody truth but he cannot know it' . . ."

In form, I suppose, this is not a modern saying. We do not speak of "embodying" truth or, indeed of "embodying" anything else. But in intention, as I hope we can agree, it is entirely modern. Only a modern man could be concerned, at his life's end, with the problem of the possibility of *knowing* truth. And there

is also something else about this statement which is modern —
something else which touches closely upon the question I have
set myself in these remarks. What appears here, and in the most
poignant terms, is not merely modern man's concern with the
possibility of knowing, but modern man's hunger for belief as
well. What appears, indeed what is glimpsed or almost glimpsed,
is the nature of that hunger. Consider what it is that Yeats believes he has found: what it is that he has "wanted" and has
"found." He has concluded, after a life-time spent in the pursuit, through poetry and through philosophy, of knowledge, that
man cannot *know* truth. But he has concluded also — and
it satisfies him — that man can *embody* truth. Now the key
word here is not the ambiguous word "embody" which may
mean many things. The key word is the word "man." *Man* can
embody truth. This is no resolution of the problems of truth in
supernatural terms or even in terms of faith. This is a resolution
in terms of man himself, *man's* capacity in his own being to embody. And what it suggests, since the resolution satisfies the
questioner — satisfies him at the most crucial moment of his
questioning life — is this: That the hunger to believe was at the
end, and had indeed always been, a hunger to believe somehow,
some way, in himself *as knower.*

But this, of course, is precisely what we should have expected
had we considered what it means to face life as modern man
does face it in terms of knowledge. To attempt to resolve the
mystery by knowing is to make an underlying assumption which
most of us take for granted or merely ignore: the assumption not
only that the mystery will yield to knowledge but that *man* can
make it yield. From this point of view, the whole enormous
edifice of modern science rests upon belief, whether the scien-

tists so recognize or not. It rests upon belief in man. And so too
does that other, perhaps greater, edifice raised upon man's other
means of knowledge — art. It is understandable therefore, indeed it is more than understandable, that a man who had spent his
life in the pursuit of the kind of knowledge to which poetry is
the key, should have lived it also in a hunger to believe in man.

It was not an easy belief to come to or to hold. To believe in
man as men of our generation must believe is not to glorify man
or to put him in place of God or otherwise to blind ourselves to
the realities of human life. Yeats never attempted to conceal from
himself the fact that human life is, in its condition, tragic. Indeed
he early came to the conclusion that men only begin to live
when they have come to understand how wholly tragic their
lives are. And neither did he attempt to gloze over or to conceal
the sordidness of human existence. The belief in man for which
he thirsted and to which eventually he attained was a belief
in man, a belief in man's life, *in spite* of misery and *in spite* of
death.

That such a belief is difficult, no one was more aware than
Yeats himself. The sardonic third section of "Vacillation" ends
with a credo which a Stoic might well have regarded as rigorous:

> *No longer in Lethean foliage caught*
> *Begin the preparation for your death*
> *And from the fortieth winter by that thought*
> *Test every work of intellect or faith*
> *And everything that your own hands have wrought*
> *And call those works extravagance of breath*
> *That are not suited for such men as come*
> *Proud, open-eyed and laughing to the tomb.*

Proud of what? Proud of being man — but not with that famous pride which led to the expulsion from Eden and so to death. This pride accepts the fact of death and all the suffering and is proud notwithstanding. This pride is "open-eyed." It comes "laughing to the tomb." It accepts life — the whole of life which includes the death that ends it. It shuts its eyes to nothing. And it laughs; not grimly endures but laughs.

For most of us such a discipline, such a belief, is perhaps too self-sustained and self-sustaining to be acceptable. We want not so much to believe ourselves as to be supported by belief, surrounded by it, borne up by it from without. But Yeats came ultimately to the conclusion that it was precisely this discipline of spirit which justified life at its highest and greatest: at its most creative.

"Lapis Lazuli," one of his last poems, ends with three old Chinese seated in a little "half-way house" on a mountain staring out over "all the tragic scene."

> *One asks for mournful melodies;*
> *Accomplished fingers begin to play.*
> *Their eyes mid many wrinkles, their eyes,*
> *Their ancient, glittering eyes, are gay.*

Philosophers may take exception to any such conclusion as to the nature of man, but Yeats, after all, is not writing philosophy, he is making images of experience. It is true in experience, whatever it may be in philosophy, that creative men have about them, even when their lives are as tragic as the life of John Keats, a gaiety such as the gaiety which pervades Keats's letters. And it is true also that the old and wise who see, who really see, have in their eyes precisely such an ancient, glittering gaiety as

Yeats describes. One thinks of Whitehead and of Justice Frankfurter and Robert Frost. Yeats had reason in his own life to believe that men at their best, men who can *make*, men who can *know*, are able to face the tragedy of living and dying, not with patience, not with courage, but with a welcoming acceptance which justifies not only life but man. Out of those reasons, and out of his own extraordinary powers as a poet, he created for himself at the end the belief in man which gave him, as he put it in that letter, "what I wanted." It was a belief *in spite of*, not a belief *because*, but for that very reason it was a belief that soared. The last stanza of the second of "Two Songs From A Play" shows how high it soared:

> *Everything that man esteems*
> *Endures a moment or a day.*
> *Love's pleasure drives his love away,*
> *The painter's brush consumes his dreams;*
> *The herald's cry, the soldier's tread*
> *Exhaust his glory and his might:*
> *Whatever flames upon the night*
> *Man's own resinous heart has fed.*

How far Yeats's words can speak to our condition each one of us must answer for himself. He began where most of us, I assume, begin: with the passion to know which characterizes the mentality of our time. He asked himself the question which those of us who think at all must sooner or later ask ourselves — whether knowledge of meaningful truth is possible. He discovered in himself the need for a *belief* which could make that knowledge possible. He found that belief in a rigorous and difficult faith in man. None of us may follow the same road. But one conclusion may, I think, be drawn from these poems of Yeats which will have significance for us all. Those who think that our hunger for belief is a hunger for ready-made answers are wrong. Dogma, whether political or social or philosophical or theological, cannot satisfy a generation which assumes as its basic assumption that mankind can know. What the young wish, if I understand their minds at all, what they are hungry for, what they must have, is a belief which derives from their own experience of the world and which makes sense of that experience. They will not be satisfied with beliefs imposed upon their lives like official stamps upon a passport. They must come to their beliefs themselves and as themselves and for themselves. Above all they must come to a belief in life, in their own lives, in their own living of their lives: such a belief as Yeats put into words in the epitaph he wrote for his grave in Drumcliff Churchyard: that epitaph in which he sends those who come to mourn for him back from grave to life, bidding them look on life and death together with a cold, an indifferent eye — a man's eye bold in the knowledge that a man must live to die, must die, but having *lived:*

> *Cast a cold eye*
> *On life, on death.*
> *Horseman, pass by!*

Poetry and Journalism

1958

POETRY AND JOURNALISM don't meet in the contemporary
mind. If they are related at all they are related as opposites. No
poet likes to be called a journalist and as for journalists, the suggestion that their work is poetry is resented. Nevertheless there is
something to be said for a comparison between the two in an age
in which journalism has overrun the earth leaving poetry little but
its pride — and not always much of that. For the pride of poetry
is to be an art and even art is not beyond the modern
journalist's ambition. Journalism is the stepchild of history — if
it is not, indeed, its foster father — and history, you will recall,
had a muse of its own as far back as Parnassus. No one would
claim that the usual news story is a work of art, at least in the ordinary sense of that term. But no one would deny either that
great works of journalism exist and that when they exist they exist
within a discipline of their own — a discipline which reveals itself, as the disciplines of art always reveal themselves, in form.
The style of a great work of journalism is not, as the glib phrase
goes, the man. The style of a great work of journalism is the man
in terms of the purpose — the man working at the utmost intensity of which he is capable toward an end to which he is wholly

committed. But this, of course, is precisely the characteristic of
the style of any work of art — the precise characteristic which
distinguishes a work of art from a mere indulgence of personality
on the one hand or an impersonal "job" on the other. The
young critic who recently remarked that the magazine article or
newspaper story has become, with us, a more effective form than
the novel, may or may not be right, but the recognition that the
newspaper story or the magazine article is capable of a form
comparable to the great form of fiction is as just as it is belated.

   You cannot, in other words, distinguish journalism from
poetry merely by saying that one is an art and the other isn't.
And neither, I think, can you justify their antipodal relationship
by the device used in most college catalogues where courses in
expository writing are courses in expository writing, but
courses in the writing of poems are courses in creative writing.
The theory would be, I imagine, that the poet is supposed to
create a world in his poems whereas the journalist is supposed
not to create one: to stick as closely as he can to the world he's
got. This means that the poet makes something new, but the
journalist describes something old, or, in any case, something that
has already happened — for, if it hasn't already happened, he is
no journalist. More precisely, this means that the journalist se-
lects — for obviously selection is necessary if the story is to
have a beginning and an end — from among things that already
are — events that have in fact befallen, actions actually acted,
objects seen, sounds heard — whereas the poet must spin his
chronicle out of himself like a spider. But if we leave the theory
and look at the practice — specific poems, specific journalisms —
will this distinction as between creative and selective hold? Is
the poet's "creation" different in kind from the journalist's "se-

lection"? Is it so different in kind that the two labors must be thought of as standing at opposite poles of the universe of discourse?

Take the first poem that walks into your mind: for of course all of us have such visitors. "Old favorites" we call them because they are free of the house and enter without knocking. Some of us — quite a few, I should guess — will find ourselves thinking of Herrick's "To Daffodils," not only because it is one of the finest of English lyrics and one of the poems most frequently taught to children, but because its tune, once echoed in the corridors of the ear, will never stop:

> *Fair daffodils we weep to see*
> *You haste away so soon.*
> *As yet the early-rising sun*
> *Has not attained his noon.*
> *Stay, stay,*
> *Until the hasting day*
> *Has run*
> *But to the even-song;*
> *And, having prayed together, we*
> *Will go with you along.*
>
> *We have short time to stay as you,*
> *We have as short a spring,*
> *As quick a growth to meet decay,*
> *As you or any thing.*
> *We die*
> *As your hours do, and dry*
> *Away,*
> *Like to the summer's rain;*
> *Or as the pearls of morning's dew,*
> *Ne'er to be found again.*

Or some of us will fish up Keats' murex because those five

long i sounds at the beginning of the "Ode on a Grecian Urn" have held an instant of our minds motionless since the day in our childhood when we first heard them:

> *Thou still unravish'd bride of quietness,*
> *Thou foster-child of Silence and slow time,*
> *Sylvan historian . . .*

But whatever poem you call back to mind — to conscious mind, for there must be scores of them lying underneath the thought like fallen columns under the tourist traffic in the Forum in Rome — whatever poem you call back to mind, the question I would put would be the same: Does your poem seem to you, as you contemplate it in your imagination, to be "created" in the sense in which we use that word of the events described in the book of Genesis? Is there not rather a selection and ordering as there is a selection and ordering in the art of history and in the practice of journalism? The selection is of a different kind — yes: things are chosen which history would find too trivial to touch and which journalism, in its passionate haste to get on with the story, would have no time for. The organization of the fragments selected is also different. Things are put together in poetry which history would never put together because of its addiction to the logic of cause and effect and which journalism would never put together because of its commitment to the lucidities of common sense. Men do not pray with daffodils in history if they care for the opinion in which posterity will hold them. But granted all this — granted, too, that the structure of words in poetry is very different, far more orderly, immeasurably more strict, than the structure of words in the prose of journalism or of history, does it really follow that the enormous gulf we have dug between the conception of journalism and the conception of poetry is explained away by calling poetry a "creative art"?

I should not say so. I should say that an examination of actual poems and actual journalisms would lead any reader to the conclusion that the difference between them, wide though it is, cannot be stated in terms of "creation." Both are *re*-creations, different in degree but not different in kind, for the material in each case is our human experience of the world and of ourselves; and not fundamentally different in method or even in purpose since the method of poetry like the method of journalism is selection from the chaotic formlessness of experience, and the purpose of both is the reordering of the fragments selected in a sequence that makes sense. It is perfectly true that the sense which poetry makes of its fragments is not the sense which journalism makes. No reporter in America or anywhere else would organize fragments of the experience of a divorce case to read: "love is not love / which alters when it alteration finds / or bends with the remover to remove: / O, no! it is an ever-fixed mark / that looks on tempests and is never shaken; / it is the star to every wandering bark, / whose worth's unknown, although his height be taken." In journalism this summation of experience is not sensible at all. It is not even true. Love, in journalism, does not "bear it out even to the edge of doom." And the opposite is also obvious. The sense which journalism makes of the life of a man and the life of a woman, or the life of a man and the lives of two women, is not sensible or even true in poetry. But the fact remains that both Shakespeare's sonnet and the news story of the broken marriage are *re*-creations of fragments selected from the confusion of human experience in an effort to give them order and make them comprehensible. The purpose in one case may merely be to make them comprehensible to human curiosity whereas the purpose in the other is very evidently to reach the human intelligence at its most perceptive and most alive: Shakespeare's sonnet has undertones of irony which only a most subtly listening ear can hear. But in both cases and however different their levels, the end is comprehension, understanding.

Some will regard this statement as a depreciation of poetry. Creation has a grander sound than *re*-creation and is undoubtedly, if we may accept the evidence of the book of Genesis, more difficult. But poetry, despite the almost magical powers of the greatest poets, is a human labor and what humanity most desperately needs is not the creation of new worlds, but the *re*-creation, in terms of human comprehension, of the world we have, and it is to this task that all the arts are committed. Indeed it is for this reason that the arts go on from generation to generation in spite of the fact that Phidias has already carved and Homer has already sung. The Creation, we are informed, was accomplished in seven days with Sunday off, but the *re*-creation will never be accomplished because it is always to be accomplished anew for each new generation of living men. To hold the vast, whirling, humming, buzzing, boggling confusion of the Greek world still long enough to see it is not to hold the vast, whirling, humming, buzzing, boggling confusion of our world still. New charms are necessary, new spells, new artifices. Whether they know it or not, the young men foregather in Paris in one generation, in San Francisco in another, because the world goes round, the light changes, and the old jugs will not carry living water. New jugs must be devised which the generation past will reject as monstrosities and the generation to come will, when it arrives, reject for other reasons: as banalities and bores.

But the essential point is that this labor does not differ in kind from the continuing labor of generations of journalists and historians who also face a new and turning world and who must also find new words. The materials of poetry, whatever the miracles accomplished with them, are gathered where the materials of history, present and past, are gathered, in what Keats called the arable field of events. Poetry transforms these materials by a faculty the use of which is discouraged in journalism, the faculty of imagination, but the product of the metamorphosis is not an opposite thing from the product of the process known in journalism as reporting. A poem is not what our grandfathers used to say it was: a "fancy" as opposed to the sober "facts" of practical men. For one thing, the constructions of the imagination are not "fancies" and never were. For another, "facts" are not what our grandfathers supposed them to be in those happy far-off Victorian generations when science picked "facts" out of life like grits out of porridge and marshaled them in patterns on a page. The formal conveniences of modern theoretical physics do not, as Einstein himself has told us, correspond to events in the real world.

But this paradox of physics is apparently easier to grasp than the far simpler truth that the *re*-creations of the imagination *do* correspond to the experience of the real world. Poetry may take liberties with the materials of that experience which history and journalism are not free to take. It may translate them into unexpected and even improbable forms. But it neither will nor can disguise their origins in experience, for the moment it did so it would cease to be an art. It would become a sorcery, a magic. Those Grecian centaurs, half man, half horse — those Oriental mother goddesses all arms and breasts — derive from nature. It is only the arrangement of the parts which is unnatural. The parts themselves, the horse, the man, the arms, the breasts, have been discovered in the world the senses know. Even what we call "abstraction" in the art of our own day is not new creation in the sense in which the world of Genesis is new. Vision reduced to line, balance, color, proportion, is still vision and stilll belongs in a world in which line and balance and color and proportion exist.

Indeed, this dependence of poetry, of all art, on human experience of the actual world is only made the more obvious by the attempts of art, which have been frequent in our time, to escape from the actual world. Poems, for example, which derive from the subconscious mind, as the poems of the early Surrealists did or purported to do, are still poems of experience and still poems composed by a process of selection from among the moments of experience. The only difference is that the selecting sieve is set up, or is supposed to be set up, somewhere outside the conscious mind. But the poem does not become, in consequence, a parentless, a pristine creation. On the contrary, it is even more obviously and immediately derived from the common human reality than a poem made, as the Greeks made poems, under the selective directon of a conscious intelligence. The proof lies in the experiments of those contemporary psychiatrists who have attempted to work their way back through completed poems to their roots in experience. They have made very little of the poems of, say, John Donne, but they have had a harvest home with the works of the Surrealists. A Surrealist poem is a direct recording of the experiencing mind on the tape of speech and all that need be done to make one's way to the unhappy childhood or the illicit love is to play the recording back. John Donne is another matter. The conscious act of art is there to make a mechanical playback impossible. All you will get if you try is that series of garbled screams and whinnies with which the amateurs of tape recordings are familiar.

But one need not go to the Surrealists or their successors to make the point. The most apparently "fanciful" of all familiar poems will testify, if you will truly read them, that their fancies are no less substantial, no less true, no less (if the word is still permitted) real — at least no less authenticated by experience — than the most substantial "facts." Consider Prospero's great trope in *The Tempest* — those cloud-capped towers, gorgeous palaces, solemn temples, the great globe itself which "like this insubstantial pageant faded," dissolve — "leave not a rack behind." Consider Rimbaud's pianos in the Alps, his hares praying to the rainbow through the spider's web, his little boy waving his arms to the weathervanes after the Deluge had subsided, in the *Illuminations*. Compare these extravagant "fancies" with the "hard facts" of history and journalism. You will find it difficult, I think, to say just what the substantial difference is. You may even find yourself concluding that, if anything, the "fancies" are harder than the "facts." We are — we are indeed — such stuff as dreams are made on and any man who has not yet learned that "our little life is rounded with a sleep," has not begun to live that little life. We do, after every Deluge which drowns the world, whether for one man or for many, come upon that moment when everything is new again and possible — even the impossible: when little boys and weathervanes salute each other. There can scarcely be a man or a woman in

my generation, if he has really shared that generation's life, who
has not known that moment — and then lost it as Rimbaud's poem
loses it. Are these "fancies" not as substantial as our "facts"?
Are they not as real as murder or the World Series or Governor
Faubus, to say nothing of our China policy or a Dow-Jones average? Has anyone ever met a Dow-Jones average on a Sunday
aftenoon, or bathing, or anywhere else in the world? And as for
our China policy, would anyone know its face if it walked into
the room and sat down and arranged its smile?

 I am not suggesting that the facts of journalism are insubstantial. I am merely suggesting that there is no such difference between the "facts" of journalism and the "fancies" of poetry as
we assume when we turn them into each other's opposites. You
can prove it to yourself in either way: by reading poems or by
reading newspapers. What do you remember about that revolution some years ago in Iraq? What I remember is the account of
the assassination of the Premier, the famous desert fox, the most
powerful man in the valley of the two rivers, who was shot in
the dress of an old woman. Why do I remember that? Because
the "fact" becomes something more than fact in that telling. Because I understand something of the man — and of those who
killed him. Because the political event becomes a human event
and casts a shadow far beyond Baghdad, far beyond the desert,
far beyond the Middle East. Or take another important news
story of the same period. Why did the story of President Eisenhower's assistant, Sherman Adams, fail to arouse anything but
political passions and why is it dead now? Because it never came
alive, turned human, added to or substracted from the total of
experience. All the human improbabilities and paradoxes were
there, the contradictions between apparent character and ad-

mitted conduct, the surprises, but the human being who could
make it real never appeared. The Sherman Adams story poetry
would have told was never even shadowed. And the result is
that the tale has no life in it. It is only when the scattered and illegible fragments in which we pick up our experience of the
world are recomposed in such a way that they make sense as human experience that great journalism can result. And the same
thing is true in the same words of poetry. What poetry composes
of its fragments is more lasting than what journalism composes.
It is larger. It goes deeper. It is more meaningful. It has beauty.
But it is not contrary in kind. Poetry and journalism — to put it
in more inclusive terms, poetry and history — are not opposites
and cannot be opposites and the notion that they are is a delusion.

What really distinguishes poetry from journalism, aside from
the obvious distinctions of form — uses of words, patterns of
words, sequences of words — is not a difference in kind but a
difference in focus. Journalism is concerned with events, poetry
with feelings. Journalism is concerned with the look of the
world: poetry with the feel of the world. Journalism wishes to
tell what has happened everywhere as though the same things
had happened for every man. Poetry wishes to say what it is
like to any man to be *himself* in the presence of a particular oc-
currence as though he alone had faced it. The best definition of
journalism appears daily in the New York *Times*: "All the news
that's fit to print." The best definition of poetry is spelled out
still in Coleridge's *Biographia Literaria*: ". . . the balance or
reconcilement of discordant qualities . . . a more than usual
state of emotion with more than usual order." To separate journalism and poetry, therefore — history and poetry — to set
them up at opposite ends of the world of discourse, is to separate

seeing from the feel of seeing, emotion from the acting of emotion, knowledge from the realization of knowledge.

The poet, with us, stops his horse at twilight at the wood's edge in falling snow and yields for a moment to that longing for sleep in the cold, white, drifting stillness which is also another and a deeper longing all reflective men have known, but the journalist permits himself to see only a man in a buggy stopping in inclement weather at a remote and unlikely spot: since nothing has "happened" he publishes nothing. And the same thing is true in reverse. The journalist dodges hand grenades in the bazaar of a hot, dusty, dirty, flea-bitten desert city to report an obscure war which may be the beginning of the ultimate war, but the poet, because all this is merely "happening," does not write at all: because nothing is "felt," he has nothing to say.

I exaggerate, of course. There have been journalists of our generation — men like Elmer Davis as well as men like Ernie Pyle — who would not have separated the feel of things from the look of them if they could, and there are contemporary poets who not only felt but saw the war in Spain — saw it, in fact, far more clearly than the journalists or the foreign offices or the professional observers of world affairs. Indeed the greatest of contemporary poets was also one of the most exact and penetrating observers of the history of his time if not always the most intelligent interpreter of that history.

> *Turning and turning in the widening gyre*
> *The falcon cannot hear the falconer;*
> *Things fall apart; the center cannot hold;*
> *Mere anarchy is loosed upon the world,*
> *The blood-dimmed tide is loosed and everywhere*
> *The ceremony of innocence is drowned;*

> *The best lack all conviction while the worst*
> *Are full of passionate intensity.*

No journalist, writing of the tragic events with which the name of the late Senator McCarthy is associated, ever defined that aspect of contemporary life as precisely as Yeats had defined it some thirty years before:

> *The best lack all conviction while the worst*
> *Are full of passionate intensity.*

But Yeats is an exception in this as in many other things. And not even Yeats was able to bring the event and the feel of the event together as they were brought in Homer's time and Dante's and Shakespeare's. Journalism tends more and more with us toward an admirably dispassionate objectivity which presents the event in the colorless air of intellectual detachment at the cost of its emotional significance, and poetry, reacting to the same divisive influence but in an opposite direction, turns more and more to the emotional significance divorced from the event. I do not know that it is possible to say that this fracture of the word is bad for journalism as such, for the great modern newspapers are, as newspapers, far superior to their predecessors. They collect more news faster and present it more accurately. It is only too possible to say, however, that it is bad for poetry and bad for the civilization in which we live.

Great poems are instruments of knowledge — a knowledge carried alive into the heart by passion, but knowledge nevertheless. Feeling without knowing never made a work of art and never will. And the attempt to detach feelings from their occasions which contemporary poetry increasingly makes — to pursue feelings as themselves and for their own sakes, resolutely ignoring the events from which they derive — can only be harmful to the art. Poems so composed are like kites without strings. They cannot bear up against the carrying away of time because they have no attachment to a point in time.

But the consequences to poetry itself of its increasing inwardness are of concern, unhappily, only to poets. What the rest of us might wish to think of is the effect of all this on the civilization in which we live. It is not difficult to define. Some time ago, Mr. Lewis Mumford, certainly one of the most intelligent of living Americans, wrote a letter to the New York *Times* expressing his horror at the apathy of his countrymen in the face of the dangers inherent in our policy and conduct in the Far East. Here we were, he said, on a brink from which we might at any moment be shoved by the Chinese Nationalists or dragged by the Chinese Communists, with a war yawning before us which could only be fought by the horrible weapons of genocide and with the end of human life on the earth as a very possible consequence; and yet we neither protested nor objected. We merely sat there in a numb indifference, leaving the decision of life or death to a Secretary of State whose previous decisions or indecisions were responsible for our predicament.

It was an angry letter and one with which men of certain opinions might differ. But what struck me about it was not its statement of the facts, which seemed to me only too painfully correct, but its explanation of the reason for our national indifference to the facts. Our apathy, Mr. Munford suggested — I do not know how seriously — could only be the consequence of our enormous consumption of tranquilizers and sedatives. Only a nation doped into unreality could possibly contemplate in silence a series of events and declarations which might at any moment lead to the extermination of enormous numbers of peaceful human beings, first in Asia and then throughout the world — including the part of the world in which we live ourselves. I say I was struck by this explanation. I was struck by it because I found myself wishing the real explanation might be as simple and ironic. For the truth is, of course, that our apathy with regard to the incredible and terrifying events in Southeastern Asia is the result, not of our habits in the taking of pills, but of our habits in the thinking of thoughts. And the further truth is that this strange dislocation in the thinking of thoughts by which we can "know" what we cannot feel — by which we can "know" that the consequence of a merely diplomatic maneuver may be the atomizing of the city of Peiping and then Tokyo and then Moscow and then New York, but cannot imagine in our live emotions what this "knowing" would feel like — this dislocation is the consequence of a deeper dislocation, not only in ourselves, but in the civilization in which we exist.

For this divorce between knowing and feeling is not something we Americans can claim as our own peculiar prerogative. The Germans have exhibited the same curious capacity: the "good Germans" who "knew" about the gas ovens of the concentration camps, but were nevertheless able to live with their knowledge in tranquillity and good conscience until at the war's end they began to go, in crowded, silent audiences, to performances of *The Diary of Anne Frank*. What is wrong with us — shall we call ourselves the "good Americans"? — is precisely what is wrong with the "good Germans." We "know" what happened at Hiroshima. We have read, or read about, John Hersey's account of the results of the atomic bombing of that city. Most of us are at least aware of the specters which crawl through Dr. Hachiya's book: "Their faces and hands were burnt and swollen and great sheets of skin had peeled away from their tissues to hang down like rags on a scarecrow. They moved like a line of ants. All through the night they went past our house, but this morning they had stopped. I found them lying on both sides of the road so thick that it was impossible to pass without stepping on them." We know all this. But do we *feel* our knowledge? Could we even think about risking the possibility of a world-wide atomic war as a matter of "face" or official vanity if we did?

Nothing could better illustrate the flaw at the heart of our civilization. Nothing could more convincingly demonstrate that knowledge without feeling is not knowledge and can lead only to public irresponsibility and indifference — and conceivably to ruin. Nothing could more clearly prove that when the fact is disassociated from the feel of the fact in the minds of an entire people — in the common mind of a civilization — that people, that civilization, is in danger.

Some will think the terms I have been using are inadequate to so serious an indictment. Journalism seems to most of us a profession like another and poetry seems remote indeed from matters of such moment as the survival of the world. But the fact is, of course, that the survival of the world — at least the survival of a world which has prepared as ingeniously for its own suicide as the world we live in — depends, madmen and accidents aside, solely on the *knowledge* of the men and women who inhabit it. And that knowledge is composed precisely of the two increments which journalism and poetry provide. Information is essential to the kind of knowledge on which an opinion

relevant to our Asian situation can be based. But the feel of the
facts which that information communicates is also essential if the
knowledge and the opinions it fathers are to be trustworthy and
reliable. What has happened with us is that the first has outrun
the second. We are, as we are constantly and justly being reminded, the best-informed people on an earth which is better
informed now than it ever was before in its history. But,
though we are provided with more facts than any previous generation, we are not necessarily possessed of more knowledge of
those facts. On the contrary, we seem to be less and less capable of receiving our facts into our imaginations where they can
come alive with feeling. Benjamin Franklin's contemporaries
were not told within a few hours that some hundreds of coal
miners had been trapped in a mine in what is now Yugoslavia,
but when, after many months, the news of such a disaster at last
came through, it would have come as a human tragedy with its
human significance about it. The news of Napoleon's retreat
from Moscow would be broadcast today minute by minute,
photographed, columnized, interpreted, recorded to the last detail. When Napoleon actually turned back, the news was
brought to New York in a brig commanded by my great-grandfather months after the event and in an individual witness's report. But it loomed in the New York newspapers of the next
morning like news from Troy, which, in a sense, it was. What
the Greeks knew about Troy, they knew through a man's slow
telling.

I am not deploring the advances of journalism. They are
miraculous. No man who has grown used to the news coverage
of an expertly managed paper could live without it. But every
improvement, and particularly every improvement made possi-

ble by mechanical invention, exacts its price, as we are discovering in our increasingly mechanized country. Often the price is exacted at the cost of nature, sometimes at the cost of human nature. The extraordinary advance in the supply of information in the United States and through the West is of the latter kind. We are deluged with facts, but we have lost, or are losing, our human ability to feel them. Which means that we have lost or are losing our ability to comprehend the facts of our experience as poetry comprehends them, re-created and made real in the imagination. Poetry still survives with us: survives with vigor and inventiveness, throwing up new masters capable of standing with the old. But the *poem* has lost its power in men's minds. We have not discarded the art as Herbert Spencer thought we would when the machine had come to flower, but we have impaired the practice of the skill the art can give, the skill of feeling truly and so truly knowing. We know with the head now, by the facts, by the abstractions. We seem unable to know as Shakespeare knew who made King Lear cry out to blinded Gloucester on the heath: ". . . you see how this world goes," and Gloucester answers: "I see it feelingly."

Why we are thus impotent, I do not know. I know only that this impotence exists and that it is dangerous: increasingly dangerous. I know, too, or think I know, that, whatever the underlying cause of the divorce of feeling from knowing, that divorce reveals itself most vividly in the strange and ignorant belief that the life of the imagination lies at an opposite pole from the life of the inquiring mind — that men can live and know and master their experience of this darkling earth by accumulating information and no more. Men who believe that have, in effect, surrendered their responsibilities as men. They have gone over to the enemy — to those unhappy hordes, victims of the new and terrible tyranny of our time, who are not meant to know for themselves and with their whole beings, but only to accept the daily ration of news and hates which Peiping or Moscow issues to them. Slavery begins when men give up the human need to know with the whole heart — to know for themselves — to bear the burden for themselves — the "burden," as Wordsworth called it, "of the mystery." To acquiesce, as the Russians and the Chinese and the Poles — even the Hungarians — have had to acquiesce, in someone else's knowing is to acquiesce in someone else's deciding, and at that point, whatever the society is called, it is not free. The real defense of freedom is imagination, that feeling-life of the mind which *actually* knows because it involves itself in its knowing, puts itself in the place where its thought goes, walks in the body of the little Negro girl who feels the spittle dribbling on her cheek, follows in that line of ants whose skin is ragged tatters. The man who knows with his heart knows himself to be a man, feels as himself, cannot be silenced. He is free no matter where he lives, as Boris Pasternak poignantly showed that he was free even in Russia. The man who knows with his mind only, who will not commit himself beyond his wits, who will not feel the thing he knows, or know the thing he feels — that man has no freedom anywhere. He is tugged by the string of whatever is told him, maneuvered by slogans. Sooner or later his life will seem indifferent to him, something managed by others, and he will acquiesce in the management, think about it as little as possible, occupy himself with the only things near enough to seem real — his car, his front lawn, those shadows on the television screen — symbolic shadows.

To me — not many others think so — the real crisis in the

life of our society is the crisis of the life of the imagination. Far
more than we need an intercontinental missile or a moral rearma-
ment or a religious revival, we need to come alive again, to re-
cover the virility of the imagination on which all earlier civilizations have been based: Coleridge's "synthetic and magical power
by which "the whole soul of man" may be brought to activity,
and knowledge may be *known*.

II

State of
the Union

Changes in the Weather

1956

NOTHING is more difficult to make sense of than the weather. Not only is it continually and inexplicably changing but even when you have it you cannot be altogether certain what it is. You will get one weather system, one human climate, in one decade and then, for no reason anyone can really explain, you will get another and before you are well accustomed to that you will have a third. There was a spell before the First World War of what the French describe as *beau fixe*, an uninterrupted succession of blue skies and white clouds when everything was certain and secure and firmly anchored to its own shadow and children grew up in the houses in which they were born and their fathers came home every afternoon on the five-fifteen, driving down from the station behind a pair of bouncing bays who knew the road by heart and Sunday dinner took two hours to eat and there were still foxes in the ravines and Canada geese in the spring fogs and a buffalo robe in the sleigh which smelled of General Custer.

People remember that sunny season even now with nostalgia and longing and write sad stories about how it is gone, altogether gone, the sky gray, the leaves scattered from the oaks, the old house torn down and the stable turned into a duplex apartment.

After the war, and for no reason anyone could give, there was a wholly different human climate. There was what we call the Twenties (as though the calendar were to blame for it) when human life, at least in our part of the world, was one long jazz-lit midnight entirely populated by the young or by those who ought to have been young, and the moon came up behind Notre Dame and went down behind Les Halles, or anyway Sullivan Street, and the man at the next table was a great novelist or a famous painter and you couldn't dance in the streets for the millionaires who were dancing there already, and children were up at all hours because they didn't know where to go to bed and half of every college class were stockbrokers and the other half didn't bother either. People write about that time too with nostalgia and longing — but not, you will notice, those who were in it. Those who were in it, those who are still alive who were in it, write about something else.

Because after the Twenties the climate changed again and men and women who were dressed for dancing in the midnight streets began to look oddly out of fashion. That was the Thirties when nobody was young any longer and next to nobody was rich and a great many people had nothing at all to do and almost as many had less than they should have had to eat and there was room to spare in the subways and scarcely a seat in the parks and the heart smoldered with indignation like a peat fire under-ground in the wet moss and the dead leaves but smoldered too with a kind of fiery hope so that men and women walked the streets together or sat around tables together and talked of a new world, a new and better beginning, and tried to make it happen in a theater somewhere, or in a fresco on a post-office wall, or a government plan to refinance farmers or to get the textile industry off its back. People write of the Thirties too but not with nostalgia, and certainly not with love. When they write about the Thirties now they write confessionals explaining how inexperienced they were then and how hopelessly hopeful they were and how naïve.

So that the Thirties are gone as the Twenties are, only farther, and a Second World War has followed the First taking most of the decade of the Forties with it, and a new time has followed the old, and the question asks itself again. What's the weather? If you take your question to the politicians, you will be told that the Fifties, the American Fifties at least — and the Sixties after them and undoubtedly the Seventies and perhaps even the Eighties — are not a period in which things are to be done but a period in which things are to be kept from being done, a kind of chronological barbed wire fence to keep history away, a margin of time in which to "contain" the Russians by arms if the Russians make use of arms and to "contain" the Russians by economic means if the Russians resort to economic means but in any case and whatever the method to "contain" the Russians.

And the journalists, if you ask them, will tell you that the Fifties are years without describable faces, that they cut no figure against the stars, that they are neither one thing nor the other. They are boom years as the Twenties never were boom years, and they are troubled years as the Thirties never were troubled, but neither the boom nor the trouble seems real. The prosperity hasn't headed in the glass as it did thirty years ago. It hasn't effervesced. It isn't exciting. And the same thing, they will tell you, is true of the troubles of the Fifties. They are terrible troubles, anguishing troubles, worse troubles than the Thirties ever knew — a whole civilization precariously balanced upon a quaking crust above an ultimate destruction. But somehow the troubles do not *work* as they did twenty years ago. They do not goad the country into hopeful action. They sink into the time instead like something water-logged in the soul which makes men mean instead of candid, timid instead of determined, suspicious of each other instead of courageous and firm.

But the most revealing answer will come, if you should put your question to them, from the writers. It may or may not be the sole function of art to hold a mirror up to nature but it is only in the reflection of art that the character of any time is ever truly seen, as earlier epochs of all sorts and kinds bear witness. The Twenties were scarcely under way before T. S. Eliot had composed their dirge and they were still young when Scott Fitzgerald began his portraits of their people. As a matter of fact, they had not even commenced when Ezra Pound conceived, in his *Hugh Selwyn Mauberley*, the songs they would be obliged to sing. And the Thirties were quite as vividly rendered. Dos Passos had guessed their climate before the rains began, and his prognostications were subsequently verified by a body of writers so numerous that they were unable, when the Thirties ended, to find common transportation forward into the succeeding years. But when it comes to the Fifties the mirrors all go blank. Novels, some of them excellent novels, have been written in this country in the Fifties but no significant novel I can think of *of* the Fifties. Poems, good poems, have been written but no *Mauberley*, no *Waste Land*: nothing which even undertakes the task to which *Mauberley* and *The Waste Land* addressed themselves.

Now, if this were a country and a time, as the avant garde keep chanting from their safe position at the rear of the column, in which the poet cannot function — cannot be expected to function — the blankness in the glass would be comprehensible enough. But the facts of record suggest that nothing of the kind is true: that "the poet" has functioned very well in this country and in very recent years. Only once in its history indeed has the Republic been anything like as well supplied with functioning poets in all the forms of literature as it has been in this period. One has only to think of the more obvious American names, of Eliot and Pound and Frost and Wallace Stevens and Marianne Moore, of Hemingway and Faulkner and Thornton Wilder, to be quite certain that it is not for lack of adequate witnesses that the world around us has no image. Think if you can of Sandburg's *The People, Yes* back in the Thirties and how the look and feel of a generation is there and the continent behind it, far off, vast to the horizon. Poets who can produce work of that power and comprehensiveness are not silent today because they lack the capacity or the opportunity to speak.

But what then is the explanation? It will be found, I think, not in a lack of competent writers but in a dislocation of the generation as a whole, a total failure to comprehend the time, to sense the weather in the streets. There can be few examples in the chronicles anywhere of a more confused and contradictory relationship between event and response, between historical situation and psychological consequence, than the example our generation offers. The historical situation is familiar enough. Not since the carvings on the rocks began has the human world changed so fast or in so many directions or over so vast an area as in the decade since the ending of the Second World War. Political change is on such a scale and of such a character that the maps of fifteen years ago are meaningless over the greater part of entire continents, and maps of any kind are incapable of expressing the political actualities in certain portions of the earth.

Military change is even more revolutionary. We are told by

military experts that the advance, if that is the appropriate word, in military weapons has pushed the techniques of General Eisenhower's Normandy Landings back into the era of the Battle of Missionary Ridge. As for economic change, developments there are so extraordinary that the term "Industrial Revolution" seems scarcely applicable any longer to those moderate and leisurely events of the eighteenth and nineteenth centuries to which we were taught to apply it. And all these changes, furthermore, economic, political and military, are merely the outward and visible signs of an inward and human alteration in the patterns of the lives of men. Millennial ways of working and sleeping and eating and thinking are changing or have changed in every part of the primitive world and in parts which are very far from primitive, and the whole relation of men to the earth and to what lies beyond the earth is changing with them.

And yet it is precisely this time of ours which my generation in the United States has chosen to regard as a final and perfected epoch, an American "way of life," to be defended at all costs against any and every change including, particularly including, changes under way in the rest of the world, or that part of it at least beyond the Urals. Where earlier generations of Americans, facing an undiscovered future, lived in the expectation of change, my generation lives in an accomplished present and looks forward to the familiarity of a past where change is irrelevant. We know that modifications, some of them modifications of the most radical character, are taking place in the industrial process even in the United States but we regard them as developments, not revolutions. As to modifications elsewhere throughout the world members of my generation make no secret of their belief that political and social and economic change is merely a Communist conspiracy and that, if only the Russians could be forced to cease their conniving, history — American history at least — would stand forever still on the golden peak of 1955.

That this belief confuses effect and cause, that it violently exaggerates the power and influence of Communism and that it relegates the United States to the ranks of the passive and therefore senile nations does not seem to trouble those who hold it. Change of any critical character is so abhorrent to the contemporary American mind that it regards all change as conspiratorial and hence morally iniquitous. One of the most astute political observers of the time has summed this attitude up by saying that what most Americans really want is for everything to stay the way it is, only, perhaps, a little more so. Our domestic and foreign policy would seem to bear him out. It is the-world-the-way-it-is we Americans undertake to preserve at home and the-world-the-way-it-is-at-home we undertake to protect by our activities abroad. For the policy of containment in its various forms is not merely an affirmation of the iniquity of Communism: it is an affirmation also of the self-sufficiency of the United States.

Now the insistent attachment of my generation to the present American way of living and its whole-hearted abhorrence of Communism are entirely understandable. We have reason to know, and we think our friends in such a country as, for example, France should have reason to know also, that Communism, whatever it may have been in theory, is in practice the stalest, stupidest and most brutal joke ever perpetrated on the decent aspirations of the human spirit. And as for the way we live in the United States, though it has its faults, ours is at least the first economy in history to provide mankind in general with mankind's dearest wish: a degree of leisure.

Furthermore, though we may be almost as materialistic as our critics say we are, and though our cities are certainly uglier than cities have a right to be, we have nevertheless some inkling of the uses to which leisure might be put. Our arts, that is to say, have exhibited a vitality which the arts of no other contemporary country, and least of all the Communist provinces, have surpassed. So that the vehemence of our loyalty and the heartiness of our detestation are understandable enough.

But what is not understandable is the image my generation has formed of the contemporary world. What is not understandable is the image of a static America in a changing time: the strangely romantic notion that the United States exists, or should exist, or can be made to exist, somewhere outside or in remove from the social and economic and political actualities of the decade; that it can deal with the enormous forces now at play in the world merely by resisting one of their most distorted manifestations; that it can surround the future with arms and dominate the racing world by standing still. These are not only delusions: they are dangerous delusions — dangerous in the public world and dangerous also in the private world of the human heart.

The public danger is familiar. What it comes down to is the risk that we will abdicate to the Russians if we have not already abdicated, the leadership of the modern revolution and thus the power to shape the emerging world. Looking at that revolution from the point of view of our wholly imaginary isolation in time and space, and permitting ourselves to believe that all this stir and change is in some way Russian in inspiration, we devote our principal energies to the military containment of the Communist powers and offer economic leadership and assistance to the rest of the world, when we offer it at all, only to those nations which will take our side, or which we hope will take our side, in the expected conflict.

Unhappily for this policy, social and economic revolutions cannot be herded from the flanks. They can only be led from the front. And Maginot Lines are even less useful in political than in military campaigns. No one should doubt by this late date that the future belongs to those who can lead, and thereby shape, the social and industrial forces now in movement throughout the world.

But the public danger is not the only danger of our obstinate attempt to impose upon a changing world a static image. There is a private danger also. For a number of years now I have been watching young men and young women for whom I deeply cared making, or attempting to make, their peace with the prospect beyond the roofs of Cambridge.

Part of the trouble, I have no doubt, is the iron condition-precedent which the necessities of their country impose upon their lives: the young men have their military duty to perform before they can begin to think with certainty of their own careers. Part of the trouble, also, is the warning given them by their elders that even after their military duty is completed the life of their generation will be one of waiting and watching, of matching weapon with weapon, of remaining constantly alert and eternally prepared until at some unforeseen and unforeseeable moment Communist imperialism will collapse. But these considerations and others like them are only part of the difficulty. What troubles these young men and women far more than the military obligation is the difficulty of making sense of the image of the age they have inherited from their elders.

They do not doubt, any more than their elders doubt, that Communism is a scourge and an affliction which must be opposed. But our conception of the age — the conception of my generation — as an epoch of resistance, an era merely of defense, lacks meaning for them. They have no conviction of the reality of such a time and no certainty that they can act upon it — no certainty that there will be anything, indeed, in such a time on which to act. Neither pole of our commitment quite convinces them. They do not recognize their imagined America in our loyalty to a finished, final order which exists to stay the same — a "way of life" which is the way things are. And as for the scourge of Communism, they cannot altogether believe that it is by raising walls against the world, by denying the tremendous tides running in Asia and in Africa, by shouting "Those who are not with us are against us!" as though the difference between human liberty and human degradation were no more than a choosing of political sides — they cannot altogether believe that it is by such an effort they will accomplish their labor and their destiny. A new generation needs room to turn around in, needs the breath of possibility, the chance of choice. And the image of the world we give them leaves no room for choice.

The Conquest of
the United States

1949

SOMETIME along in the nineteen-eighties, when the world
has left us as far behind as we have left the years that followed
the First World War, somebody is going to publish a piece called
The Nineteen Forties. I hope to be dead at the time.*

The subject of this piece will be the conquest of the United
States by the Russians. It will begin more or less as follows: —

Never in the history of the world was one people as completely dominated, intellectually and morally, by another as the
people of the United States by the people of Russia in the four
years from 1946 through 1949. American foreign policy was a
mirror image of Russian foreign policy: whatever the Russians
did, we did in reverse. American domestic politics were conducted under a kind of upside-down Russian veto: no man could
be elected to public office unless he was on record as detesting
the Russians, and no proposal could be enacted, from a peace
plan at one end to a military budget at the other, unless it could
be demonstrated that the Russians wouldn't like it. American
political controversy was controversy sung to the Russian tune;

* *Pravda*, which devoted a column to this article, warmly endorsed the hope.

left-wing movements attacked right-wing movements not on American issues but on Russian issues, and right-wing movements replied with the same arguments turned round about.

American education was Russian education backward: ignorance of Communism was the principal educational objective recognized by politicians and the general press, and the first qualification demanded of a teacher was that he should not be a Communist himself, should not have met persons who might have been Communists, and should never have read books which could tell him what Communism was. American intellectual life revolved around Russian intellectual life: writers stopped writing and convoked enormous meetings in expensive hotels to talk about Russia for days at a time, with the result that the problems of American culture (if that self-conscious and overfingered word is still in use in 1980) became reflections of the problems of Russian culture. Even religious dogma was Russian dogma inside out: the first duty of a good Christian in the United States in those years was not to love his enemies but to hate the Communists — after which he was told to pray for them if he could.

All this, moreover — so the story will go on — all this took place not in a time of national weakness or decay but precisely at the moment when the United States, having engineered a tremendous triumph, and fought its way to a brilliant victory in the greatest of all wars, had reached the highest point of world power ever achieved by a single state. The American national income had doubled and doubled again in a generation. The American standard of living was far in advance of any other, including — including particularly — the Russian. The American industrial potential balanced, and overbalanced, that of the rest of the industrial world. American technological supremacy was so obvious that it was taken for granted, and American products were so far superior that they were used or copied everywhere on earth.

It was not, in other words, a weak and declining people, caught in the expanding shadow of history's new master, which gave up its independent mind, contracted its national will to the dry negation of the will of others, and threw away the historic initiative which, in the lives of nations as in the lives of men, is the key to greatness. It was the most powerful people in the world — a people still young in a continent still new — a people which, only a generation before, had been regarded as brash to the point of arrogance, cocksure to the verge of folly, and so wholly certain of its future and itself that travelers wrote books about the national assurance. It was the nation, in brief, which had been chiefly famous among other nations because it conceived of its present not in terms of its past but of its future — the nation which spoke with a straight face and with entire sincerity of the American Dream.

It ought to be possible for a good historian with a lively sense of the ridiculous to amuse himself and his readers for some pages with variations on that theme. But what will be hardest for us to take — those of us who are left around — will not be the ridicule of our successors but their sympathetic understanding. For it is unlikely that any future account of the prodigious paradox of our conduct will fail to reach the conclusion that we lost our way as a people, and hitched ourselves backward to the Russian star, primarily because we were unable to think.

We were unable, that is, to understand the nature of the

crisis in which we were caught or the character of the role we were called upon to play. Instead, we confused one of several consequences of the crisis with the crisis itself, enlarged upon a necessary police operation until it became not only *a* national policy but *the* national policy, and chained ourselves, as a sort of vast sea anchor, to the purposes and policies of a rival state. Even the Marshall Plan, which, in its beginnings, was a courageous and positive proposal, responsive to the realities of the world situation, became in press and Congress, under the influence of our fears, a negative and defensive operation.

As to the nature of the crisis, it will be noted that the general opinion held among us, however individuals might dissent, was the opinion that the troubles of our age were international in character; that they had been precipitated by the rise of Communism; that Communism was a great new revolutionary force; that the way to resolve the crisis, therefore, was to resist and contain and presumably strangle the Communist revolution.

As to the role we were called to play, we had persuaded ourselves that this labor of resistance and containment must take precedence over everything else, and that purely American objectives and purposes, including the great traditional objectives of American life, must not only be subordinated to the accomplishment of the task of containment but even, in certain cases, sacrificed to it.

All this, our historians will observe, was uninformed and unintelligent. The crisis in which we were caught was not new but had been produced by the cumulative changes of many centuries. It was not a crisis in international relations but a crisis in civilization, a crisis in culture, a crisis in the condition of man. That crisis had not been precipitated by the rise of Communism, which was, indeed, one of its consequences, or by a conspiracy in the Kremlin, which was one of its incidents, but by a tragic lag between the disintegration of one order of society — the petering out of one historical era — and the flowering of another.

Communism, finally, was not a new revolutionary force but one of several forms of authoritarian reaction, political, philosophical, and clerical, headed back toward the disintegrating order of society and competing with one another for the domination of that disappearing world. The true revolutionary force in our epoch — the force moving not backward toward the disintegrating age, but forward toward the age which had not yet begun — was the force which had been released at the end of the eighteenth century and the beginning of the nineteenth by the words and actions of a few men, most of them Americans.

The belief that the world crisis could be resolved merely by resisting and containing Communism was, therefore, a delusive belief; and the conclusion that the realization of the historic American purpose must be deferred and subordinated to the defeat of the Russian purpose was not only a false conclusion but a betrayal of the life of the Republic.

We shall hardly be in a position — those of us who live that long — to refute this damaging indictment. No one but the ignorant man or the fanatic really believes even now that Communism is the origin of our ills. We know perfectly well, whatever we may read in the general run of our newspapers or hear from the noisier commentators on the air, that the real difficulty of our time goes deeper than Russian imperialism or Communist fraud. The real difficulty touches life itself, not merely the manipulation of life. It involves a conflict not between nations but between worlds: a dying world not altogether dead; a new world conceived but not yet born.

The dying world is the world which reached its highest European integration in the Middle Ages: the world in which men were able to realize themselves and fulfill their lives as members of the closely knit body of a city, or a church, or a state, or a feudal or institutional structure of some kind. This world began to decay with the Renaissance and has disintegrated with a rapidly accelerated momentum over the years which included the two great world wars. The new world is the world in which men, exiled from an institutional security and an institutional fulfillment, will learn to realize themselves as whole and individual human beings answerable to their consciences. The new world, though it was foreseen and its possibility declared a hundred and seventy years ago, has yet to be established. The limbo in which we live is the interval between the two.

But if this is true the theory propounded by the Communists and their authoritarian rivals, that Communism is a revolutionary force, collapses. A revolutionary force, as distinguished from a reactionary force, is one which moves not backward against the flow of change but forward with it. It is a force which dares to take the revolutionary risk of trusting the flowering of the tree, the meandering of the current. The whole movement of human life, violently accelerated over the last few centuries, has been a movement toward the separation of the individual consciousness from the common consciousness, the common sleep, the animal sleep — a movement toward the differentiation of the individual from the community of the tribe, and, before that, from the community of the "natural" life of universal instinct.

Communism is not a force which moves with that current. On the contrary, Communism, like its authoritarian rivals, seeks to cure the sickness of the condition of man by turning back against the current of human evolution to that decaying city of hierarchical and disciplined order in which mankind, at certain sacrifices of manhood, may find seclusion and retreat.

The one force which can claim the revolutionary title in the world we live in, the one force which can claim to move in the direction of life, is the force that Jefferson put into words. Later Americans have, it is true, betrayed that force, both in terms and actions. Its vocabulary has been appropriated again and again for private advantage. Its victories have been corrupted by hypocrisy and cynicism and selfishness. Its articles of faith have been made the catechism of a faithless commercialism. Its central concept of the dignity of the individual, grown cancerous on occasion, has swollen to the morbid and malignant figure of irresponsible and grasping power — the "rugged individual" whom some still think of as American. But though the hope has been betrayed and forgotten in one generation and another, the living seed remains: the seed remains and grows. It is this seed, this influence, this force, this force of revolution, which is the living thing in the Republic. Without it, the United States is so much land, so many people, such and such an accumulation of wealth. With it the United States is a stage upon the journey of mankind.

It is not only, however, because we have been wrong and fainthearted in our thinking that we shall be blamed by those who come after us. It is not only because we had no reason to subordinate our own purposes to the defeat of Russian purposes and thus to surrender to Russia the initiative we had always held before. We shall be blamed also because the negative and defensive attitude of mind to which we have committed the Republic is mistaken and mischievous and evil in itself. It is mistaken because it is incapable of achieving even its own negative purpose. It is mischievous because it has choked up the deep springs of the moral life of the nation. It is evil because it has deprived the world of the thing the world most needed — a positive and believable alternative to the grim choice the authoritarians hold before mankind.

The inadequacy of the position we have taken, even within its own narrow and negative purpose, is only too obvious. Neither Communism nor any other body of positive belief can be overcome in a period of world-wide dissatisfaction and unrest merely by denying it, or by offering, as a substitute, the world of things as they are. It can be fought only by facing it with a true alternative. And the true alternative to Communism is not the world of things as they are; nor, even more certainly, is it some other kind of authoritarianism.

The real choice is the choice between all forms of authoritarianism on the one side and, on the other, the dream of a whole and responsible human freedom. The real conflict, in other words, the underlying conflict, is not the struggle between the Kremlin and the West which the press associations report from day to day. The real conflict is the conflict between world reaction, which preaches submission to authority, whether of a state or a man or a party or a church, and world revolution which is still, however the various reactionaries may attempt to confuse the issue, the revolution of the individual, the revolution of the whole man.

Stated in terms of structure, the real alternatives are, at the one pole, a cellular, authoritarian society in which individual human beings may live their lives through the life of the society as a whole, and at the other, a world of individual men, whose relation to each other, in the freedom of their individuality, will create a society in which each can live as himself.

For the United States in such a situation to adopt a wholly negative policy aimed at the containment of Communism is not only to fail in the effort to defeat Communism but to miss the real American objective as well; and, worse still, to obstruct one form of authoritarian reaction to the advantage of others. Having unwisely elected to forgo our own purposes as a people, and to resist the purposes of the Russians, we have found ourselves, not once but many times in the past four years, befriending those who hate the revolution of the individual as violently as the Communists hate it. And not only abroad but here at home. For, by putting the hatred and fear of Russia first we have opened the sacred center of our lives, our most essential freedoms — the freedoms of mind and thought — to those among us who have always hated those freedoms and who know well how to use our fear of Russia as a mask to cover their disguised attacks. The spread of legalized thought control from points of infection in the Congress to state legislature after state legislature across the country is not the work of chance. It is the work of freedom-hating men. And we have laid the nation open to them by our fears.

The second vice of the morbid and negative national opinion we have accepted in these years — its mischievous influence on our spiritual life — may be judged by other evidence, no less obvious to those who wish to see it. The soul of a people is the image it cherishes of itself; the aspect in which it sees itself against the past; the attributes to which its future conduct must respond. To destroy that image is to destroy, in a very real sense, the identity of the nation, for to destroy the image is to destroy the

means by which the nation recognizes what it is and what it has
to do. But the image a people holds of itself is created not by
words alone or myths but by its actions. Unless the actions are
appropriate to the image, the image is blurred. If the actions
deny the image, the image is destroyed.

What is happening in the United States under the impact of
the negative and defensive and often frightened opinion of these
years is the falsification of the image the American people have
long cherished of themselves as beginners and begetters, chang-
ers and challengers, creators and accomplishers. A people who
have thought of themselves for a hundred and fifty years as having purposes of their own for the changing of the world cannot
learn overnight to think of themselves as the resisters of another's
purposes without beginning to wonder who they are. A people
who have been real to themselves because they were *for* something cannot continue to be real to themselves when they find
they are merely *against* something.

They begin to ask questions. Who are they then? Are they
still the journeying restless nation to which the future was a direction on a map and the duty of the son was to turn his back on
his father's gateposts, or have they turned around and headed
the other way? Are they still the new nation of discoverers and
inventors who were never satisfied to leave things as they were
but remade the world in every generation, or are they an old
nation now of protectors and preservers whose passion is to keep
things as they used to be? Are they still the young champions of
freedom in the west who warned the Holy Alliance to leave the
fires of revolutionary freedom alone to burn as they might on
this continent, or have they joined those who put the fires out?

The old words of freedom and revolution are still around,

louder than ever, but somehow they are not the same. Revolution, which was once a word spoken with pride by every American who had the right to claim it, has become a word spoken with timidity and doubt and even loathing. And freedom which, in the old days, was something you *used* has now become something you *save* — something you put away and protect like your other possessions — like a deed or a bond in a bank. The true test of freedom is in its *use*. It has no other test. But freedom in this sick and melancholy time of ours has become, not a thing to use, but a thing to defend.

Even the word American has changed. The American once was a man bound to his country and his fellows by a common belief in something, not yet realized, that he loved. Now he is a man — or there are those who tell him he is a man — bound to his country and the rest by a common hatred of something looming that he fears.

What has been happening to the people of the United States in the last few years is something that can destroy the inward vitality of the nation if we let it go on. It is possible for writers of a certain journalistic mentality to look at the change and rejoice in it as proof that we have grown up as a country, that we have faced the harsh realities of life at last and that we have now become a great power. But a people which recognizes its unity only in its opposition to another people, which understands its purpose only in its resistance to another purpose, is not a people which has a unity or a purpose of its own. And it is not a great people whatever its power or its wealth. The great nations in the history of the world have been the nations which proposed, the nations which asserted, the nations which conceived. The United States was such a nation when it knew its mind and declared its belief and acted to create the world it wanted.

From the American point of view, then, the severest indictment of this generation of men and women will be the charge that we falsified the American image and thus undermined the spiritual integrity of the nation. But there will be other accusations from other quarters and some of them will be even harsher than our own. There will be the judgment of the men of conscience and concern and honest mind in every country who, when all the arguments are in, write down the verdicts. And what they will say of us will certainly be this: that we had it in our power at a critical moment in history, when the whole future of humanity hung in balance, to present a true and hopeful alternative to the iron choice with which the world was faced and that we did not do it; that we did not do it even though the true alternative was the course to which our whole past and our entire tradition had committed us; that instead of doing it we built a wall against one half the evil but not against the other, and made the wall still higher by tearing down for its construction some of the dearest of our own beliefs.

It will be difficult for us to answer that charge in whatever tribunal of the future such verdicts are debated. We can argue with great conviction that we had no choice, in the face of Russian threats of force and Russian conspiracies of fraud, but to arm ourselves and to resist. And it is true that we had no choice. But it is true also — and no one who remembers what has been said in the American press and the American Senate, in these days, can deny that it is true — that our policy in this situation was not merely to put ourselves in a position to resist and then go on about our American purpose: on the contrary our purpose and our policy *became* resistance.

Resistance to the Russians became an end and object in itself. And the result was a declaration of political bankruptcy such as few great nations in the course of history have ever confessed to. When Senators, urging recognition and aid for Franco, argued that that enemy of everything this republic is or has ever stood for deserved our friendship because he had fought the Communists and Russia, they said in effect that what we believe in is nothing, but what we hate is the gateway to our minds.

No one in his senses denies that Russian fraud, Russian lies, Russian militarism, Russian imperialism, Russian stupidity and fanaticism and greed left us no choice but to rearm. But no one in his senses can deny either that we made of this necessity the excuse for a failure to achieve a policy of our own. That failure may well turn out to have been the costliest blunder in our history.

What needed to be done in the years immediately following the second war is obvious even now. What needed to be done both for the purposes of peace and for the hope of human life was to break the impotent and issueless deadlock, the total spiritual impasse, between the two authoritarianisms of right and left by declaring, as alternative to them both, a free man's solution of the problems of this time. To the shrill bat voices of those who cry out from the direction of Franco's Spain on the one side and Stalin's Moscow on the other that the world has no choice but to choose between them, and that peace between them is impossible — to these shrill and cynical and brutal voices there should have been a man's voice answering, like Ulysses' above Hell's offering of blood, to tell them both they lied.

The answer to the "inevitable choice" between the authoritarianisms with their heartless promise of a bigoted and bloody war is the answer implicit in the American proposition. The answer is that there is also another choice: a man's choice: one man's choice. What was needed was to *make* this answer. What was needed was to declare, with the full and reasoned conviction of a great people, that there was still a man's way out of the wreck of our disasters; that the revolution of the individual, far from being finished, had not yet begun; that the words of that revolution were not merely words but meanings also; that the meanings could be given and could be understood. *What was needed was a redeclaration of the revolution of the individual in terms which would have realistic meaning in this time.* Only one nation in the world was capable of that act and the nation was our own. And we did nothing. We built walls.

It will not be possible for us to argue, when the finger of time is leveled against us, that we did not see what needed to be done. The wisest and soberest and most realistic statesman of our generation warned us three years ago that the job we had to do — the job we had to do whether there were Communists around or not — was to make freedom a reality in the post-war world; and Henry L. Stimson did not speak alone.

Neither will it be possible for us to plead that there was nothing we could *do* — nothing we could do as a people: that a people cannot think itself through problems such as these: that the labor of redefining, of implementing, the revolution of the individual in a modern industrial society is a labor of such difficulty that only the technicians of industry and politics can accomplish it: that to ask an entire nation, but an act of choice, an act of will, to make freedom a reality under the conditions of contemporary life is to talk in rhetoric, not reason. It is true of course that the labor is difficult; nothing more so. It is true that it will require much technical skill, political, industrial, mechanical, and economic. But it is not true that it is the technical difficulty that stands in the way. What really stands in the way is the moral difficulty, the difficulty of choice, the difficulty which only the people, acting as a people, can remove.

No intelligent man believes that technical difficulties are insurmountable — and least of all in a country of great natural wealth, a high level of administrative and technological intelligence, and large reserves of skilled labor. If the people of such a country were determined to hammer out a political and industrial and economic order in which individual men — all men as individuals — should be capable of living and working in dignity and freedom and self-respect with an adequate opportunity for the realization of their full potentialities as human beings the thing could be done. It makes a great deal of difference, as Bishop Berkeley observed, whether you put truth in the first place or in the second. It makes a great deal of difference whether you say that your objective is a free society but that you wish first to be safe, or first to be comfortable or first to be something else, or whether you say that *your objective is a free society*.

Certainly the political problems, difficult and delicate though they may be, are not insoluble. Some, like the control or the liquidation of monopolies which stand in the way of individual initiative, have a long history in this country. Others, like the struggle to liberate individuals from the degrading fear of racial discrimination or unemployment or old age or sickness, are less familiar — at least in the United States. Still others, like the overriding question of the relation between individual freedom and the intervention of the state, have a meaning for our generation which they did not have for generations before. But only a man who did not wish to find an answer to questions such as these would argue that no answer can be found.

And what is true of the political difficulties is true also of the industrial. Even the greatest of the industrial obstacles to individual freedom — the mechanization of the machine-worker — could be removed if the freedom of the individual became the first business of society. There is no lack of mechanical inventiveness, as the proliferation of new machines and new machine methods demonstrates. Unwanted gadgets are produced with the most astonishing originality and brilliance. Machines and methods which would restore to the men who work them a measure of their former manhood, their former mastery, could be developed with equal skill if industry were determined to discover and produce them.

No, it is not the technical problem requiring special knowledge and unusual skill which stands in the way of the great alternative of freedom. It is not the failure of the engineers or the economists or the political philosophers to devise the new form of a free society which has robbed us of our initiative as a people. We cannot excuse or justify ourselves by complaining that no one has told us what to do. The real obstacle is the obstacle of ends, not means. The real obstacle is the obstacle of will, not method. Those who follow us and observe our failures will say we did not wish sufficiently for freedom. And what they say will be true.

Freedom — individual freedom — is always a hard choice. With us, in a world in which the old established order, weakened by the earthquakes of four centuries, has all but collapsed, it has become a choice which many men find it impossible to make. For to choose individual freedom now is to choose, not a common struggle aginst the masters of an ordered world, but a lonely journey, each man for himself, across the ruin and the rubble which that world has left. To choose the revolution of the individual now is to choose not revolutionary armies and open battles but singleness and duty in a broken world.

It is not remarkable, therefore, that many of those of our generation who should have been champions of the revolution of the individual — poets, writers, men whose first necessity is freedom — have been unable to accept the burden: have turned back instead to one or the other of the authoritarianisms where they can stretch the painted canvas tent of dogma between them and the empty sky where once the roofs were. But though it is possible to understand why many of the best have left us, and why great numbers of the American people have given up the lonely pursuit of liberty for the safer assurance of discipline and peace, it is not possible for that reason to forgive their desertion, or to justify it, or to forget that it is through them and their default that the world has lost the great and positive affirmation it so desperately needed.

We are at that point in our moral history as a people at which we have failed, for the first time in a moment of decision, to assert our moral purpose. We have not yet denied that purpose but we have failed to assert it. We have not yet changed the direction of our national life but we have lost our momentum, we have lost our initiative. We have not yet rejected our role as a revolutionary people moving with the great revolutionary current of history but we have ceased to move, we have begun to resist, to oppose. It does not require a prophet to see that we have come to a moment of critical decision — a decision which is none the less critical because it may be taken unaware.

If we do nothing, if we continue to stand where the Forties have left us, we will have taken one decision, we will have ceased to be what we were and we will inevitably become something else, something very different, something the founders of the republic would not recognize and surely would not love. Only by action, only by moral action, only by moral action at the highest level — only by affirmative recommitment to the revolution of the individual which was the vital and creative impulse of our national life at the beginning of our history — only by these means can we regain ourselves.

"National Purpose"

1960

THAT something has gone wrong in America most of us know. We are richer than any nation before us. We have more Things in our garages and kitchens and cellars than Louis Quatorze had in the whole of Versailles. We have come nearer to the suppression of grinding poverty than even the Utopians thought seriously possible. We have wiped out many of the pests and scourges which afflicted humanity. We have lengthened men's lives and protected their infancy. We have advanced science to the edges of the inexplicable and hoisted our technology to the moon itself. We are in a state of growth and flux and change in which cities flow out into countryside and countryside moves into cities and new industries are born and old industries vanish and the customs of generations alter and fathers speak different languages from their sons. In brief, we are prosperous, lively, successful, inventive, diligent — but nevertheless and notwithstanding, something is wrong and we know it.

The trouble seems to be that we don't feel right with ourselves or with the country. We have lost our way in the woods. We don't know where we are going as a people. We have even set up a public commission to discover our national purpose and have begun to discuss the problem in articles such as this. All of which is peculiar since we have, of course, the most precisely articulated statement of national policy ever adopted by any people in the whole of human history. It is the purpose put into words by the most lucid mind of that most lucid century, the eighteenth, and adopted on the Fourth of July in 1776 as a declaration of the existence and national intent of a new nation.

Not only is it a famous statement of purpose: it is also an admirable statement of purpose. Prior to July 4, 1776, the national purpose of nations had been to dominate: to dominate at least their neighbors and their rivals and, wherever possible, to dominate the world. The American national purpose was the opposite: to liberate from domination; to set men free. *All* men, to Thomas Jefferson, were created equal. *All* men were endowed by their Creator with certain inalienable rights. Among these rights were life, liberty and the pursuit of happiness. It was the existence of these rights which justified American independence from King George and justified also the revolution which would have to be fought for that independence. It was the existence of these rights which would provide a foundation for the government to be established when independence was secure.

We not only *have* a national purpose: we have one of such aspiration, such potentiality, such power of hope that we refer to it — or used to — as the American Dream. We were dedicated from our beginnings to the proposition that we existed not merely to exist but to be free, and the dedication was real in spite of the fact that it took us three generations and a bloody war to practice our preachment within our own frontiers. It was real in spite of the fact that its practice is still a delusion.

To be free is not, perhaps, a political program in the modern

sense, but from the point of view of a new nation it may be something better. The weakness of political programs — Five Year
Plans and the like — is that they can be achieved. But human
freedom can never be achieved because human freedom is a con-
tinuously evolving condition. It is infinite in its possibilities —
as infinite as the human soul which it enfranchises. The nation
which seeks it and persists in its search will move through history
as a ship moves on a compass course toward a constantly opening horizon.

And America did move steadily on before it lost headway in
the generation in which we live. The extraordinary feel of live-
ness which the Americans communicated, whether agreeably or
not, to their early European visitors came from that sense of national expectation. We were never a very philosophical people
politically after Jefferson and his contemporaries left us. We
were practical men who took instruction from the things we saw
and heard and did. But the purpose defined in our Declaration
was a reality to us notwithstanding. It gave us *aim* as the continent gave us *scope*, and the old American character with its almost anarchic passion for idiosyncrasy and difference was the
child of both. Those Missouri militiamen Francis Parkman describes in *The Oregon Trail* slogging west to the war with Mex-
ico, each in his own rig and each in his own way, could have con-
stituted an army nowhere else. When, at Sacramento, a drunken
officer commanded his company to halt and a private yelled
"Charge!" the company charged, knocking five times their number of Mexicans out of prepared entrenchments. The anarchy
didn't matter because they were all headed in the same direction
and the name of that direction was West — or freedom. They
had a future in common and they had a purpose in common and

the purpose was the enfranchisement of men — of all men — to think for themselves, speak for themselves, govern themselves, pursue happiness for themselves and so become themselves.

Why then do we need to rediscover what our national purpose is? Because the words of the Declaration in its superb housing in the National Archives have become archival words, words out of history? Because the Bill of Rights of the American Constitution belongs, like the Magna Carta, in an airtight case? No one who reads the newspapers could think so. There has never been a time when courts and Congress devoted more of their attention to the constitutional guarantees of individual freedom than they do today, and as for the Declaration of Independence, its language is more alive in the middle of the twentieth century than it was even when it was written. It is not Communism, however Communism may attempt to exploit them, which has begotten the new nations of Asia and Africa or the new nationalistic stirrings in South America and the Caribbean and even in Europe. The Marxist dream is a dream of economic machinery, not of living men: of a universal order and system, not a proliferation of nationalities. No, the dream which has set the jungle and the cane on fire is different and older. It is Thomas Jefferson's dream — the dream which he and his contemporaries believed would change the world. It *is* changing the world — and not later than one might expect. Two hundred years is a short time in the history of dreams.

If the American Dream is out of date today it is out of date only in America — only in America and in the Communist countries in which the political police have extinguished it. But is it really out of date in America? Is its power to direct and draw us really so faint that we are lost in the blaze of our own prosperity and must enlist the aid of learned men to tell us where the future lies?

Have we lost our sense of purpose or have we merely lost touch with it? Have we rejected the arduous labor to which our beginnings committed us? Or are we merely confused and bewildered by the volcanic upheavals which have changed the landscapes of our lives? Or is it neither rejection nor confusion? Is it nothing more than the flatulence and fat of an overfed people whose children prepare at the milk-shake counter for coronary occlusions in middle age? Are we simply too thick through the middle to dream?

I doubt for myself that we have rejected the American Dream or have even thought of rejecting it. There are minorities, of course, who have little enthusiasm for the actualities of the American commitment to freedom, but this is largely because they do not understand what the struggle it culminated was all about. Certain areas on the fringes of Europe were preserved by their geographical location from the necessity of living through the crisis of the Western mind which we call the Reformation, and American stock from these areas tends to find the master-mistress idea of the American Revolution — the idea which raised it from a minor war for independence to a world event — incomprehensible if not actually misguided. It is not a question of religion. Catholics from the heart of the European continent understand Jefferson as well as any Protestant. It is a question of geography. Men and women whose ancestors were not obliged to fight the battle for or against freedom of conscience cannot for the life of them understand why censorship should be considered evil or why authority is not preferable to freedom.

But all this does not add up to a rejection of the American dedi-

cation to liberty — the American dedication to the enfranchisement of the human spirit. The Irish Catholics, who are among
the most persistent and politically powerful advocates of increasing censorship in the U.S., and who are brought up to submit
to clerical authority in matters which the American tradition
reserves to the individual conscience, are nevertheless among the
most fervent of American patriots. And if their enthusiasm for
freedom of the mind is restrained, their passion for freedom of
the man is glorious. Only if a separate system of education should
be used to perpetuate the historical ignorance and moral obtuse-
ness on which fear of freedom of the mind is based would the
danger of the rejection of the American Dream from this quarter become serious. As for the rest, the only wholehearted rejection comes from the Marxists with their curiously childish notion that it is more realistic and more intelligent to talk about economic machinery than about men. But the Marxists, both Mr.
Hoovers to the contrary notwithstanding, have no perceptible
influence on American opinion.

I cannot believe that we have *rejected* the purpose on which
our Republic was founded. Neither can I believe that our present purposelessness results from our economic fat and our spiritual indolence. It is not because we are too comfotable that the
dream has left us. It is true, I suppose, that we eat better — at
least more — than any nation ever has. It is true too that there
are streaks of American fat, some of it very ugly fat, and that it
shows most unbecomingly at certain points in New York and
Miami and along the California coast. But the whole country
is not lost in a sluggish, sun-oiled sleep beneath a beach umbrella,
dreaming of More and More. We have our share, and more than
our share, of mink coats and prestige cars and expense account

restaurants and oil millionaires, but America is not made of such as these. We are an affluent society, but not affluent to the point of spiritual sloth.

Most American young women, almost regardless of income, work harder in their homes and with their children than their mothers or their grandmothers had to. For one thing, domestic servants have all but disappeared and no machine can serve a meal or mind a baby. For another there are more babies than there have been for generations. For still another, the rising generation is better educated than its parents were and more concerned with the serious business of life — the life of the mind. To watch your daughter-in-law taking care of her own house, bringing up four children, running the Parent-Teacher Association, singing in the church choir and finding time nevertheless to read the books she wants to read and hear the music she wants to hear and see the plays she can afford to, is a salutary thing. She may think more about machines and gadgets than you ever did but that is largely because there are more machines and gadgets to think about.

No one who has taught, as I have been doing for the past few years, can very seriously doubt that the generation on the way up is more intelligent than the generation now falling back. And as for the materialism about which we talk so much, it is worth remembering that the popular whipping boy of the moment among the intelligent young is precisely "Madison Avenue," that mythical advertising copy writer who is supposed to persuade us to wallow in cosmetics and tail-fin cars. We may be drowning in Things, but the best of our sons and daughters like it even less than we do.

What then has gone wrong? The answer, I submit, is fairly

obvious and will be found where one would expect to find it: in
the two great wars which have changed so much beside. The first
world war altered not only our position in the world but our attitude toward ourselves and toward our business as a people.
Having won a war to "make the world safe for democracy,"
we began to act as though democracy itself had been won — as
though there was nothing left for us to do but enjoy ourselves:
make money in the stock market, gin in the bathtub and whoopee
in the streets. The American journey had been completed. The
American goal was reached. We had emerged from the long
trek westward to find ourselves on the Plateau of Permanent
Prosperity. We were *there!* It took the disaster of 1929
and the long depression which followed to knock that fantasy
out of our heads, but the damage had been done. We had lost
touch with the driving force of our own history.

The effect of the second war was different — and the same.
The second war estranged us from our genius as a people. We
fought it because we realized that our dream of human liberty
could not survive in the slave state Hitler was imposing on the
world. We won it with no such illusions as had plagued us twenty-five years before: there was another slave state behind the one
we had detested. But though we did not repeat the folly of the
Twenties we repeated the delusion of the Twenties. We acted
again as though freedom were an accomplished fact. We no
longer thought of it as safe but we made a comparable mistake:
we thought of it as something which could be protected by building walls around it to contain its enemy.

But the truth is, of course, that freedom is never an accomplished fact. It is always a process. Which is why the drafters of
the Declaration spoke of the *pursuit* of happiness: they knew
their Thucydides and therefore knew that "the secret of happi-

ness is freedom and the secret of freedom, courage." The only way freedom can be defended is not by fencing it in but by enlarging it, exercising it. Though we did defend freedom by exercising it through the Marshall Plan in Europe, we did not, for understandable reasons involving the colonial holdings of our allies, defend freedom by exercising it in Asia and Africa where the future is about to be decided.

The results have been hurtful to the world and to ourselves. How hurtful they have been to the world we can see in Cuba where a needed and necessary and hopeful revolution against an insufferable dictatorship has chosen the Russian solution of its economic difficulties rather than ours. We have tried to explain that ominous fact to ourselves in the schoolgirl vocabulary of the McCarthy years, but not even those who see Communist conspiracies underneath everyone else's bed have contended that the Cuban people were tricked or policed into their enthusiasm for their revolution. On the contrary the people appear to have outrun the government in their eagerness for the new order. What this means is obvious. What this means is that the wave of the future, to the great majority of Cubans, is the Russian wave, not the American. That fact, and its implications for the rest of Latin America, to say nothing of Africa and Asia, is the fact we should be looking at, hard and long. If the Russian purpose seems more vigorous and more promising to the newly liberated peoples of the world than the American purpose, then we have indeed lost the "battle for men's minds" of which we talk so much.

As for ourselves, the hurt has been precisely the loss of a sense of national purpose. To engage, as we have over the past fifteen years, in programs having as their end and aim not action to further a purpose of our own but *counter*action to frustrate a purpose of the Russians is to invite just such a state of mind. A nation cannot be sure even of its own identity when it lives its history in a mirror.

What, then, is the issue in this debate? What is the problem? Not to *discover* our national purpose but to *exercise* it. Which means, ultimately, to exercise it for its own sake, not for the defeat of those who have a different purpose. There is a vast difference between strengthening the enemies of our enemies because they are against what we are against, and supporting the hopes of mankind because we too believe in them, because they are our hopes also. The fields of action in the two cases may be the same: Africa and Asia and Latin America. The tools of action —military assistance and above all economic and industrial and scientific aid — may look alike. But the actions will be wholly different. The first course of action surrenders initiative to the Russians and accepts the Russian hypothesis that Communism is the new force moving in the world. The second asserts what is palpably true, that the new force moving in the world is the force we set in motion, the force which gave us, almost two centuries ago, our liberating mission. The first is costly. The second will be more costly still. But the second, because it recaptures for the cause of freedom the initiative which belongs to it and restores to the country the confidence it has lost, is capable of succeeding. The first, because it can never be anything but a policy of resistance, can only continue to resist and to accomplish nothing more.

There are those, I know, who will reply that the liberation of humanity, the freedom of man and mind, is nothing but a dream. They are right. It is the American Dream.

The Unimagined America

1943

THE WHOLE HISTORY of our continent is a history of the imagination. Men imagined land beyond the sea and found it. No force of terror, no pressure of population, drove our ancestors across this continent. They came, as the great explorers crossed the Atlantic, because of the imagination of their minds — because they imagined a better, a more beautiful, a freer, happier world; because they were men not only of courage, not only of strength and hardiness, but of warm and vivid desire; because they desired; because they had the power to desire.

And what was true of the continent was true of the Republic. Because our forefathers were able to conceive a free man's government, they were able to create it. Because those who lived before us in this nation were able to imagine a new thing, a thing unheard of in the world before, a thing the skeptical and tired men who did not trust in dreams had not been able to imagine, they erected on this continent the first society in which mankind was to be free, all mankind.

The courage of the Declaration of Independence is a far greater courage than the bravery of those who risked their necks to sign it. The courage of the Declaration of Independence is the courage of the act of the imagination. Jefferson's document is an image of a life, a plan of life, a dream — indeed a dream.

But our right to live as we imagine men should live is not a right drawn from dreaming only. We have, and know we have, the abundant means to bring our dreams to pass — to create for ourselves whatever world we have the courage to desire. We have the metal and the men to take this country down, if we please to take it down, and to build it again as we please to build it. We have the tools and the skill and the intelligence to take our cities apart and to put them together, to lead our roads and rivers where we please to lead them, to build our houses where we want our houses, to brighten the air, to clean the wind, to live as men in this Republic, free men, should be living. We have the power and the courage and the resources of goodwill and decency and common understanding — a long experience of decency and common understanding — to enable us to live, not in this continent alone but in the world, as citizens in common of the world, with many others.

We have the power and the courage and the resources of experience to create a nation such as men have never seen. And, more than that, we have the moment of creation in our hands. Our forefathers, when they came to the New England valleys or the Appalachian meadows, girdled the trees and dragged the roots into fences and built themselves shelters and, so roughly sheltered, farmed the land for their necessities. Then, later, when there were means to do it, when there was time, when the occasion offered, they burned the tangled roots and rebuilt their fences and their houses — but rebuilt them with a difference: rebuilt them as villages, as neighborhoods; rebuilt them with those lovely streets, those schools, those churches which still speak of their conception of the world they wanted. When the means offered, when the time offered, men created, on the clearings of the early useful farms, the towns that made New England and the Alleghenies.

Now is the time for the re-creation, the rebuilding, not of the villages and towns but of a nation. Our necessities have been accomplished as men have always accomplished their necessities — with wastefulness, with ugliness, with cruelty, as well as with the food of harvests. Our necessities have been accomplished with the roots of the broken trees along the fences, the rough shelters, the lonely lives. Now is the time to build the continent itself — to take down and to rebuild; and not the houses and the cities only, but the life itself, raising upon the ready land the brotherhood that can employ it and delight in it and use it as a people such as ours should use it.

We stand at the moment of the building of great lives, for the war's end and our victory in the war will throw that moment and the means before us. But to seize the moment and the means we must agree to seize them: we must recognize the task we have to do. And we have not recognized it. When we speak of our destiny today, we speak still in terms of the agricultural and sparsely settled nation Thomas Jefferson and his contemporaries had in mind. The ideal landscape of America which Jefferson painted hangs unaltered in the American imagination — a clean, small landscape with its isolated figures, its pleasant barns, its self-reliant rooftrees, its horizons clear of the smoke and the fumes of cities, its air still, its frontiers protected by month-wide oceans, year-wide wildernesses. No later hand has touched it, except Lincoln's maybe, deepening the shadow, widening the sky, broadening the acreage in the name of freedom, giving the parts a wholeness that in brighter, sharper light they lacked. For fifty years and longer it has been a landscape of a world no man living could expect to see, a landscape no American could bring to being, a dream — but of the past, and not the future.

And yet we keep this image in our minds. This, and not the world beyond us, is the world we turn to: the lost, nostalgic image of a world that was the future to a generation dead a hundred years. No other image has been made to take its place. No one has dreamed a new American dream of the new America — the industrial nation of the huge machines, the limitless earth, the vast and skillful population, the mountains of copper and iron, the mile-long plants, the delicate laboratories, the tremendous dams. No one has imagined this America — what its life should be; what life it should lead with its great wealth and the tools in its hands and the men to employ them.

The plants and the factories and their products have been celebrated often enough — perhaps too often. The statistics have been added up. The camera has held its mirror to the great machines. But the central question we have yet to ask. What are they *for*, these plants and products, these statistics? *What are they for in terms of a nation of men* — in Jefferson's terms?

.

There are men who believe there is no answer. There are men, and among the wisest of our time, who do not believe that an image of this new America can be conceived — who do not believe in a world of plenty; do not believe in it with their hearts whatever their senses tell them; do not believe that the lives of men can be good lives in the industrialized society which alone makes plenty possible.

Judge Learned Hand spoke not for Mr. Justice Brandeis alone, but for many others, when he summarized the Justice's position as resting on the strong belief that "most of our positive ills have directly resulted from great size. With it has indeed come the magic of modern communication and quick transport; but out of these has come the sinister apparatus of mass suggestion and mass production. . . . The herd is regaining its ancient and evil primacy. . . . These many inventions are a step backward . . . our security has actually diminished as our demands have become more exacting: our comforts we purchase at the cost of a softer fiber, a feebler will, and an infantile suggestibility."

And in the concluding sentences of his noble tribute to the great Justice, Judge Hand used words which many of the best of his contemporaries would speak after him without the alteration of a syllable: "You may build your Towers of Babel to the clouds; you may contrive ingeniously to circumvent Nature by devices beyond even the understanding of all but a handful; you may provide endless distractions to escape the tedium of your barren lives; you may rummage the whole planet for your ease and comfort. It shall avail you nothing; the more you struggle the more deeply you will be enmeshed."

They are eloquent words and noble words. They respond to a strong strain in the American character. But are they necessarily and inevitably true? Is it inevitable that men who contrive ingeniously to circumvent nature should live tedious and barren lives and fall into the fatness of the spirit we, as well as Justice Brandeis, have seen and hated? Is it inconceivable that men should achieve a life with the machines as disciplined and honorable and as free as the life that Jefferson believed they could achieve with mules and oxen? Is it certain that the human spirit

can survive and flourish only in a world where need and hardship
drive with stinging whips?

Is the fault with the machines or with ourselves? Is it because
we have automobiles to ride in, because we can purchase certain
commodities easily, because our presses can turn out tons of
printed paper in a day, that our fiber is soft, our will feeble, our
suggestibility infantile? Or is it because we do not use these
things as we should use them — because we have not made them
serve our moral purpose as a people, but only our private comfort?

Is the whole question indeed not a question of ourselves instead of our devices? Is it not for us to *say* how these devices,
these inventions, should be used? Does their use not rest upon
the purpose of their use? And does the purpose not depend
upon our power to conceive the purpose — our power as a people to conceive the purpose of the tools we use; our power as a
people to conceive and to imagine?

A hundred and fifty years ago de Crèvecoeur asked a famous
question which has echoes now: "What then is the American,
this new man?" But what then *is* he? What then is he now? A
man incapable of the act of the imagination, or a man to whom
it is native and natural? A man to dare the dream of plenty with
all its risks and dangers, or a man to hold to the old nostalgic landscape with the simple virtues safely forced upon him by the necessary self-denial?

A man who has the courage — or the foolishness perhaps —
to think a nation may have physical abundance and still retain,
or still not lose, its soul? Or a man to accept the shamefaced verdict of the twenty years just past and return to the discipline
of want and hunger?

A man who has the hardihood or the courage to believe that
the machines which have enslaved his fathers will make his
children free — free as no human beings in the world have yet
known freedom; free of the twisting miseries and hungers;
free to become themselves? Or a man to reject the hope of
that enfranchised freedom and to seek his independence in the
ancient narrow circle of his old dependence on himself?

Which of these two men is the American? A while ago we
should have said the American character was self-evident: a restless man, a great builder and maker and shaper, a man delighting
in size and height and dimensions — the world's tallest, the
town's biggest. A man never satisfied — never — with anything:
his house or the town where his grandfather settled or his father's profession or even his own, for that matter. An inveterate
voyager and changer and finder. A man naturally hopeful; a
believing man, believing that things progress, that things get for-
warder. A skillful man with contraptions of one kind and another — machines, engines, various devices: familiar with all of
them. A man of certain unquestioned convictions — of a strong,
natural attachment to certain ideas and to certain ideals. But
first of all and foremost of all a restless man and a believing man,
a builder and changer of things and of nations.

We should have said, a generation back, there was no possible
doubt or question of the will and power of this nation to pro-
pose the kind of future for itself which would employ the means
of plenty for a human purpose. We should have said the principal characteristic of the American people was a confidence in the
future and themselves — confidence that the future was the
thing they'd make it. I cannot think, for myself, we have so
changed that we do not believe this now. I cannot believe we

are so changed that we will let ourselves go with the drag and the current of history — that we will let the future happen to us as the future happens to chips on a river or sheep in a blizzard. I cannot believe we have so changed that we do not believe in ourselves and the future.

And yet we have not done what must be done if we believe the future is the thing we'll make it. We have not named that future.

And the time is short.

A View of Oxford,
Mississippi

1963

MOST THINGS, public things, happen and go by and you forget about them, but not the Mississippi riots. Not for me, anyway, and I don't suppose I'm alone. There must be other Americans who find those faces in their minds as I do — flickering, twisted faces on long gone television screens and still there, still staring. You wonder why.

Not, I'm pretty sure, for the usual reason, the reason we've decided to give ourselves: not because we were shocked by the open defiance of the law. Southern segregationists, including Southern segregationist lawyers, including Southern segregationist lawyers who have actually read law, have been shouting defiance of the law for years, declaring that the Congress is the sole lawmaking body under the Constitution, that what the Congress means by its laws is for every citizen to decide for himself according to his locality and his inclination, and that the interpretations of the laws by the federal courts in general, and by the Supreme Court in particular, are irrelevant, impertinent, and immaterial, *Marbury v. Madison* and its innumerable successors to the contrary notwithstanding.

I am not suggesting that anyone outside the foggier bayous of

Alabama or Louisiana or South Carolina or Mississippi has taken these contentions seriously. I am merely noting that we had heard them before the Oxford riots as we had heard, too, that the doctrine of nullification is still sound doctrine, that John C. Calhoun is the father and fountain of pure constitutional thought, and that the Civil War has been repealed. What was said in Jackson, in other words, and shouted at Oxford was not new and could scarcely have astonished us. Most of it, indeed, went back a hundred years or more. An anonymous professor at the University of Mississippi told the New York *Times* that "sources of information on the thinking of the rest of the nation were shut off" in that state in 1830, at which time "the state's leaders ceased to react to public issues in terms of established fact but were governed instead by the orthodox view," and, in brief, "stopped thinking."

The date may surprise us. It is difficult — or is it? — to think of Faulkner, who spent his life in Mississippi, writing out of a deepfreeze a century old. But the argument itself sounds plausible. A state in which a decision of the highest American court can seriously be called a "Communist conspiracy" must necessarily be a state which has been out of touch with history for a rather long time. And a local mentality which can actually read, to say nothing of write, pronouncements like those which appeared in the *Clarion Leader and Jackson Daily News* at the time of the riots is obviously a mentality which only the Boston fudge manufacturer who invented the John Birch Society could regard as in any sense contemporaneous.

The same thing may be said of the violence which pronouncements such as these excited. That, too, should have been foreseen. Elsewhere in the Republic one might be surprised to find a

governor who approved the lawlessness he was sworn to suppress, but not in Mississippi, where there were two kinds of law.
And elsewhere one might be shocked by state police officers who
deserted federal officials in a situation of obvious and increasing
danger, but not in Mississippi, where federal officials and state
policemen are on opposite sides. Once an entire state has se-
ceded from history — which is, in a sense, to secede from reason — almost anything can happen. Even Governor Ross Barnett. Even the sudden and inexplicable timidity of Ross Barnett's
state police.

But if the governor of Mississippi was foreseeable in the light
of his history or lack of it, and if the defiance was familiar, what
was it that astonished us in Oxford? Why were we shocked
into silence by that Sunday's news? Why did we spend the days
and nights that followed fiddling with our television sets, watching the faces of little crowds of students on the university cam-
pus, following the slight, grave figure of the man who was the
center of it all as he moved in and out of doors and corridors with
federal marshals at his side and jeers and spitting catcalls in his
ears? Why is it that those scenes come back and back and the
heart sinks and a heavy apprehension haunts our minds, an apprehension which was not there before — was never, as long as
I can remember, there before?

I think, for myself, what shocked me, sickened me, was the
black pit of public hatred into which I looked. I had known, of
course, that racial hatred existed in this country as it exists elsewhere. I could hardly have helped but know it after the events
of my own lifetime. But, whether because of the kind of life I
have lived or because of some failure of my own understanding,
I had always thought of this hatred as something exceptional,

something transient, something which would disappear with the illiteracy and poverty and ignorance out of which it came.

I knew, of course, that there were presumably educated and visibly well-to-do men and women in the South and elsewhere who looked down on Negroes, because I had met such men and women. I knew there were college graduates with enough intelligence to write books who believed, or said they believed, that all Negroes are biologically inferior to all whites. I realized there were people who called themselves Christians who *knew* that God intended the black man to be a hewer of wood and a drawer of water to the white man, any white man of any qualifications or none — particularly none. But I also believed these people to be what they so obviously were — waifs and strays from the great process of history who needed to find somebody or other to look down on in order to look up to themselves. And I never doubted that in an actual test between these petulant opinions on the one side and the Republic on the other the opinions would wither away in shame and disappear. But what happened in Oxford was that they did not wither away. They stared back at you out of young men's faces ugly with spite. They spat back at you out of the faces of middle-aged men whose words would have been incredible if you had not heard them. And it was the Republic which gave ground. In spite of the decisiveness of the President and the courage of the marshals, it was the Republic which gave ground.

For the real confrontation in Mississippi was not a confrontation between federal marshals and a mob. It was not a confrontation between the President of the United States and the local governor. It was not even a confrontation between the Constitution and the doctrine of nullification. It was a confrontation between the Republic itself, the great idea on which the Republic is founded, and the one idea which may, someday, destroy it.

"All politics," as Valèry once said, "presuppose an idea of man." But only the United States, among the nations of history, was brought into being by an explicit and reasoned idea of man to which it was dedicated and on which it was to stand. It is not the second of July, 1776, when the thirteen colonies declared themselves absolved of all allegiance to the British crown, which we celebrate as our national anniversary. It is the fourth day of July. It is the fourth day of July because America, as the delegates to the Continental Congress well understood, did not begin with the repudiation of British rule. It began with the assertion of the American idea. And it was on the fourth that the American idea was spelled out. At the beginning of the Revolution and down through the first bloodshed at Lexington and Concord there had been no talk of independence and no desire for it. What the Colonists wanted was *British* liberty in America. Only when the Tory ministers made it clear that there would be no British liberty in America — that liberty, if the Colonists were to have it, must be American liberty — did independence become a national objective, and even then independence was a means rather than an end. Liberty was still the prime concern, and until American liberty was defined, a new liberty for a new people in a new world, America had not begun.

It was for no sentimental or idealistic reason, in other words, that the old fathers celebrated the American festival not on the anniversary of American independence but on the anniversary of the declaration of the American idea. For the American idea, quite literally and realistically, *is* America. If we had not held these truths to be self-evident, if we had not believed that all men are created equal, if we had not believed that they are endowed, all of them, with certain unalienable rights, we would never have become America, whatever else we might have become.

But if this is what America is, then it is less difficult perhaps to understand why Oxford shocked us, for what looked out of those flickering faces was the antithesis of America — the passionate repudiation of the American proposition, and thus the implicit rejection of America itself. What we saw in those faces, heard in those words, was not hatred of James Meredith. Not a single student in the University of Mississippi had ever seen James Meredith to know him as a human being before that night. Not a single member of the mob could have told you what he looked like. He was a Negro, and that was enough. But to hate a man because he is a Negro is to hate an abstraction. And to hate an abstraction is to hate an idea. And to hate the particular idea the mob at Oxford hated is to deny America. For the idea those young men and those old men hated was precisely and literally the idea on which this Republic was founded, the idea that any man may claim his equal manhood in this country, his unalienable right. What the mob at Oxford hated was the intolerable idea that this different human being should claim a manhood equal to their own.

Insurrection, a congressman called the Oxford riots. And insurrection they were in the strict legal sense of that term — a revolt against lawful authority. But to those who still love this Republic they were far worse than insurrection; they were subversion. And not subversion in the current witch-hunting sense, which sniffs with terror at every dissenting view, but subversion in the honest meaning of that word — subversion of the country itself. For America cannot survive if the American idea is repudiated. Nations are not made by territory. Nations are made by commitments of mind and loyalties of heart, and the nobler the commitment of the mind, the higher the loyalty of the heart, the greater the nation. If the American proposition is no longer the proposition to which the American heart and mind were committed at our beginning, then America is finished, and the only question left is when America will fall.

Not soon, you will say. We survived for the first three generations of our history with slaves and masters, and thereafter we survived for a century with segregation and lynchings and all the rest of it, and as for the American idea, it is not our treatment of Negroes alone which has menaced it. Millions of Americans whose forebears came to the United States in the last century and the beginning of this came from countries where the American idea was strange and outlandish and where even the basic conception of self-government was unknown, with the result that there are pockets of opinion in the country even now in which the right of a citizen to exercise his American privilege — to make up his own mind for himself and say what he thinks — is deprecated; where censorship flourishes. All this, of course, is true. The American idea has had to struggle for survival for close to two hundred years, and not always against lynch mobs and White Citizens Committees.

But there is a great difference between ignorance of the American idea or misconception of it or even indifference to it on the one side, and denial, denunciation of it on the other. The woman who tries to expurgate her local library of books she does not like and to tell her fellow citizens what they may believe or learn regards herself as a good American — usually as a better American than anyone else. But the man who attempts to deprive other men of the equality of manhood to which the American idea entitles them has no illusions about himself or his relation to the American proposition. Hatred comes first with him, and everything else comes after — including his country's laws, his country's order, and his country itself.

No, it was not the openness of the defiance of the law that shocked me. It was the openness of the hatred, the open recklessness as to the effect of the hatred on anything or everything — United States marshals, United States troops, and the fundamental moral and human belief in which and by which the United States exists. Like a tragedy in which the clown prepares the scene, the great American drama of belief in man moved toward collision with the contempt for man which is its opposite. And before the night was over the people of the United States and of the world — but most immediately the people of the United States — had learned that a considerable body of Americans reject, violently reject, the American idea.

It was a sobering realization and one that should continue to be sobering for a long time to come. Before the Oxford riots we had been aware that our actions as a people did not always chime with our words. Our words described us as an open society, a free world, a bulwark of liberty. Our actions sometimes confessed that there were many Americans to whom our society was not open, many Americans to whom our world was not altogether free, many Americans whose liberty had fences around it. But our distress in these contradictions was more embarrassment than anything else. They lost us propaganda battles, and occasionally they made us feel like fools, but we were sure of ourselves notwithstanding — sure of our own integrity and sure, above all, that our hypocrisy was nothing compared with the hypocrisy of the Russians and the Chinese, to whom peace means war, conquest is liberation, and democracy is the police. Oxford changed all that. Oxford was not a mere propaganda victory for our enemies. Oxford was a defeat for ourselves.

A Decent Respect

1965

SOMETHING NEEDS to be said about the position in which the United States has been placed in world opinion by the war in Vietnam and the intervention in the Dominican Republic. The events themselves have been discussed at length by critics and defenders of American policy; their effect on the general attitude toward the United States of the peoples of the world is of equal if not greater importance. In its first public act after independence the American nation acknowledged "a decent respect to the opinions of mankind." The reasons which moved the Continental Congress to adopt that phrase in its famous Declaration are still operative today.

What has happened in Vietnam and Santo Domingo is simply that the conception of America — the conception which has held throughout my lifetime — has changed. I do not say that it has changed everywhere, but it has been altered certainly in the minds of many of our friends in Europe and Latin America, in the official statements of at least one government allied to our own, and in the actions, as well as in the words, of some of our own people, particularly the generation now of college age.

It is not easy to put the change into words. No man knows

precisely what others think of him or of his nation: those in my generation, for example, who fell in love with France in their youth were not in love with the same France that Frenchmen think of. But one thing can be said about the French conception of Americans at that time: whatever else we were we were idealists — and rather fatuous idealists at that. We were their allies, yes, and they liked us for that, though they thought we might have come a little sooner. But we were also a nation given to enormous words and lofty ideas and humanitarian theories. We had Fourteen Points on which we meant to build a League of Nations to save the world and we went up to the front talking about a war to end war — a war to make the world safe for democracy. The French didn't smile — not then at least: too many Americans died with those words in their mouths. But they had their own notion of us and they kept it. We were a young nation and we fought quite well once we got the hang of the fighting, but our thoughts were too large for our mouths; we believed too much in humanity and such abstractions as international justice and international organizations and the possibility of universal peace. It was all in Clemenceau's face as he rode beside Wilson through those yelling crowds.

And twenty-five years later, though much had changed, though the Hitler war was a necessary war to cleanse the earth of an intolerable evil rather than a commercial struggle translated into noble terms, though our part was a greater part, though we led now and no longer followed, the conception was much the same. Again we were a nation that fought well — better perhaps. Again we died — more of us this time, many more. But still we talked in the old way about freedom — Four Freedoms this time — about human decency, about the hope for an enduring peace. And this time, when the war ended, we not only proposed an international organization; we presented a plan already hammered out in preliminary talks with our principal allies, and the plan was adopted. We were still the innocents, the idealists. We even believed, for as long as events would let us, in the good will of those on the other side of the Carpathians who had fought beside us to bring Hitler down.

So that the composite picture somehow endured. It survived Hiroshima, though not unaltered. It was enhanced by the Korean War, where the aggressor was self-confessed and where most of the nations of the United Nations were on our side. It was not harmed — if anything it was helped — by twenty years of the most persistent and abusive propaganda from Moscow and Peking; to indict a nation as an "imperialist aggressor" in a vocabulary in which "liberation" means subjugation and a "people's democracy" is a police state injures it neither in its own nor in its neighbors' eyes — if I may paraphrase Mr. Yeats.

I do not mean to suggest that this portrait of America, composed by fifty years of history and two world wars, was wholly flattering. No nation is universally admired until time has left it 2500 years behind, and even then there will be Alcibiades in the stern of the ship and Socrates's murderers. We had our critics — as many critics, indeed, as we had contemporaries. We were too rich. We talked in a rather childish way about brinkmanship, like two boys daring each other to walk out on a railroad trestle. Our principal exports — tourists and Coca-Cola — were not everywhere well received. Nevertheless, the essential figure was still the figure Wilson had presented — Wilson and that innocent doughboy of the First World War. We were on the side of the angels, however far below. We still talked in the vocabulary of the vast ideal and backed it up with enormous gifts of goods and money. And above all, though we had more power than any nation in the history of the world had ever had, we still refrained from the use of power except as a deterrent.

And then the picture changed. It changed first, or almost changed, at the Bay of Pigs, where, at the last moment, we did not use our planes. It changed four years later, first in Vietnam and then in Santo Domingo: we bombed North Vietnam and we occupied Santo Domingo with American troops. In both cases, of course, we explained our actions as preventive. We bombed North Vietnam because we believed the bombing would prevent the further invasion of South Vietnam by the Communists; we occupied Santo Domingo to forestall a Communist seizure of the Dominican Republic. But in both cases our explanations were overshadowed by our acts. What the world saw was the exercise of power: the use of American troops for the first time since the bad old days of gunboat diplomacy to impose our will on a Latin American country; the use of American bombers against a nation with which we were not at war.

With that spectacle the feel of America in the world's mind began to change. It is still changing. And not abroad alone but here as well. The famous "teach-ins" in universities across the country, where our normally silent students spent long angry nights, were not, as the participants sometimes seemed to think, debates on foreign policy. They were searchings of the national conscience.

Men differ, of course, and will doubtless continue to differ about the rights and wrongs of these great questions, the wisdom or unwisdom of our decisions, the accuracy of our intelligence, the effectiveness, in terms of their own purposes, of the measures adopted. But about the *fact* of the consequences of all this on the world's opinion of America there is no room for difference. We have changed in the world's eyes. And the one question that matters in this connection is whether the world is right — whether we have actually changed.

Do Vietnam and the Dominican Republic mean that we are no longer that idealistic nation of the First World War — no longer a people attached to those enormous phrases, those almost inexpressible aspirations which impose their own sometimes quixotic laws of self-restraint? Have our ways of thinking and of feeling altered? Are we "realistic" now? "Hardheaded"? Indifferent to those opinions of mankind which our progenitors put in the first sentence of their first communication to the world?

There are men in the United States, distinguished and influential men, who think we are and should be — who think we have concerned ourselves too often and too long with those opinions. We have been softened, they say, by our sensitiveness to the reactions of others. We consider, not what we have to do, but what the world thinks of what we have to do. And the result is preoccupation with the opinions of others, the kind of preoccupation which the advertising industry has exploited with such humiliating consequences.

There is truth in this: too much truth for comfort. The exploitation of a decent human concern for others to bully men and women into buying mouthwash is one of the least lovely things in American life. And the corruption of language which accompanies it is another. Take, for example, the word "image," which was once a word of art employed with rigorous precision by disciplined poets who knew exactly what they meant by it.

It has now become a trade term of the advertising agencies used in a muzzy, fuzzy, girlish sort of way to mean what people think of you — or more precisely what they will think if you don't use a particular deodorant or a certain soap or the brand of China policy advocated by the Daughters of the American Revolution. Nobody thinks of a man any more — only the "image" of a man. Nobody thinks of a policy — only of the "image" of a policy. Sooner or later no one will think of the Republic either — only of the "image" of the Republic — how the United States would look in a full-page ad.

But it is one thing to tell the people of the United States that they should think less, collectively and individually, about their "image" and another thing altogether to tell them that the opinions of mankind should be ignored. There is no good reason why we in this country should wish to be loved for our every action, to smell sweet in every nose, but there *are* reasons why we should want the world's respect. For the world's respect is a part, and an essential part, of any nation's respect for itself.

So that there is no escape by that road from the insistent question. *Do* our actions in Vietnam and Santo Domingo indicate that we have outgrown our old concern, our old idealism and innocence of belief, our visionary streak? It is wholly possible. Nations, like men, grow harder-headed as they grow older, more skeptical of their early aspirations, and we have lived for a long time in a climate of abstract principle, of a high and noble rhetoric.

It is possible that we have changed. But I for one would doubt that it is true; I would doubt it as an American; I would doubt it even more as an American writer. There is a great deal in American life, as there is a great deal in the modern life of any

country, which its writers deplore. There is vulgarity everywhere. There is ignorance and hatred — and not only in the
deep South. Our relations with each other lack richness and
tenderness. We die without death, like modern men in other
countries, after lives without living. Our cities are monstrous.
Our suburbs are worse. Our countryside, one of the loveliest
on earth, may well be lost in another generation. All this is obvious. But what is also obvious, if you look closely and listen well,
is the persistence of a human warmth, a human meaning that
nothing has killed in almost 200 years and that nothing is likely
to kill — not even the long, cold, inescapable struggle of this
generation of Americans — not even the blunders they may
well make in winning it.

At the darkest and most desperate moment in our history,
Abraham Lincoln, on his way to Washington to be inaugu-
rated as President of a disintegrating nation, stopped at Independence Hall in Philadelphia, the small brick building where
these hopes began. He had often wondered, he said, what it was
that had held the states so long together in the past. Certainly it
was not war — the war of independence with the mother country. There was something else, something more, and now he
thought he had discovered what it was. It was something in the
Declaration, he said, which had been drafted eighty-five years
before within those rooms, something which promised liberty
"not alone to the people of this country but also to the
world . . . ," something that promised "that in due time the
weights should be lifted from the shoulders of all men."

It was a strange thing to say, if you stop to think of it, with
all that darkness on the horizon just ahead. But it was true
and history proved it true. What has always held this country

together is an idea — a dream if you will — a large and abstract thought of the sort the realistic and the sophisticated may reject but humankind can hold to. That idea, I think we may be certain, we will never lose because we cannot lose it and remain a nation. And the opposite is also true. As long as we remain a nation that idea will be under the "image," the face beneath the painted face.

III

The Second
Civil War

A Dedication

1956

ONE DEDICATES a new library in the United States today because the building of a new library in the United States today
is itself an act of dedication. It commits a man or an institution or a community to one side rather than the other side of the
profound spiritual struggle in which our generation is engaged
— the spiritual civil war, if I may call it that, which quietly but
bitterly divides the country.

The reason will be obvious to anyone who considers what
a library actually is — or, rather, what the word has come to
mean on our continent over the past half century or so. We can
no longer use it to designate those towering rooms, lined from
floor to ceiling with yellow leather, which our houses used to
contain because our houses no longer contain them, and no
one would think of using it to describe the four-foot shelf behind
the television screen where six best sellers, still in their dust
jackets, lean against a pair of roller skates. A library to us is
something more and something different. It is many books, but
it is also many *kinds* of books; as many books of as many kinds
as can be gathered. Where the private library of the eighteenth
and nineteenth centuries was a *selection*, the library as we think

of it, the academic or public library of the twentieth century, is a *col*lection. Where once the criterion of choice was one man's preference of the books which interested him or with which he felt comfortable, today the criterion of choice is a disinterested completeness within the limits of a practicable relevance. Where once a library admitted only those books of which its owner approved, excluding all those whose language offended him or whose doctrines contradicted his own, today a library — what we call a library — includes every book which falls within the limits of the library's concern and the library's means whether it pleases the librarian or not and whether or not its conclusions agree with his.

A library's subject field may be limited: some of the finest libraries in the United States today are what librarians call special libraries. But to no aggregation of books, no matter what its scope, do we accord that proud title if it determines its content by other criteria than those of substance and relevance. The honor of the modern American librarian is the completeness as well as the worth of his collection. He would no more suppress a relevant and substantial book because it was offensive to himself personally or to his employer or to those who attempt to influence his employer than a college scientist would suppress a part of the evidence of his laboratory because it disappointed his preconceptions or disturbed the board of overseers or outraged the convictions of the loudest alumni. A modern American librarian regards himself as a trustee of the printed record of his civilization, or of so much of it as his means and his mission permit him to collect, and he would regard any exclusion from his collection of a relevant book or class of books as a falsification of the record and a breach of trust.

The consequence is that any library — any institution we would call a library — any institution called a library whose opening decent men would solemnize — will inevitably contain books with whose arguments and conclusions many Americans, even, conceivably, all Americans, will violently disagree, as well as books whose language and whose observations of human conduct millions of us will find offensive. There will be books on political theory, all kinds of political theory including the political theory of Karl Marx. There will be books on religion, all kinds of religion including the religion of cannibals and of Protestants like myself. There will be books on art, all kinds of art including the art which produces apoplexy among Senators. There will be books in which the observation of life includes the observation of love, and books in which the observation of love keeps the eyelid open long after most of us would modestly have closed it. There will be all sorts and kinds of books having nothing whatever in common with each other but the fact that it is these books — these and the others that could be added to them if means permitted — which contain among themselves the vast and various record of human perception, human speculation, human questioning, human doubt, human wonder, human creativeness which constitutes our human civilization.

To open a library, a modern American library, to its public of students or citizens is therefore to open a kind of Pandora's box. Hope is here, beauty is here, wisdom is here, but there are other stinging buzzing things beside. There are doubts which may not have been felt before. There are questions which may never have been asked. There are old errors long since recognized as such and new errors which might conceivably be truths. There are windows into corridors of the soul which have

not yet been entered and glimpses into miraculous labyrinths of
the body which have not been guessed at, and shadows and
shinings of emotions never sensed or seen. And all these whirling, humming things, moreover, even the best of them, even
beauty, even wisdom, may be dangerous. Men have been driven
mad by too much truth. Men have been debauched by beauty.
And as for the power of error, no one doubts that it exists and
that mankind is wonderfully vulnerable to it. Have we not the
spectacle in our own day of half the world persuaded to accept
the slavery of the self?

So that the opening of a library is, in the most literal sense of
the term, an invitation to danger. But it is also something more
than that, and it is the something more I wish to speak of. Carleton College does not merely invite its students to risk themselves
in this new building. It assures them at the same time — and
it assures the world as well — that it believes the risk thus taken
is the road to life. It affirms by this stone and steel and glass that
it is a good and desirable thing for men and women, young as
well as old, to have access to books of all kinds and of all opinions and to come to their own conclusions; that it is a good and
desirable thing for men and women, young as well as old, to examine heretical arguments as well as orthodox arguments and to
decide for themseles which is right and which is wrong; that it
is a good and desirable thing for men and women, young as well
as old, to learn how life has looked to all kinds and conditions
of observers of life, the despairing as well as the hopeful, the
sensuous as well as the ascetic, and to determine for themselves
which aspect of life is true and which aspect of life is misconception: which is abhorrent and which is beautiful.

And it is precisely in this affirmation that the dedication we

are seeking here consists. For to affirm what the opening of
this library affirms is to commit oneself to one of the deepest
and most courageous of all human beliefs. It is to commit oneself to a belief in the intelligence and the power to discriminate
of the human mind. If you assert that all the opinions, all the
perceptions, all the visions, all the arguments, all the images, are
to be made available, insofar as you can gather them, to any mind
which wishes to search them out, you are asserting at the same
time that you believe the mind which searches them out is capable of judging among them and arriving at sensible conclusions.
You are putting your trust, that is to say, not in indoctrination
and dogma — not in the conclusions of other and earlier men
which have now achieved the authority of accepted doctrine
— but in the mind itself which is the instrument of all conclusions, and in the act of mind, which is also an act of spirit, by
which the image of the world, generation after generation, is
re-created.

Stated in the usual commonplaces of philosophic discourse this
dedication may seem neither particularly daring nor particularly
new. Belief in the freedom of the mind — for this, I suppose, is
what the philosophers would call it — is something of a platitude
in Western dialectic. Theoretically we all of us believe in the
freedom of the mind, if for no other reason than that the Communists don't believe in it. Theoretically, also, we are all of us
aware that our Republic was founded upon a belief in the freedom of the mind and that the fundamental law which holds our
Republic together guarantees that freedom. All this, however,
is theory only. There is also fact. And fact tells a very different
story. The fact is that the official philosophic agreement of all
Americans on the principle of freedom of the mind covers a pro-

found and bitter disagreement which, since the Second War, has divided us far more deeply than most of us are willing to admit. There are few Americans as yet who are willing openly to attack the Constitution and the tradition of individual liberty which it incorporates. But there have been increasing numbers of our fellow citizens who have questioned in recent years the specific constitutional guarantees of individual freedom established in the Bill of Rights. And a surprising proportion of our people are today engaged in activities, such as the attempted suppression of books and opinions by boycott and by economic pressures of various kinds, which openly violate the spirit if not the letter of the constitutions of the Federal Government and the several states.

In this situation the affirmation of belief in the freedom of the inquiring mind which the opening of a new library implies is anything but an affirmation of the obvious. On the contrary it is an affirmation which some Americans would regard, if they spelled its implications out, as an impudent affront. Here is a city, here is a college, which says to its citizens or its students: you may read what you please even if what you choose is *Das Kapital* or D. H. Lawrence or the *Ulysses* of Joyce. You may know whatever you choose to know; even the facts of Soviet life; even the reveries of Molly Bloom. You may read and you may know because you have a right as a free man to read and know — because your intelligence depends on your reading and knowing — because the safety of the Republic depends on your intelligence. This, to the boycotter and suppressor, is dangerous and subversive talk. He does not believe in intelligence; what he believes in is the Truth and the Truth he knows already. As for the Republic, if the Republic needs to be saved, the Marines will save it or the F.B.I. or a Congressional Committee. There is no need for the citizens, young or old, to read opinions other than the accepted opinions, or to imagine life in terms other than the accepted terms, and the institution which invites them to do either is un-American.

One wonders, incidentally, what these people think, if they ever do think, of the seal and symbol of the country for which they claim to speak. The eagle is a bird chiefly notable for the catholicity of its vision. It hangs at a great height in clear air where a whole valley, a whole mountain, is spread out beneath it, and nothing stirs in all that countryside which it does not see. Its passion is to see. Its life is to see. That other, clumsy, grounded bird which deals with every new experience of the world by covering its eyes with sand and exposing its nude enormous anatomy to the weapons and the wind was never considered worthy of a place on the great seal of the United States until our time. Today it has become the symbol of the selectors of textbooks in a number of American states and the emblem of most veterans' committees. But the eagle is still aloft there in the federal air. Will it stay, one wonders, when it sees these other clumsy frightened creatures burrowing with their beaks and chins to hide the actualities of the earth?

But this, as I say, is an incidental matter. What concerns us here — and we may thank God for it — is not the folly of the frightened but the meaning of the act of faith. The frightened are important to us only because they make the act of faith come clear. And how clear they make it come! One has only to consider what is really in issue between the offerers of books and the withholders of books to see what the offering of books, the making available of books, means to this Republic and to the free civilization in which this Republic exists. To withhold books, to suppress books, to censor books, to deny the people of a town or of a state or of the country the right to read books as they choose to read them, is to question the basic assumption of all self-government which is the assumption that the people are capable of governing themselves: that the people, that is to say, are capable of examining the evidence for themselves and making up their own minds and coming to their own conclusions. The unstated pretension of all those who undertake to withhold books is the pretension that someone else knows better than the people: that the Chicago Archdiocesan Council of Catholic Women with its monthly blacklist of books knows better than the people; that the police chiefs of various towns and cities with their extra-legal threats to booksellers and libraries know better than the people; that the Attorney General of Massachusetts, should a bill pass directing him to establish a code "regulating and defining the permissive content of books, pamphlets, etc.," would know better than the people. It is the nerve center, the heart, of democracy which is struck at by these practices and measures, for the heart of democracy is the right of a people to make up their minds for themselves. And, by the same sign, it is democracy itself, at its heart, at its center, which is strengthened whenever a free choice of books is made available to the people — whenever the people are told in their towns, in their colleges: Here are the books! Read them as you please! Make up your own minds! Determine your own destiny! Be free!

It is for this reason that the opening of a new library is no longer the merely architectural event which it would have been in the days when Andrew Carnegie was dotting the American landscape with those placid domes of his. What were once peaceful establishments, secluding themselves behind their marble animals and their metal mottoes and the enormous names of those happy authors whom they chose for more or less eternal remembrance, have become strong points and pill-boxes along the extended and dangerous frontier where the future of free institutions is being fought out, day after day, in minor skirmishes rarely noticed in the public press and tactfully deprecated when they are recorded at all in the various professional publications. It would be difficult, I think, to overestimate the debt owed by the party of freedom in the United States today to the unknown and unsung librarians who, with little backing from their fellow citizens, and with less economic security than would encourage most of the rest of us to be brave, have held an exposed and vulnerable front through ten of the most dangerous years in the history of American liberty.

The changed situation is reflected in nothing more dramatically than in the changed status of the men and women who work in libraries. Fifty years ago no one would have questioned the assertion that the fundamental qualification of the librarian is objectivity: fifty years ago most librarians were objective — and looked it. But when, in February of this year, Mr. Quincy Mumford, the Librarian of Congress, laid down objectivity as the prime requirement of a Library employee, there was an immediate and sharp reaction which, because of the circumstances surrounding the statement, had repercussions in the press. Dr. Albert Sprague Coolidge, son of the Library's greatest private benefactor, Mrs. Elizabeth Sprague Coolidge, had been invited by the Library to serve on the advisory committee for the Coolidge Foundation but had subsequently been passed over. In explaining the reasons for this curious sequence of events, the official *Information Bulletin* of the Library of Congress stated in its issue of February 6 that "The Librarian felt that Dr. Coolidge's past associations and activities, entirely aside from the 'loyalty' or 'security' issue, would impair that objectivity in the fulfillment of his duties that one has a right to expect of a public employee, even in an advisory capacity on cultural matters."

Made by a less distinguished librarian than Mr. Mumford and in a case of less importance than that of Dr. Coolidge, this would not perhaps have been regarded by the press as a particularly remarkable statement. Made in the circumstances in which it was made and by the man who made it, it was felt to be remarkable indeed. And obviously it was, for what it clearly implied was that a man is not suitable for work in a library who has taken sides on public issues. There was, as Mr. Mumford went out of his way to state, and as those who have been associated with Dr. Coolidge well knew, no question whatever of disloyalty. Dr. Coolidge had been an effective and outspoken anti-Communist and anti-authoritarian all his life and Mr. Mumford was fully aware of that fact: "Dr. Coolidge," the *Bulletin* says, "has not been labeled a security risk by the Library of Congress either in private or in public." What was wrong was merely that Dr. Coolidge had joined organizations and taken positions which lined him up to be counted on one side — what men who love freedom would generally regard as the right side — of controversial public issues.

Now I have the greatest respect for Mr. Mumford. He came to the Library of Congress originally on my invitation: to head the new Processing Department following the reorganization of the Library in 1940 and 1941. I know at first hand his devotion, his intelligence, and his professional skill. I have not the slightest doubt that he acted reluctantly in the Coolidge matter and that the step he took was the step he believed right. Nevertheless I cannot help wondering whether he fully considered the implications of his reasoning and above all whether he related it to the actual, present situation of the profession he leads. That his ruling would automatically exclude at least one former Librarian of Congress from the Library's service in the future is doubtless irrelevant and immaterial since that Librarian is very fully employed elsewhere. But it is not irrelevant and it is not immaterial that the statement as it stands would exclude a great many others including particularly the most respected librarians in the country. No librarian who believes in the freedom guaranteed by the Constitution, and who detests authoritarianism, can avoid taking positions on controversial issues; indeed on the most controversial of all issues — for the issue of the freedom of the mind in America today is precisely that. He must believe in that freedom or he cannot be an honest librarian, and, if he believes in it, and acts on his belief, he can hardly hope to avoid contention. He may avoid such associations as Dr. Coolidge seems to have chosen but he cannot avoid decision. And whenever he decides that a book which somebody wants suppressed shall not be suppressed, whenever he decides that a magazine which somebody wants discontinued shall not be discontinued, he will have ceased to be "objective." He will have taken sides. He will have become a controversial figure, and as such will no longer be a desirable employee under the Librarian's rule.

I am completely certain that Mr. Mumford intended no such consequence. He knows, as any man must know who has that great institution in his charge, that the Library of Congress is the custodian of something more than a large number of books and pamphlets, maps and manuscripts. It is the custodian also of the cultural consequences. Had Herbert Putnam and his predecessors not accomplished the still inexplicable miracle of turning a modest legislative library into the national library of the United States, Washington would be a very different city and the federal government a very different government. Had Elizabeth Sprague Coolidge never given the Library of Congress its Coolidge Auditorium and made possible the magnificent concerts of music, new as well as old, which the Auditorium provides — had the Archive of American Folksong never been established in the Library's Music Division — the history of American music would have been a very different history. It is quite inconceivable that such an institution should now revert to a doctrine of library management, and therefore of library function, which seeks to neutralize belief and courage. The gelded librarian is a sacrifice which only McCarthyism demands, and McCarthyism in decay need not now be handed its dearest victim.

Rather, the whole energy of the profession should be directed in the opposite sense. Librarians should be encouraged to despise neutrality when neutrality interferes with the performance of their duties as librarians. They should be encouraged to believe positively and combatively in those principles of a free society in which they must believe to keep their libraries whole and sane. They should be brought to see that you cannot keep an even hand, a neutral hand, between right and wrong in the running of a library in a country and a time like ours. There are certain issues as to which objectivity, if objectivity means unwillingness to take a positive position, is impossible to a decent man in a critical period, and the issue of human freedom is one of them. You cannot be neutral on that issue anywhere in the world we live in and least of all can you be neutral on it in a library. You are for it or you are against it and if you are silent you are against. The test of a man's fitness for service in a library in the United States today is not, therefore, his lack of opinions. It is the kind of opinions he holds and the courage with which he holds them. If you believe in the use of books to indoctrinate — which is to say, in the suppression of certain books in order to leave available only the views expressed in certain others — you have no place in an American library however well fitted you may be for service in a library in Czechoslovakia or Spain. If you believe in free and equal access to all substantial books regardless of their views, and if you are willing to assert your belief in words and to defend it in action, the profession, if you are otherwise qualified, should welcome you.

And it is my conviction that it will. I do not believe that American libraries will adopt the rule laid down, or seemingly laid down, in the Coolidge case. The word "objectivitity" is, of course, a tempting word. It seems to offer a way of disposing of a troublesome problem without quite facing it. "Objectivity" is one of the *good* words of our contemporary vocabulary. Scientists are objective about their findings. Judges are objective in their opinions. Great newspapers are distinguished from newspapers which call themselves great by the objectivity of their presentation of the news. When we are called objective we are pleased, and when we refer to others in the same terms we mean to compliment them. The word raises a standard to which our scientifically minded generation can repair as the men of the Nineties repaired to "passion" and the men of the eighteenth century to "sensibility." But like all *good* words, "objectivity" has another side, and American librarians know it. It connotes a quality — a suppression of personal commitment and personal feeling — which is admirable in a journalist reporting the news or a scientist observing an experiment or a judge judging a case, but which is anything but admirable when there is a cause to defend or a battle to be fought. A general who was objective about the outcome of a campaign might be a great military technician, but he would be a soldier of limited usefulness. And a librarian who was objective about the survival of the tradition of free inquiry on which Western civilization is founded might be an admirable administrator, but his services to the human spirit in a place and time like ours would be negligible or worse.

The great American libraries have given courageous proof over the past few years that this kind of objectivity does not tempt them. And the Library of Congress itself, I feel reasonably certain, has no intention of deserting the principle. Indeed, I have good reasons for believing that the Library of Congress regards itself as standing firm in the faith despite the unfortunate language of its statement of policy in the Coolidge case. The Library of Congress, I am reliably informed, used the word "objectivity" in that ruling as a synonym for "good judgment" (a tribute to the influence of the scientists in our society) meaning no more than that a man who would join the organizations Sprague Coolidge had joined could not be counted on to exercise discrimination in advising the Library on the music to be played at Sprague Coolidge's mother's concerts and similar matters. If this is so, the position should perhaps be clarified. Good judgment is a desirable characteristic in a library employee as in anyone else — though it may well be doubted whether the soundness of a man's aesthetic sense can be determined by the orthodoxy of his political affiliations: if it could, few of the great artists and writers and musicians who have provided the contents of our libraries and museums would be employable in their management. But sound judgment as a euphemism for an unwillingness to take sides on fundamental moral and intellectual issues is not desirable anywhere in a free society and least of all in the libraries which house its memory and its conscience.

One cannot be objective in that sense and be the champion of a cause, and every American librarian worthy of the name is today the champion of a cause. It is, to my mind, the noblest of all causes for it is the cause of man, or more precisely the cause of the inquiring mind by which man has come to be. But noblest or not, it is nevertheless a cause — a struggle — not yet won: a struggle which can never perhaps be won for good and all. There are always in any society, even a society founded in the love of freedom, men and women who do not wish to be free themselves and who fear the practice of freedom in others — men and women who long for the comfort of a spiritual and intellectual authority in their own lives and who would feel more comfortable still if they could also impose it on the lives of others. As long as such people exist — and they show no sign of disappearing from the earth, even the American earth — the fight to subvert freedom will continue. And as long as the fight to subvert freedom continues, libraries must be strong points of defense.

It is not as a strong point that we regard this peaceful building on the day of its dedication. But it is one notwithstanding, and will continue to be one for a long, long time to come. Young men and women will find defenses for the freedom of the mind in this place by finding here what freedom of the mind can mean. And a whole countryside will know that one more bulwark has been raised against ignorance and bigotry and fear: a tower which will not yield. That dedication is in the stones themselves. We do no more than name it.

The Teacher's Faith

1952

SOME MONTHS AGO, when the faculty of Yale University was under attack for its religious and economic beliefs, one of the most widely read American magazines published an editorial analysis of the controversy. On the economic count judgment was entered for the defendants. The views of the Department of Economics at Yale were blameless. Not only was there no basis for charging that students were picking up dangerous ideas: there was little basis for charging that they were picking up any ideas whatever. On the religious count, however, the verdict was in doubt. The editors had gone to New Haven. They had interviewed members of the faculty, church-goers and non-church-goers alike. They had found common agreement that teachers, like other citizens of the Republic, are entitled to hold whatever religious opinions they please — including no religious opinions. And they were troubled. Apparently, the editors wrote, all the faculty of Yale University believed in was academic freedom. The implication was pretty obvious that academic freedom isn't much of a faith.

That opinion, teachers themselves seem increasingly to share. Challenged by the advocates of positive religious instruction in the schools, they conduct themselves not as champions of a great cause but as apologists for a half-discredited theory. Told that their tradition is "secular" and therefore no longer adequate to a world of conflicts such as ours, they accept the charge and justify the practice, if they justify it at all, on other grounds. Instead of challenging their challengers and making the issue what it really is — the issue of the spiritual and educational validity of the concept of academic freedom — they raise constitutional or political objections to the changes proposed and thus surrender the field where the battle must be fought.

The fundamental question is the question of the *meaning* of a faith in academic freedom. Academic freedom is not, as so many Americans seem to suppose, a special freedom for the academies, a professional freedom for teachers alone, the violation of which can harm no one else. Academic freedom is the fundamental freedom of us all: a freedom which is called academic not because it is limited to the schools and colleges but because it finds in the schools and colleges its most characteristic and most critical expression. It is "academic" freedom because it describes the freedom of the individual mind, and because schools and colleges have a particular responsibility for the individual mind. It is "academic" freedom because it is a freedom which, unless it exists in the academies, will not exist at all.

When a man asserts that he believes in academic freedom he is not asserting that he believes in special guild advantages for teachers. He is making a fundamental affirmation about all mankind — to my mind, the most fundamental affirmation a man upon this earth, and dealing with the things of earth, can make.

Any believer in freedom believes, of course, and of necessity, in man. He has no alternative. He has nowhere else to go. He has rejected the pretension of the ruler to rule for the people, and the pretension of the censor to think for the people, and the pretension of the church to believe for the people, and he is left with the people themselves — which is to say, with the individual human beings who compose the people. Wishing to be free himself he asserts his belief in the right and capacity of all men to enjoy freedom.

But with the believer in freedom who makes his affirmation in terms of the human mind and the things with which the human mind is concerned, the commitment is not general but precise and not implicit but express. In affirming that he believes in the freedom of the schools, such a man is declaring that he believes in the freedom of every human mind. And in declaring that he believes in the freedom of every human mind he is declaring, explicitly and unequivocally, that he believes in three things: the uniqueness and worth of the individual human being; the power of the truth to prevail; and the human future.

No man who did not believe in the future could declare that the minds of men must be free to discover the future. No man who did not believe in the power of the truth to prevail could declare that the minds of men must be free to find the truth for themselves. No man who did not believe in the dignity and worth of the human individual could declare that a man must be free to be himself.

These are tremendous commitments for any man to make. They are tremendous commitments indeed for the teacher — for the man who accepts in the practice of his life a measure of responsibility for their realization. But to affirm a belief in academic freedom is to make just these commitments. It is for this reason that the belief in academic freedom of the faculty of Yale

University — and of the thousands of other teachers who feel as that faculty feels — is not a secondary or an inadequate belief. On the contrary it is a belief which goes to the heart of the whole commitment to freedom. No honest or conscientious man could undertake to teach in a free society who did not hold it. And no man who truly held it could ever be false to the freedom in which such a society is conceived.

But all this, conclusive though it may seem to many of us, will not persuade those skeptical editors or the millions of Americans who think, apparently, as they think. It is not the commitment of the faculty of Yale University to freedom which these people question. It is the fact that the commitment is a commitment to freedom *only*. Academic freedom is all very well, they are saying — a belief in academic freedom is, of course, admirable enough among teachers — but freedom is not a faith. And what this country needs — what this country needs, above all, in its present troubles — is faith. The sickness of our time is materialism. If we are to survive in our struggle with the materialistic philosophy of our enemies we must give our children a faith in values superior to the values of Marxism. We must give them a devotion to spiritual things. And we must give it in the schools.

This is the substance of the position as one meets it again and again in print, on the public platform and in the resolutions of trustees and boards of education and legislative committees. Its implications are rarely spelled out as explicitly as they were in the attack on Yale University, but the implications are nevertheless there. What they come down to, in all such cases, is a demand that something "more" be required of the country's teachers than a belief in freedom of the mind. Not all critics of the colleges and schools would substitute for a belief in academic freedom a belief in a particular religious creed. Some apparently ask nothing more than that the country's teachers should believe in *some* religion and that their religious belief should *somehow* be communicated in their teaching. But whatever the form of the suggestion, there is always involved, explicitly or implicitly, the proposal that teachers be required to believe, *as teachers*, in something "more" than academic freedom. Academic freedom, it is insisted over and over again, is a purely secular conception. Western man must find his refuge in a belief in God. And the schools must help prepare that refuge for him.

To meet contentions of this character with constitutional objections is not intelligent. The fact that the end result of any such revolution in our educational system might very possibly be an establishment of religion such as the Constitution forbids — even the fact that many who support that revolution undoubtedly desire just such a consequence — is not an adequate answer. If the reasons for the revolution are as compelling as we are told they are — if it is only by surrendering the tradition of intellectual freedom on which our institutions are founded that the moral and spiritual health of the country can be assured — then the Constitution cannot be permitted to stand in the way.

The real issue is not a legal issue — even a constitutional issue. The real issue is the issue of substance: Is it, or is it not, true on the facts and on the probabilities that a substitution of positive instruction in matters of belief for the traditional reliance on freedom of inquiry is necessary if we are to survive as a free people?

That some reawakening of the spiritual life of our people is needed and desperately needed, no observant and sensitive man will deny. The world is sick and the name of its sickness is indeed materialism. Not only as a defense against Marxist propaganda, but for nearer and more urgent reasons, there must be some renewal of belief in the spiritual possibilities of man: of belief in the meaning and the richness of his other life. But is it by the means now proposed that this renewed conviction will be found? Is it by qualifying our old belief in freedom in the schools that we will find our souls again? Is it true in fact that the belief in freedom is a merely secular belief? Is it true in probability that a religious test for teachers would increase the religious consciousness of the people?

The answer to both questions, in my judgment, is very clear. It is *not* true that belief in the freedom of the human mind is a merely secular belief — a belief having no concern with the life of the human spirit. On the contrary, it is to the freely and boldly inquiring human mind, from the days of the first prophets and visionaries to the days of the latest poets and scientists and seers, that the noblest and most exalted possibilities of the human spirit have been revealed. And neither is it true that the substitution of religious tests and religious teaching for academic freedom in the country's colleges and schools would enhance the spirituality of the nation. On the contrary any such practice would almost certainly have an opposite effect. It would beget skeptics, not persuade them. And it would destroy a great part of the power of American schools to serve the cause of freedom.

Let us look at this latter proposition first. The real proof of any experience is the experience itself. Even in teaching. Even in the teaching of spiritual truth. Indeed, above all, in the teaching of spiritual truth. Tell a child often enough that he must believe in God without giving him any reason to believe, in his own experience, and you will persuade him of nothing but the fact that *you* believe in God — or that you say you do. But let your students feel their own freedom as responsible beings to accept or to reject, and bring them face to face in that sense of freedom with a free and honest man in the trials and turnings of his life, and you will find that the realization of the spiritual experience may occur even in a classroom. It is in freedom that children as well as men accept the truth, for in freedom they find it for themselves. It is in his own experience that a child learns: his experience of the things of the mind when the things of the mind are in question; his experience of the things of the spirit when it is the spirit that must be answered.

The moment you introduce the element of compulsion, whether legal compulsion or social compulsion or that shameful compulsion of economic blackmail which is now so prevalent in the country — the moment you introduce the element of compulsion into matters of belief, all this is altered. If the teacher is no longer free he is no longer wholly a man. So long as he stands before his class responsible to his freedom and himself, answerable to his conscience and the truth, he is himself a part of the experience his students share. Once it is understood and known that he *must* believe to be a teacher, then what he says as teacher is no longer necessarily what he means as man. He may serve, as teachers serve in Soviet Russia or in Franco Spain, as a conveyor of dogma. He can scarcely serve as teachers have been expected to serve in the past in the United States, as an educator of men. And as for his students, though they may accept his declarations of belief on authority, they will not accept them in their lives. The Christian West is full of dishonest and immoral politicians, shameless demagogues, corrupt public officials, cynical and disreputable men of business, gangsters and common criminals who profess belief in Christianity and membership, even active membership, in the church. It is not by formal protestations of belief in God that the West will be saved from the cancer of materialism — or the world either. It is by the live experience of the soul.

But the revolutionary proposal now made to us is not only unacceptable because of its practical ineffectiveness. It is unacceptable also because it is founded in a complete misconception of the tradition it would supplant. Why believers in the American tradition of education have not challenged the repeatedly made assertion that the American conception of academic freedom is a merely secular conception — meaning a merely worldly conception — I do not pretend to understand. Secular in one sense of the word academic freedom undoubtedly is: those who believe in academic freedom do not consider that it is the teacher's function to teach the dogmas of a church merely because they are its dogmas. But secular in the sense in which the word is used in the current controversy, the conception of academic freedom — the conception of the freedom of the mind — certainly is not. It is not a conception allied to materialism, nor a conception which denies the possibility of spiritual belief. On the contrary it is a conception founded upon the observed truth that it is in the struggles which the believer in intellectual freedom accepts for himself that true belief, honest belief, living belief is found. There are men who live by the free mind who have never found certainty beyond the certainty of the questions they must ask. But there are also believers in the freedom of the mind — thousands of them — who have fought their way to conclusions which stand like rocks upon the frontiers of the human spirit.

The choice before us is not the old false choice between the spirit and the mind. The choice is not the choice between academic freedom and religious belief. The choice is a choice be-

tween the *kind* of conviction to which a man comes in the freedom of his own search for truth and the responsibility of his
own conscience, and the *kind* of conviction to which a man
comes under the direction of the belief of others — particularly
others in authority. You can come to spiritual truth in either
way. In this country we have put our trust in the former. Our
frontiers were settled, our institutions were shaped, our books
were written, by men who came in their own way to their own
truth and lived it. It is difficult to think of a great American name
which was not the name of a man of this kind. Lincoln's was.
Emerson's was. Melville's was. Adams's was. Jefferson's was.
Franklin's was. Whitman's was. So were the names of the
founders of the great industries, the designers of the great techniques, the builders, the makers.

You do not, it is true, arrive at *conformity* by freeing men in
their youth to find their truth for themselves. But conformity
was never, after Colonial times, what we wanted in this country.
We wanted individual consciences, not doctrinal agreement. We
wanted men, not creeds. We were increasingly doubtful, as we
observed ourselves and our history, that men become religious
because they repeat a common form of words, even the noblest.
We were increasingly convinced that it is not by religious instruction in the schools that a Christian people becomes Christian. And we were convinced of this not alone because our
numerous Christian denominations could not agree among themselves on the beliefs which should be taught, but for other reasons also — reasons of conscience, reasons of human respect.
Believing in the individual man, in the individual mind, we believed in that man's right — in that mind's right — to ask his
questions for himself and find his answers.

The real question, as I see it, is not whether we should now replace our old trust in man and mind with a new trust in doctrine and authority, requiring our teachers to make a confession of religious belief, and to impose that belief upon their students if they can: there is no sound argument in either theory or practice for such a betrayal of our past. The real question is why such a proposal has been made — why publications of influence have supported it — why great numbers of Americans appear to be indifferent to the consequences it would have, both for their country and themselves.

The obvious answer to that question would, I suppose, be Communism. The lie, the deception, the fraud, the conspiracy, which Communism is, we would be told, has changed the world. It is no longer possible to believe in the future; all we can now do is to oppose our doctrine to Communist doctrine, fighting the battle for men's minds, not by *freeing* their minds, but by *conditioning* them. It is a position we have all heard argued. The difficulty with it is that it makes nothing but rhetorical sense — and little enough of that. So far as the power of the truth goes, there is no reason whatever to believe that the moral nature of man has been perverted by Soviet propaganda anywhere beyond the reach of the Soviet police. So far as the people are concerned, the whole notion that they can no longer be trusted is cowardly, contemptible and unworthy.

The McCarthys and McCarrans among us, ignorant of the deep roots of the American tradition, may doubt the ability of a free people to resist Communism but no one else should doubt it. Communist influence, even in those quarters where the Communist appeal might be expected to be greatest, is feeble and faltering. But even if all this were not so — even if the American Communist Party were as large as the Italian, even if Communist propaganda had succeeded in altering human nature, even if the prophecies of Karl Marx had all been proven, it would still be true that no more disastrous defense against Communism could possibly be devised than the defense now proposed to us. What we are defending against Communism is freedom — freedom of the individual human being. Freedom, like everything else affecting the human spirit, is a process. It is not a thing. It is not a possession. It is not a doctrine. It cannot be protected, in the current phrase, by holding on to what we have, by freezing our way of life. It can be protected only by exercising it. The defense of freedom under attack is more freedom. "The process," Whitehead said, "is the reality," and of nothing is that definition truer than of freedom. The moment a free people puts its trust, not in the process of freedom, but in the dogmas which it regards as expressing the finalities of freedom, just at that moment it has surrendered the reality of its cause and the meaning of its life.

Schools have a role to play — teachers have a role to play — in the struggle of individual freedom against institutional authority; in the struggle of the human spirit against the formulas; in the struggle of life against materalism. No one, indeed, has a more important role to play than the teacher. But his role — his role in this republic at least — is not to commit his students to belief. His role is to commit them to the human experience — to the experience of the human mind and the human soul — in the profound and never questioning confidence that if they truly taste of that experience, if they truly see the choices of their lives, they — they themselves — will choose. In that confidence political freedom was conceived. In that confidence the institutions of human freedom were established. In that confidence the faith of those who teach the free is founded.

The Worm at Heart

1952

UNTIL THE PUBLICATION of Niebuhr's *The Irony of American History* no responsible American writer had, to my knowledge, centered his attention upon the American belief in man as the key to the moral and intellectual crisis in which we live. It makes no difference that Niebuhr's book is written to persuade us that we should now repent of our belief in man. What is important is Niebuhr's identification of the real issue under all the meaningless talk as the issue of our own beliefs, not the beliefs of our enemies. In his discussion of that issue he is, as I see it, wrong: as wrong as it is possible for a wholly honest and highly intelligent man to be. But he has made it possible to transfer the Great Debate, over which so much journalistic ink has been so pointlessly spilled, from the world of nightmare to the world of waking.

Niebuhr's position is explicitly put: "Our modern liberal culture, of which American civilization is such an unalloyed exemplar, is involved in many ironic refutations of its original pretensions of virtue, wisdom and power"; history has now caught up with us and only by contrition and by repentence of our original beliefs can we avoid disaster; "our success in world politics" — which means, of course, our survival as a world power — "necessitates a disavowal of the pretentious elements of our original dream." The real issue, in other words, is the American dream itself, the dream of man. What is wrong with us as a people, in Niebuhr's view, is our failure to perceive, consciously or unconsciously, that the fundamental proposition upon which our nation was founded was "pretentious" and that it has been refuted by history: that we must now renounce it.

But the usefulness of Niebuhr's book is not only that it replaces false issues with real. Its even greater usefulness is that it makes a debate of the real issue possible. Those who have taken Niebuhr's position in the past have generally been Catholics whose political convictions, on this fundamental point, could not be debated without the counter-charge that the tenets of their faith had been challenged. Niebuhr is not only a Protestant but a man whose life has been honorably devoted to liberal causes. His thesis can be challenged without challenging anything but itself. When a man of Niebuhr's intelligence, distinction and established reputation as a liberal attacks the American proposition in the context of the present crisis in American fortunes the attack can be made, and should be made, the occasion for a searching examination of the claims of those who question the American cause.

That Niebuhr's objective is the heart of that cause cannot be in doubt. His attack is directed at the American tradition itself, at the holy of holies, at the aspiration which, because we have never been able to put it into the language of legal draftsmanship, we have called the American Dream. Our "pretension" is our belief in man. Our weakness as a people, in Niebuhr's view, is our rejection of the conception of human weakness and vileness comprised in the doctrine of Original Sin. We Americans have refused "to accept the fact that the whole drama of history is enacted in a frame of meaning too large for human comprehension or management." And history has found us out. History has demonstrated that the heart of the American Dream is delusion.

The "irony" of Niebuhr's title is the irony of the fact that it was the American Dream itself — the aspiring hope with which we began our history — which prepared our present difficulties. And the assumption on which the whole indictment stands is, therefore, an assumption as to the nature of the American Dream. What is that assumption? It is implicit in the argument throughout and quite clearly revealed in such a sentence as this: "Our difficulty as a nation is that we must now learn that prosperity is not simply coordinated to virtue, that virtue is not simply coordinated to historic destiny and that happiness is no simple possibility of human experience." The American Dream of Niebuhr's indictment is, in other words, the fantasy that the prosperous are the good, that the good will inherit the earth and that happiness is something you can buy on the installment plan. The American belief in man thus becomes a belief in a mere economic integer: man as getter, man as consumer. And the tradition of liberalism becomes, in consequence, a fatuous materialism which knows nothing of the infinite possibilities of life.

Now, it is only too obvious that there have been Americans, as there still are Americans, who talk as though the American Dream were precisely what Niebuhr says it is. No one who investigates that submerged continent of American literature which is produced in the advertising agencies can be ignorant of the underlying assumption of its authors, that the cause to which we are committed in the mortal struggle of our time is a cause which can be precisely equated with "the American way of life," and that "the American way of life" finds its perfect expression, not in noble action, nor in wise meditation, but in the possession of a new car or a larger refrigerator.

But it is not to the advertising agencies one would expect a serious writer to go for light upon the fundamental aspirations of his fellow citizens. The deepest aspirations of a people are commonly expressed in those occasional and lucky words of its greatest men which have found a common acceptance, not so much because they were true when they were spoken, as because the assent of many men and women over generations of time has made them true. They are spelled out in the words of the founders and the defenders which the people have remembered. In this country they are to be found sometimes in Jefferson's words, sometimes in Franklin's, in Lincoln's, in Emerson's, in Ahab's on the enormous sea. And what they come down to, as one brings them all together, is not a fantasy of man as a getter of wealth, or of man as a consumer of wealth, or of man as the beneficiary of a merely material happiness, but a dream of man as man: a dream of the illimitable capacities of man which holds that human beings, if they are free to think for themselves and judge for themselves, *are capable of governing themselves:* a dream of the ineradicable dignity of man which holds that neither state nor church nor any other institution or authority has the right to shape men's minds and souls because men's minds and men's souls are capable of shaping themselves: a dream of the boundless possibilities of human knowledge and human imagination which holds that the future of mankind is not circumscribed by finality but may be opened out, from generation to generation, into continents never yet conceived.

Niebuhr's error, and the error of the many men who see the American liberal tradition as he sees it, is quite simply, that he misconceives the character of the American belief in man. You will find him speaking of our "confidence in happiness as the end of life and in prosperity as the basis of happiness." You will find him writing of the United States as a nation "which thought it an easy matter to distinguish between justice and injustice and believed itself to be peculiarly innocent" or as "a culture which knew nothing of sin and guilt." And as you read you will find yourself wondering what nation, at what period of its history, he has in mind. Is it of the long, tortured struggle of the Puritan conscience in New England he is thinking when he puts us down as a nation which knew nothing of sin and guilt? Is it the agony of the Civil War he has in mind when he speaks of us as a culture which thought it an easy matter to distinguish between justice and injustice? Are those naïve victims of an infantile hallucination of material happiness of whom he writes the great figures of the generation of the Revolution: a group of men whose experience of the vicissitudes of life, and whose knowledge of the world, was as varied as their intelligence was remarkable?

The fundamental weakness of the argument is the weakness of the whole case against the American tradition. The weakness is the arbitrary assumption that liberalism is a timeserving faith which cannot touch, and therefore cannot satisfy, men's souls — that liberalism, because it rejects the claims of the several orthodoxies to tell men what they must believe, believes, itself, in nothing but material things. There could hardly be a more distorted reading of American history or of the

American character. As a people we have always, and with good reason, regarded the motivation of our national life as spiritual. Our devotion to the ideal of human individuality is a spiritual devotion. Niebuhr himself justly observes, though he fails to make the just application of his observation, that "the concept of the value and dignity of the individual . . . is finally meaningful only in a religious dimension." It is not otherwise asserted by the American Proposition. Anyone who thinks our belief in the individual human being is a purely worldly belief can know little, actually, either of our literature or of our life. We may put the proposition in secular terms in a political Declaration of Independence but that Declaration shortly becomes a sacred text from which the soul draws meanings.

It may very well be true that a fatuous optimism and a crass materialism have been characteristic American weaknesses: we have been no more successful in realizing our highest aspirations than others in realizing theirs. It is undoubtedly true, also, that the history of the last fifty years has mercilessly exposed the fatuousness of the notion that material prosperity is a proof of virtue and that happiness can be acquired wholesale. But it is not by the human shortcomings of its practice that one judges an ideal, whether it be the ideal of a church or the ideal of a society. Before a man can be heard to argue that the American Dream itself has been discredited by the events of history he must first define that dream *as it is dreamed*. If it is the American belief in man he wishes to attack, not the failure of some of us to make good the faith in man, he must state that faith in its noblest, not its cheapest, terms. If it is the American liberal tradition he wishes to destroy he must spell that tradition out in its spiritual strength, not its material weakness. No man is at liberty to assume that an ideal belief is responsible for a discreditable reality until he has stated the ideal belief as a believable ideal.

The proposition which the discreditors of the American liberal tradition must establish if they wish to succeed is the proposition that the belief in man *which Lincoln put into words* has been refuted by the history of our time. That proposition will not stand up. Lincoln's belief in man is the one triumphant cause of the world we live in. Even the Communists have been obliged to make their appeal to populations they have not yet subjugated in its name, concealing by every trick of deceit and rhetoric the authoritarian actuality of their regime. As for ourselves, our principal weakness in world affairs today is precisely the doubt of considerable portions of the world's population that we really believe in the faith we have so long and consistently declared.

The lesson of Niebuhr's book is simple and salutary. The American tradition is not in danger from those who attack the fundamental proposition on which it rests. It is not in danger from those who question openly the belief in man. Its real peril is the peril created by those who use the national hatred of Communism as a wooden horse for the destruction of the American cause. Its real peril is the peril created by the increasing numbers of Americans who, in their unthinking and unfounded fear of Communist propaganda and Communist seductions, have lost their faith in the ability of a free people to govern themselves. Open challenge to the American proposition can be debated in the open and overcome. Loss of faith in the American proposition is a secret sickness which can bring the country down.

The Alternative

1955

GRANTED THAT McCarthyism was a mass psychosis or something very like it, why did the sane citizens of the Republic tolerate it as long as they did? Throughout the McCarthy period, though freedom was in issue for all of us, the issue for all of us was not freedom. For most of us it was fear, it was hatred. Why did we put hate and fear above the love of freedom? Was it because our love of freedom, our belief in freedom, had degenerated?

There is evidence — evidence worthy of the most respectful attention — to support that conclusion: evidence which comes from men whose past devotion to freedom is notorious and whose hostility to McCarthyism and everything the word implies is a matter of public record. Mr. Walter Lippmann, who is certainly one of the most perceptive readers of the American mind, has published a book which can only be described as a retreat from the idea of freedom as that idea has been understood in this Republic. The thesis of his *The Public Philosophy* is this:

The democratic powers, with the United States as principal example, have suffered a precipitate and catastrophic decline in power and prestige. This decline has been brought about by the failure of the democratic machinery of government — a failure which Mr. Lippmann dates from 1917. What happened in that year was that the strain of "hyperbolic" war became too great for the governments involved: they ran out of "imperium," lost control of the war (meaning that they lost the power to end it by diplomatic means) and were reduced to submitting the issue to their peoples — which, in turn, meant that the issue had to be framed in terms of such absolutes as the people are capable of understanding — "war to end war," "war to make the world safe for democracy," and, twenty years later, war for the "four freedoms."

The result of all this was that no real peace could be made either in 1918 or in 1945 and that public opinion (or at least the pressure groups which exploit public opinion) has, ever since, exercised too much direct influence on the democratic governments. The governments can no longer effectively govern and their power and influence have gone down in consequence. The trouble is, in brief, that the people have played too large and too immediate a part in the direction or the attempted direction of their own affairs. There has been too much democracy and therefore too little government and the consequences may be very serious. "A continuing practical failure to govern," writes Mr. Lippmann, "will lead . . . to counterrevolutionary measures for the establishment of strong government."

What is the alternative? "The alternative," Mr. Lippmann tells us, "is to withstand and to reverse the descent towards counterrevolution. It is a much harder way. It demands popular assent to radical measures which will restore government strong enough to govern, strong enough to resist the encroachment of the assemblies and of mass opinions and strong enough to guarantee private liberty against the pressure of the masses." And what are these radical measures? What is this much harder way? Mr. Lippmann states it eloquently in words which will be widely read and deeply pondered. What it comes down to is the substitution, for the idea of greatest possible individual freedom to which we have been committed in this country since the end of the eighteenth century, of the idea of Natural Law, or what Mr. Lippmann prefers to call, "the Public Philosophy" — "the postulate that there is a rational order of things in which it is possible, by sincere inquiry and rational debate, to distinguish the true and the false, the right and the wrong." If democratic societies would accept the universal values of Natural Law as binding on all, government would be freed from its subservience to mass opinion since it could then appeal from mass opinion to the eternal precepts, and would be in a position to act on its own best judgment.

Now, the proposition from which Mr. Lippmann departs — the proposition that the democratization of war in 1917 was a mistake — will undoubtedly excite some debate. In Wilson's time and in Roosevelt's it was generally believed that the participation of the people in the determination of the great issue of war or peace, far from precipitating the collapse of democratic governments, promised a stronger and more effective democracy. The management of the great questions of war and peace by the bureaucrats of the Foreign Office and the Quai d'Orsay and the State Department, however logical it may have been in the political and dynastic wars of earlier centuries, seemed to men of my generation inappropriate to a time of vast world conflicts in which not professional armies but the people themselves were participants. We repeated with relish Clemenceau's remark that war was too serious a business to be left to the generals, and we spent a great measure of our youthful passion berating the diplomats and the politicians who, after the First World War was won, fumbled the peace and betrayed the hopes of the men and women who had fought it. The formulations of intent, which Mr. Lippmann now dismisses as "absolutes" incapable of realization by the diplomats and the politicians, were valued by men in danger and women in despair precisely for that reason. Men will die for peace and freedom but not for the terms of a treaty, and it was the conviction of my generation in the war of its youth and the war of its middle age that the American government and the governments of the free world had made some progress toward a more effective democracy by the recognition of that fact.

But the importance of Mr. Lippmann's book lies not in its history but in its philosophy, and particularly in the relation of its philosophy to the contemporary concept of freedom in the United States. For the concept of freedom is the real subject of Mr. Lippmann's argument. His concern is with "modern men who find in freedom from the constraints of the ancestral order an intolerable loss of guidance and support," who find "that the burden of freedom is too great an anxiety": "men who rise up against freedom, unable to cope with its insoluble difficulties and unable to endure the denial of communion in public and common truths." These modern men, says Mr. Lippmann, "have found no answer to their need and no remedy for their anguish in the principles and practice of freedom as they have known them in the liberal democracies of this century."

Readers of Mr. Lippmann's book may question whether he or anyone else is in a position to make so vast a statement as this last, but, whatever its universal truth, the particular truth of the declaration for Mr. Lippmann himself is evident. True freedom, to Mr. Lippmann, is not the freedom of the liberal democracies. True freedom "was founded on the postulate that there was a universal order on which all reasonable men were agreed: *within that public agreement* on the fundamentals and on the ultimates, it was safe to permit, and it would be desirable to encourage, dissent and dispute." True freedom for Mr. Lippmann, in other words, is freedom to think as you please and say as you think provided what you say and think falls within the periphery of what all reasonable men agree to be fundamentally and ultimately true. The basic philosophy of liberalism — the belief in the liberation of the individual human spirit to find its own way to enlightenment and truth — is thus rejected, and not only rejected but denounced. It is, in Mr. Lippmann's opinion, mere "Jacobin ideology." Worse than that, it is comparable to the doctrine of the totalitarian states, Communist as well as Fascist. Like the doctrine of the totalitarian states, the popular doctrine of what Mr. Lippmann calls "the mass democracies" rests upon the proposition that men may shape their own destiny and are capable of realizing their dreams of the good life. But this proposition, says *The Public Philosophy*, is arrogance, and the belief on which it rests is delusion. Men are not gods and cannot establish heaven on earth. The claim that they can leads to disaster. It leads from Rousseau and the Jacobins to Marx and on to Lenin and Hitler and Stalin — and, it would appear, to "the mass democracies." It leads from a political religion to a popular religion based on the rise of the masses to power and so to "an everlasting war with the human condition: war with the finitude of man." The true Way is not this Way. The true Way is by submission and acceptance: acceptance of our mortal lot, and submission, if not to an elite who can govern for us (Mr. Lippmann does not say so), at least to the rule of those eternal postulates which fix the limits of finite human action and establish order in our mortal lives.

Now what is significant here is not the plea for a return to Natural Law. That plea has been heard again and again from Catholic philosophers over the course of many years. What is significant here is the revulsion against "mass" democracy of a writer whose career has been closely associated with the development of democratic ideas in our generation, and whose views have generally been found to be expressive of the opinions of an influential section of the American people. Mr. Lippmann's gloomy account of the present state and future prospects of the Western democracies will not surprise his readers: many of them will have had similar thoughts. Some will even agree with his conclusion that "the people have acquired power which they are incapable of exercising." A few, though not, I think, many, will go along with Mr. Lippmann's judgment that "prevailing public opinion" in the Western democracies over the last thirty years or so has been persistently wrong: "wrong at the critical junctures." But no reader who feels deeply about the democratic tradition will be able to avoid a sense of shock when he perceives what is actually being said by this distinguished democratic writer about the heart of the democratic philosophy and the democratic life — about freedom itself.

We know — we can scarcely avoid knowing — that there are millions of modern men who fear freedom or are frightened of the loneliness it implies or prefer to have their lives lived for them. If it were not so Hitler could never have come to power nor could the Communist states have survived. We have commonly assumed, however, that those who felt this way about the responsibilities of freedom were men who had not long been free — men whose families had lived for centuries in Germany or Italy or the old Austrian Empire or the empire of the Czars. We have even made the same observation about the increasing numbers of our own fellow citizens who press for conformity of opinion and the censorship of ideas: many of them, we notice, are relatively recent arrivals from countries where church or state has long been accustomed to police the minds of the people. What is novel in Mr. Lippmann's account is the fact that it is one of the most habituated of democratic journalists who advances the contention that true freedom in America ended with the end of the recognition of Natural Law in the late eighteenth century, and that the whole conception of the boundless liberty of the individual human spirit to which our own Republic has since been committed is a wrong steer, a tragic error.

It is one thing for an American, thoroughly familiar with the American situation, to assert that our position is dangerous and our society far from perfect. Most of us are aware that mass vulgarity afflicts our culture and mass hysteria our politics and that the government of the Republic is increasingly difficult. It is another thing altogether for such a commentator to assert that the ideas which have made a nation of us — the ideas which have shaped our development since the beginning of the nineteenth century — are pernicious ideas which should now be renounced: that the modern democratic belief in the greatest possible individual freedom itself is false doctrine.

But for all the concern it will arouse among the believers in modern democracy, Mr. Lippmann's is nevertheless a book

which should serve them well, for it reveals in the most dramatic
and personal way the nature of the influences which draw even
the best of free men back from freedom in our time. What motivates Mr. Lippmann is not distrust of freedom as such: he protests his attachment to it often and with obvious sincerity. What
motivates Mr. Lippmann is the conviction that the idea of full
individual freedom and the idea of effective community are irreconcilable ideas and that there is therefore an ineluctable
choice between them: that in that choice community must be
preferred. He is unwilling or unable to believe that no such
painful choice may be necessary: that full individual freedom
may conceivably lead to a community of its own, effective in a
new and different way. The decision for him is a decision between individual freedom as we now know it and the form of
community with which we have present literary familiarity —
the community of the Roman and the Medieval periods. And
between those two alternatives he does not hesitate. He will
willingly sacrifice a large measure of individual freedom, including the future hope for its further development, in order to return to a society of order and reason held together by the
restraints of the eternal verities. The road to the happy town-
land, as he sees it, is the road not by way of individual freedom
but by way of like-mindedness and mutual agreement on the
fundamental things. If we can agree among ourselves as to the
Good and the True — if we can shame or silence those who have
a different True or another Good — we will be *together;* we
will no longer feel alone; our house will stand.

The importance of Mr. Lippman's book is thus its demonstration, whether intentional or not, of the nature of the real issue
before our generation in the United States. The immediate and

present danger to American freedom is not the danger from without: the danger that it will be overwhelmed by the Communist conspiracy in one form or another. The immediate and present danger is the danger that the dream of American freedom will be subordinated to some other dream by men within the country who consider that they are acting for freedom's good and for the good of the Republic. Communism has no standing in the United States and its adherents have no influence, but the adherents of the doctrine of the ineluctable choice between community and freedom are numerous and influential and the dream of community they promulgate is a seductive dream in a time like ours — a dream which drags powerfully at the hearts of those who have lost, or those who have not yet learned, the difficult hope of which human freedom is the ultimate expression.

In a time when the dangers are dark and threatening and terrible like dangers in a nightmare, when the decisions are indecisive, when action, like nightmare action, seems to have no consequences, seems to move without motion like a runner in the sand — in such a time, the temptation to give up the long labor of liberty is a powerful temptation, and the vision of community becomes a vision which enchants. For the vision of community, being a vision from the past, is inevitably a vision in which everything is sure, everything is certain. Actions in the past have consequences. The sun shines from behind. To go back — back into the twelfth century, back into the world of Rome — is to go back into the light. And the longing for that distant light can be very strong.

It is for this reason that the apparent deterioration of our attachment to the idea of freedom must so concern us all. Unless we are truly committed to the forward dream of freedom, that other dream — the dream of the awakening into the past — may entice us, and if it does our greatness as a people will be over. No one truly wakes into the past. All any nation can wake into is what the past was when it too had still to be lived — darkness and danger and difficulty and only so much light as those who live in it can find. We Americans cannot wake into the state of mind which produced the great postulates of the medieval world: we can only continue, wherever we are, in dream or in reality, to struggle for the postulates which pertain to us. And these we will not find unless we are ourselves. We will be most ourselves when we are freest to discover who we are.

What is wrong, that is to say, with the dream of past community is the fact that it is not a dream but a remembrance. Mr. Lippmann's book ends in the sand because he has mistaken the direction of history. The flow of human life is not backward toward closer and closer association but forward toward greater and greater individuality. Man's journey is a journey from the remote insensibility of the jelly of his biological beginnings toward the fulfillment of consciousness, and the fulfillment of consciousness is an individual, not a herd, achievement. As his biological destiny is emergence in and to himself, so too is man's spiritual destiny. Ever-increasing consciousness, which means ever-increasing individual consciousness, which means ever-increasing individuality, is the law of human gravity and it cannot be reversed. Particular generations may dread their emergence into individuality and loneliness as our generation dreads it. They may attempt to stampede backward into the warmth and darkness and protection of conformity as millions in Europe and Asia have done in our time, and as an increasing number of our fellow citizens would do here if they could drag the rest of us with them. But the flow of life is in the other direction. The mind can no more return to its womb than can the body. It can only go on — on in increasing intelligence when it can but, whether in intelligence or not, still on.

What we are really witnessing in our time, despite the outcries and the polemics, is not a vast human protest against a wrong steer into a hundred and fifty years of mistaken individual freedom, but a small human boggling in the face of a series of startling and decisive steps toward individuality — steps imposed in part at least by new techniques which tend to free men from their direct dependence on family and clan and tribe. The modern city is a lonely place and the modern universe is lonelier: men who fear loneliness wrap conformity around their souls and attempt to wrap it around their neighbors' also. But the evidence of the contemporary arts — and there is no other dependable evidence of the condition of the human soul in any age — is convincing proof that the human journey has not, for that reason, ended or turned back. On the contrary, as the arts suggest, it has never before pressed on so urgently toward individuality and individual freedom. " 'The Discovery and Colonization of Inwardness,' " writes Erich Heller, " — this might be a fitting title for the story of poetry from the Renaissance to our day." It might indeed, and never since the Renaissance have the discoverers gone deeper into that wilderness of the individual self than in our own time. Rilke is writing of Ibsen when he says: "Farther in than anyone has yet been; a door had sprung open before you, and now you were among the alembics in the firelight." Ibsen had passed through the world of action and appearance "as one crosses a vestibule" until he came to the place "where our becoming seethes and precipitates and changes color, inside." But Rilke himself had made the same far journey. And so too have the novelists — Joyce and Proust and Kafka and their successors — who seem to us most characteristic of our time. In all the modern arts of words, in modern painting, in modern music, a common impulse is at work: an impulse, almost a compulsion, to penetrate the undiscovered country of the individual human consciousness, the human self.

One may or may not like the characteristic art of our epoch. One may regard its characteristic quality as a kind of fad — a passing by-product of the investigations of Freud and Jung. There is perhaps some basis for such an opinion. Freud and Jung and their colleagues have powerfully influenced all our contemporaries, and the manner of some modern art is undoubtedly mannerism. But the fact remains that modern art did not begin with the modern psychologists: Baudelaire had written the *Fleurs du Mal* and Rimbaud had written the *Illuminations* before modern psychology was born. And the further fact is that the direction of modern art is not a direction which the modern artists alone have devised. It is not an invented or a perverse or a wayward direction. It is the direction of all conscious life, for the realization of consciousness is the end which all such life must seek. What modern art means is merely that mankind has crossed over, not secretly and surreptitiously but openly now, into that inward country. We no longer assume the superior reality of the public world of objective reason. We assume instead the deeper reality of the world within — which is to say, the world which each human individual uniquely is.

It requires very little knowledge of any modern art to understand how painful this labor of "discovery and colonization" is:

how dangerous always, how disastrous frequently. The map of the arts in our time is scored with abandoned settlements and roads that lead to nowhere. But it is not by the choice of those who attempt these discoveries that the task is hard. The task is hard in its own nature and its nature is imposed by the situation of modern man. Artists can no more give up and turn back than the rest of us, and the rest of us have no more choice than the artists. Safety lies, security lies, for us as for them, not in an attempt to return to the continent from which we came: the winds blow all one way in human history and, besides, that continent is no longer there. Safety lies, security lies, where hope lies — on ahead. It is not by renouncing individual freedom but by achieving it in the achievement of individuality that we will complete this passage in our mysterious journey. The postulates which will give us peace are not the postulates which satisfied us on another coast. They are the postulates which will express our life beyond — our life as individual human beings set free to be ourselves.

IV

Writers in
a Wrong Time

Faulkner at Stockholm

1951

TEN YEARS AGO the responsibility of the artist was an unfashionable, not to say an improper, subject in American literary circles. Attempts to discuss it in the context of Hitler's war were received with hoots of derision. The writer had no responsibility for anything but the manner of his writing. What he wrote *about* was his own business, not to be judged by his contemporaries. Flaubert had been right: "The finest books are those that have the least subject matter . . . there are no such things as either beautiful or ugly subjects . . ." There was no such thing, for the artist at least, as a choice between Europe — the tradition of the freedom of the human spirit which Europe meant — and the suffocating evil which menaced it.

In the year just past, William Faulkner, accepting the Nobel Prize in Stockholm, and using that moment "as a pinnacle" from which to speak to younger writers throughout the world, took as the text of his sermon the writer's responsibility. He began with a definition of the subject — a categorical definition. There is only one thing worth writing about: "the problems of the human heart in conflict with itself." He went on to relate that election of subject to the tragedy of the time in which he —

and each of us also — lives: the tragedy of "a general and universal physical fear so long sustained by now that we can even bear it." Unless a writer writes of "the old universal truths," the old universal truths of the human spirit, "he will write as though he stood among and watched the end of man." For his own part, Faulkner said, "I refuse to accept this. I believe that man will not merely endure" — endure, that is, as "a puny inexhaustible voice" in a ruined world — "he will prevail. He is immortal, not because he alone among creatures has an inexhaustible voice, but because he has a soul, a spirit capable of compassion and sacrifice and endurance." And having thus defined the subject and related it to the time in which he lived, Faulkner concluded by affirming, in explicit and unequivocal words, the writer's responsibility, using, not that word, but the more direct and personal word, duty: "The poet's, the writer's duty is to write about these things. It is his privilege to help man endure. . . ."

This address was received, as the world knows, without audible protest from any quarter. Quite on the contrary, it was praised even by those who had previously been loudest in their contempt for its fundamental proposition. And the question naturally presents itself: Why?

The most obvious answer is Faulkner himself. Faulkner spoke at Stockholm not only with eloquence, but with an authority which the men of ten years ago did not begin to possess. There is no writer in English more widely or more truly esteemed than William Faulkner. His views, simply because they are his views, are received with respect and examined with attention.

Another probable answer is to be found in the terminology

Faulkner employs. His proposition, though it is derived from the tragedy of his own time, is of universal application and it is stated in universal terms: few literary controversialists would undertake to deny that the poet has a generalized duty to remind man "of the courage and honor and hope and pride and compassion and pity and sacrifice which have been the glory of his past." Had Faulkner advanced this same proposition in terms of a particular crisis, the effect might have been different. To say that the poet has a responsibility for the things of the human spirit, for the glory of the human past, in the face of a particular attack upon the human spirit by a particular enemy of the human spirit, brings the general truth to a specific application which certain minds will reject. And not only because it reduces the inoffensive generalization to a precise application which may be difficult but for another and more plausible reason.

A general duty to write of the things of the spirit is clearly compatible with that paramount loyalty to his own experience which every artist accepts by the acceptance of his art. A specific duty to take the side of man, the side of the human spirit, at a *particular* moment of history, and in the face of a specific evil, is not so clearly compatible. It involves judgments of the world. There were writers, not so long ago, who regarded Fascism as something less than the spiritual destroyer which the world has now discovered it to be, and there are doubtless writers now who do not see the present struggle between spiritual freedom and repressive authoritarianism as the critical battle for the human future in which others know themselves to be engaged.

A third explanation of the shift of sentiment is probably to be found in the changes in the world itself. The last ten years must certainly have been the longest in human history. Certainly they have been the most heavily freighted with menace and premonition. Faulkner's definition of the crisis in terms of physical fear may well be mistaken. It is interesting to notice that he alters it in the little Commencement Address he gave somewhat later. "What threatens us today," he there says, "is fear. Not the atom bomb, nor even fear of it . . . Our danger is not that. Our danger is the forces in the world today which are trying to use man's fear to rob him of his individuality, his soul. . . ." But however the crisis is defined — and most survivors of the decade of McCarthy will prefer Faulkner's second definition to the first — there can be no doubt that the sense of crisis has grown more urgent from year to year since the last war. Not only our bodies — perhaps least of all our bodies — but our civilization, the whole worth and meaning of our human lives, is in danger. And, face to face with that danger, the distinctions so laboriously established by the critic and the literary philosopher between life and poetry, between art and experience, have dissolved into the unrealities out of which they were made. To *be* artist — precisely to *be artist* — a man must concern himself in our time with the things of the human spirit not only in their universal forms but in their specific, their present, agony. Like Tu Fu, he must be able to stare into the tragic face of his world and see "the bones behind those crumpled eyes."

These glimpses of reality which show the human truth behind the artifices of literary theory seem to occur in times like ours. The same Flaubert who dismissed the importance of the idea of the subject so easily in later years, wrote in 1851 to his friend Louis Bouilhet: "Beneath us the earth is trembling. Where can we place our fulcrum, even admitting that we possess the lever?

The thing we all lack is not style, nor that dexterity of finger and bow known as talent. We have a large orchestra, a rich palette, a variety of resources. We know many more tricks and dodges, probably, than were ever known before. No, what we lack is the intrinsic principle, the soul of the thing, the very idea of the subject."

One can only be grateful that, a hundred years later, at another mid-century of the human spirit, a novelist of a comparable stature found his way to the same truth and had the courage to put it into words.

The Muses' Sterner Laws

1953

THE CIVIL WAR in Spain posed a question which many writers found it difficult to answer: the question of the role of artists and poets in the face of the corruption of human values, the perversion of human intelligence and the enslavement of the human mind with which the rise of the police state threatened the entire Western world. Today that question is, if anything, more urgent than it was in the Thirties. The police state, though defeated in Europe, flourishes in Spain, from which it has spread into South America, and rages in Russia from which it has over-run all eastern Europe and the vast extent of China, with the result that civil government has been replaced by police governments in a great part of the earth and individual freedom of mind and conscience, without which civilization as we have known it is impossible, is really secure only in a shrinking area centering politically and economically around our own republic.

More menacing still, the kind of mentality which inflicted the police state on other peoples has made its appearance in American public life and even in the Congress of the United States, revealing itself in the demand, familiar in Soviet Russia and Nazi Germany, that the State should extend its controls to the intellectual and moral life of its citizens: to matters of opinion and belief.

Artists and poets who were able to satisfy themselves fifteen years ago that they had no responsibility for the sickness of the world find themselves today facing inquisition into their private lives conducted in the name, at least, of the government of the United States. And the whole problem is raised anew.

If it is to be discussed anew — and more effectively than it was in the Thirties — one point should be made at the outset: nailed to the iron door. The question of the relation of any artist to the time he lives in is a question not for his time but for his art to answer. Whatever duty he owes as artist he owes only *because* he is artist. If his art requires nothing of him in relation to his time, his time, in so far as he is artist, requires nothing. A despotic government may compel him to think one thing rather than another, to substitute for his own convictions the assertions of the regime, but the moment he accepts that compulsion he is no longer an artist: he is merely a functionary of the state.

What ought to be discussed, therefore, is not a supposed conflict of responsibilities, the one owed to a man's art, the other to society. What ought to be discusssd is the obligation of art. Does art, by its nature, impose on those who serve it a duty of any kind with reference to the public world of happening and event? Or is the nature of art such that the artist, the poet, is freed from any such duty — even from the duty acknowledged by the generality of other men? To put it in literary terms, are those critics right who, pursuing their reasons back through the mirrors of Mallarmé, discover loyalty to the art of poetry in loyalty to the inward self alone? Or was Dante right, and Tu Fu and Shakespeare, to whom loyalty to the art of poetry was loyalty not only to the inward experience of the self within the self but to the outward experience of the self within the time?

The literary generation in which a man lives may change the

fashion of his answer to that question but it will not change the question. To Coleridge the responsibility of the poet for the world of happening and event — "the close connection of poetic genius with the love of liberty and genuine reformation" — was taken for granted. But Coleridge's reasons were reasons which derived from his conception of the art itself, for to Coleridge "truth operative and by effects continually alive" was "the mistress of poets." With us, though we live in an age not unlike Coleridge's in which liberty is under attack from the same quarters and under very much the same pretexts, the close connection of poetic genius with the love of liberty and of genuine reformation is not taken for granted. Far from it. But the reasons are nevertheless reasons which derive from the art as we see the art. For we believe with Andreyev that life, in the modern world, has "gone within." We believe in consequence that the world of poetry is a world within. And in the world within, the crisis of liberty, the agony of a civilization, though they may throw shadows on the roof of the cave, throw shadows only.

It is, in other words, our modern conception of the proper place of poetry which creates the peculiar modern problem of "the responsibility of the poet." Why we choose to shut poetry up within the inward cave in a time in which the outward world is a world vast, tragic and enveloping to such a point that no human being can ignore its presence or escape its consequences is a question for the psychologists. They may perhaps inform us why we have agreed that our arts may not participate in the encounters of our lives at a point in our history when the encounters of our lives are most desperate. The question for the rest of us is simpler though still difficult enough. The question for the rest of us is whether this modern conception of the limits of the art of poetry is well considered.

It is not, needless to say, an escapist conception: a new aestheti-
cism. Our generation has been pretty well persuaded by critics
like I. A. Richards and by philosophers like Suzanne Langer that
the arts are instruments of understanding and that what they enable us to understand is our human lives and the world of feeling
and of sense in which we live them. We accept the necessary and
organic relation between life and art and are even ready, for the
most part, to include within the proper concern of the arts the
reflection, in the private cave, of the world of public and even
political experience.

We agree that what a poet, an artist, feels and may therefore,
in the Aristotelian sense, "imitate" in his art may include his sense
of the sorry world he lives in. But when we come to the consequence of feeling — even the consequence of feeling in the art
itself — the modern barrier erects itself. To feel as poet is not,
in our vocabulary, to feel as participant, even though the emotion
felt is that savage indignation in the face of injustice and cruelty
which moved Swift to unforgettable utterance. The poet with
us, the artist with us, must not be enlisted in any cause — even
the cause of human liberty — even the cause of man. Which,
perhaps, is why Yeats ended his translation of the great Dean's
epitaph with those passionate and angry words:

> *Swift has sailed into his rest;*
> *Savage indignation there*
> *Cannot lacerate his breast.*
> *Imitate him if you dare*
> *World-besotted traveller; he*
> *Served human liberty.*

World-besotted we may not be, but neither are we capable of
the imitation of Swift. Our conception of the art of poetry for-

bids it. The duty of the poet, as we see it, is to live within the cave and feel whatever moves there: not to judge or choose: above all, not to judge or choose in such a way as to affect the world outside. But are we wise — this is the question we should consider — are we wise to see the poet's duty so? Is it only *to feel* that matters in the art of poetry? Was Shaw right for once when he announced that "the main thing in determining the artistic quality of a book is not the opinions it propagates but the fact that the writer has opinions"? Is it truly unimportant in the art of letters what opinions you hold so long as you hold opinions: unimportant in the art of poetry what feelings you have if only you have feelings? Would Tu Fu have been the poet he was if the long misery of his later years, the starvation in the villages, the conscription of the children, the millions dead, had filled him with a gloating, leering satisfaction? Would Dante be revered as a poet if the few images of human virtue he met in his lifetime were jealously plunged into the pit of his hell?

The truth, of course, is that we are mistaken in our first assumption. What the art of poetry demands of those who truly practice it is not merely feeling but a *kind* of feeling. Poetry like any other art exists within and by virtue of the human condition. Its ineradicable postulate is man. A poet, an artist, must not only be capable of feeling, he must be capable of feeling as a man: of feeling as Keats felt, whom Professor Trilling has finely called the last image of health in the long sickness of Europe. The poet's labor is to bring his experience of life, his whole experience, to focus and understanding — but to *human* focus, to *human* understanding. That "universal" of Aristotle's which poetry "tends to express" and without which it is not poetry but something else is a *human* universal. Indeed the central thought of Aristotle's doctrine is precisely that: as Butcher paraphrases it, "imitative art in its highest form, namely poetry, is an expression of *the universal element in human life*." Understanding of that fact is a precondition of the practice and the criticism of every art and above all the art of poetry. A material impossibility — Aristotle again — may exist in terms of art but not a moral, a human, improbability — a violation of human expectation and understanding. It is only in its relation to "the universal element in human life" that a work of art exists as a work of art. Unless its truth is human truth it has none.

The implications for our generation are obvious. Loyalty to the art of poetry cannot be taken to justify a rejection of the human world of tragedy and choice. On the contrary, it is precisely loyalty to the art of poetry which most ineluctably imposes the acceptance of the human world. For though no external power, neither government nor institution, state nor church, may justly tell a poet *what* he is to feel, his art itself will tell him *how* he is to feel. He is to feel as man. And to feel as man is to accept the consequences of feeling. As Swift accepted them. As Milton accepted them.

Whatever in the world of happening and event affects the universal human element affects the poet in his quality as poet. He can no more be indifferent to evils which destroy the common humanity than he can be indifferent to human destiny itself, for human destiny is here in issue. Slavery — above all that worst of slaveries which constrains the minds and consciences of men — the slavery which police governments have imposed in other countries and which the police mentality seems intent on imposing here — slavery is a disaster about which those who feel as men can feel in one way only. And, feeling so, they have no choice, as men or poets either, but to accept the responsibility their passion has imposed. Tu Fu's art did not compel him to write bitterly, and at the risk of his life, of the conscription of little boys. Tu Fu's art required him to live his life awake and the rest followed. He was unable, *being poet,* to escape the vision of "the bones behind those weeping eyes."

•

It is true enough that a poet, an artist, serves his art and not a cause. He goes his own way with his own will beside him and his own truth to find. But on the great issue, on the issue of man, his truth and the truth of history are one. Or, if you prefer it that way, his truth becomes the truth of history. This, I think, is what Yeats is saying in that curious poem addressed to the men of the Nineties, the men of the aesthetic revolt, in which, after years of devotion to the Irish Nationalist cause, and at a time when he was writing political poems which Dowson and Lionel Johnson would have damned, he affirms his constant loyalty to his art: "I have kept faith, though faith was tried, / To that rock-born; rock-wandering foot . . ."

What Yeats is saying in "The Grey Rock" is that "the Muses' sterner laws" demand something more than the Muses' stricter regulations so religiously observed by his companions of the Nineties and the Cheshire Cheese. The Muses' stricter regulations — the drawn blinds, the denial of any passion that has more life in it than death — all this had been well enough for those gifted creatures who "met their ends when young" — and for Yeats young with them. But now the world has changed. Which is to say that Yeats is older. And poetry, which had once been that mirror of the Lady of Shalott which cracked from side to side if you turned your head to look at the actual water-lily, the actual plume, has become, by mere necessity, a way of knowing and understanding and facing whatever a man is obliged to know and understand and face.

Dowson and Johnson and the men of the Nineties had been loyal to the rock-born, rock-wandering foot in what they had *not* done: they had "kept the Muses' sterner laws": they had never given loud service to a cause that they might have a troop of friends. But Yeats, though he had served many causes, the cause of Ireland among them, had been loyal also. For the Muses' sterner laws are not merely the laws of exclusion. They *include* as well. And it is in what they include that they are sternest. They tell the Muses' servants not only what they must forgo, but what they must accept as well, if they are to be admitted to that excellent discipline. What they must accept is a whole life, the outward as well as the inward, "that dead young soldier in his blood" as well as "the pale unsatisfied ones" appearing and disappearing to the mind's sight in the blue depths of the sky.

The Isolation
of the American Artist

1958

IN ATHENS it was Bill Faulkner. In Paris it was Thornton
Wilder. In London it was Robert Frost himself. You can say
almost anything else about the State Department these days but
you can't say it isn't busily exporting the evidences of American
culture. Except that Thornton Wilder wasn't being exported.
There was an interview with him in the Paris edition of the New
York *Herald Tribune* along in April or May in which he was reported as saying that one of the advantages of turning sixty is that
you don't have to go lecturing around the world for the State
Department any more. Since I was turning sixty-five at the
Hotel de la Poste in Saulieu at about that time, and since I had
just come north from lecturing for the State Department in
Rome, and west from lecturing for it in Athens, the remark ran-
kled. It seemed to imply a judgment on my extra five years and
my farther wanderings. Wilder in Paris was giving it all up at the
age of sixty.

And giving it up why? Because, he said, he hadn't done it very
well! It would be difficult to think of a more inadequate justification for a great resolve. In the first place, nobody in Washington has ever suggested that it should be done very well: you just

do it. In the second, Wilder is the most felicitous talker in America on almost any subject and particularly on American culture, and it is inconceivable that, no matter where he spoke, he should have spoken badly. Even in London, where, as everyone knows, the difficulties of language are greatest and the interest in the subject least, he would have made himself understood, and on the Continent his appearances would have been triumphant.

Obviously all this was mere circumlocution. What Wilder meant was something very different. What he meant was either that the job wasn't worth doing or that it couldn't be done and therefore should not be attempted. And it was that thought that spoiled my birthday. I saw myself carrying news of American culture to the Romans and the Athenians and I blushed. In Rome I had spoken in the elegant little auditorium of the Embassy to an audience composed largely of Romans, with a scattering of young Americans; the ambassador and his staff had presumably heard about American culture before. In Athens I had appeared — that would seem to be the appropriate word — in a little downtown theater where the stage was set for a performance of *The Diary of Anne Frank* and the lights were green and the audience included, in addition to a few Embassy people and the usual American busmen, the poet Seferis, the novelist Venezis, the man of letters Katzymbalis, the painter Ghika. In both cities I had spoken on the same theme: the predicament of the American artist. And in both, it now appeared, I had wasted my time, to say nothing of the time of my listeners, and had conceivably made a fool of myself as well.

Why *should* the Romans or the Athenians care about the predicament of American artists? And how, even if they did, could you talk about it intelligibly? The Romans and the Atheni-

ans have writers of their own with their own problems.
I remembered a luncheon under a budding grape arbor in
the garden of a village inn outside Athens with the dark resin-
ated wine in the little glasses and the blue profile of Mount
Hymettus on the shining air and the big, fine voice of George
Katzymbalis reciting a poem of Seferis and Seferis sitting silent
listening, and afterwards the silence. Seferis must have known
even then that he was to go to London as ambassador with all
that bitterness of Cyprus to face and, back of him in Athens, all
that bitterness. I remembered an evening in Rome when Silone
had talked of the current newspaper sensation in words which
had us choking with laughter, but with a curious ironical sadness
in his eyes. I remembered Char, huge in the big room over his
unexpected Paris garden, talking of Rimbaud but thinking from
minute to minute of something else which pulled him back and
back into himself. A writer's life is difficult enough in any city
these days. Why take on a foreigner's troubles?

Wilder had me there, but still I couldn't give in to him altogether. It's true, you don't go abroad for the State Department
to make sympathizers for yourself. But what about your country? Isn't there something writers and artists can do abroad
which can't be done by the diplomats and the sales agents and
the bankers who are there already? It seemed to me there was,
and that almost any observant American tourist could name it.
For almost any observant American tourist who ventures beyond the grand hotels and the managed tours discovers sooner
or later that, friendly as people are, there is a sleeping dog across
the threshold. We are welcome enough to spend our dollars in
the shops, but once we try to walk into a man's life in Europe or
in Asia it's another story.

And not only because our government has played a clumsy and blundering role in Egypt and the Middle East. Governments are supposed to be stupid from time to time, and the world is ready enough to forgive the people they govern and to love them notwithstanding. What is wrong with us in our neighbors' eyes is not our government but ourselves. Or, more precisely, what is wrong is the image of ourselves the world has formed.

The dog across the threshold, to give it the name the Europeans and the Asians and the Africans call it by, is American materialism. You stumble over it everywhere you go if the talk lasts long enough and the tongues are honest. Students meet it more often than their fathers and mothers, and Fulbright Fellows, teaching in colleges and schools, more often still, but every American traveler with eyes and ears and the wit to use them learns to know the dog is there. It is not only that we Americans are richer than the rest but that we seem to like being richer. We make a point of it. When we talk, as we tend to do, about "the American Way of Life," we give the impression that we are thinking not of the freedom we have won for our minds but of the gadgets we have collected for our houses.

The impression is, of course, quite accurate. It is doubtful whether any people in history has ever thought as much and as frankly and as cheerfully about Things as we Americans have in the nineteen-fifties. For one thing, no people in history has ever had as many Things to think about as we have. Not even our American fathers and mothers. In McKinley's time materialism was the privilege of the few who could afford it. With us it has become the birthright of something approaching a majority of the population. The proof is in the election returns. The party to which the manufacturers and distributors and advertisers of

Things traditionally belong has so increased its public support
with the aid of a popular President that it now holds power by
manifest preference of the electorate rather than by prolonga-
tion of the shadow of Abraham Lincoln.

But if this is the underlying cause of the decline of what we
call our foreign relations, then the part American writers and
artists can play is fairly obvious. It becomes, indeed, a part they
cannot help but play: a part they will find themselves playing
whether they wish to or not. Artists are a kind of litmus paper
to test the degree of materialism in any society, and the work
they do and the way they live testify in spite of them or of anyone else. They exist, like the rest of us, by material means, and
they can survive a high concentration of luxury and wealth — as
they have done time and again in the history of art — but materialism of the spirit stifles them. It extinguishes their work, as it
has done in Spain, or it deprives them of their place in the society,
their influence, their effectiveness. The Russians have elevated
their artists, so long as they are obedient, to the top of the hier-
archy; but their work is mediocre. The work of Americans in
many of the arts is of the greatest significance, but what is the
artists' place? Whether they speak or whether they are silent
their actions are eloquent on that point.

The work speaks loudest, as it should. American architecture
has imposed its profiles for better or worse on the metropolitan
horizons of every continent. American music is hard to get away
from anywhere on earth, and some of it, though commonly dismissed as popular, has influenced musicians far and wide. There
are American novels which have found not only readers but imi-
tators in most of the living languages, and American novelists who
have dominated the art of fiction since Joyce died. Even in po-

etry, which is the most national because it is the least translatable of the arts, the principal influence in the English-speaking world over the past fifty years has been that of Yeats and Eliot and Pound, two of whom are Americans, while the greatest living poet today may well be another American, Robert Frost, whose work is so essentially of its own place and speech that, like certain exquisite wines, it will not translate at all.

But though the possibility for artists and writers to work in America can be demonstrated by the work itself, it is not so obviously self-evident that they have a place in American life. Seen from across the oceans in either direction, and even from beyond the Caribbean, the apparent situation of American artists and writers seems to imply the contrary. Our writers appear, from that distance, to live in a kind of domestic exile. They are noticed in the news columns when they die or when they distinguish themselves in some artistically irrelevant way such as selling a novel to the movies for more than the last novel brought, or marrying for the seventh time, but their opinions on questions of public concern are not recorded. There are, that is to say, no American Goethes. There is not even an American Sartre. There are merely — or so it looks from overseas — a number of more or less isolated individuals living quite out of the stream of American life on an island somewhere or in a foreign country or a provincial town or even an insane asylum while the great Republic speaks of itself to the world through its bankers and oilmen and corporation lawyers and generals.

Our friends abroad, needless to say, are well aware of the competence of those bankers and oilmen and generals. They do, however, find it both relevant and interesting that the most audible and authoritative voices in a Republic which once expressed itself through Whitman and Emerson should now be the voices of American men of business, and that the American people should see nothing odd in this situation. The European mind, which once observed that war is too serious an affair to be left to the generals, still believes that life is too important a business to be left to the businessmen. It still believes that great societies find their voices in their arts.

And there is other and more specific evidence which supports the impression that artists and writers play an inferior part in the present life of this country. Our friends abroad could hardly help noticing that American artists and American writers were among the principal targets of McCarthyism and that the indignities and perverse cruelties inflicted upon them were not resented by the American press and public as they would have been almost anywhere else in the non-Communist world. They noticed too that even when McCarthy was belatedly censured there was no expression of public sympathy for these particular victims and no demand that the ugly nonsense end. For, of course, it has not ended. In the vocabulary of the American moment, a vocabulary which listeners overseas find particularly revealing, writers and artists are classified as eggheads, and no one sympathizes with a broken egg: not even when the egg maintains itself with the dignity of an Arthur Miller.

Some of our fellow citizens, though holding no brief for McCarthyism, resent the conclusions drawn by Europeans from these facts. Our writers and artists, they point out, while no doubt badly treated, are not without blame themselves. Writers and artists are notorious political innocents swinging wildly from one extreme to the other, like Malraux, or canting and recanting, like Picasso. If the opinions of such people are not highly regarded in the United States, they have themselves to thank. How is the country to know from which particular soapbox a writer is addressing it?

This, of course, is a familiar self-justification; as familiar as the justification in Plato's *Republic*, where the exile of poets was also defended. But in our time and country it suffers from something worse than familiarity. It misconceives the question at issue. The question with us is not whether writers and artists change their minds. The question with us is whether the rest of the world is justified in regarding us as a materialistic people among whom artists and writers lead a second-class life or live in virtual exile. If it is, we can hardly regain its respect by arguing that we treat our writers and our artists as we do because they are political idiots. It is we who are on trial, not they. They are the witnesses.

They *must* be the witnesses, for they alone can testify credibly to the truth or falsehood of the charge. They alone know to what extent their apparent exile and their apparent inferiority are real, and they alone are in a position to confirm or deny the suffocating materialism from which we are thought abroad to suffer.

It is my personal belief that most of them, given the opportunity, would deny it. They would deny, that is to say, that American materialism, which is real enough and overreal, has yet reached the point of saturation at which the arts are in danger. They would even deny that their miseries under McCarthyism were and are wholly the consequence of a public indifference. On the contrary, many of them would willingly admit — and this would be the most telling aspect of their evidence — that the indifference was in large part *theirs:* that it was their failure to

make concerted efforts to defend themselves, rather than the
apathy of the country, which gave McCarthy his opening. They
would not merely admit it, indeed, they would boast of it. They
would tell audiences in any part of the world that, except for occasional misguided protests, they had been silent, and that they
had been silent not because the senatorial inquisitors had torn
out their tongues but because political silence is the political attitude appropriate to their calling. The American artist does not
engage in political activity even to defend himself — even to
defend the freedom by which art exists.

Not all of them, of course, would say this. There are still
American artists and writers to whom the political world is part
of the world the arts can know. But enough would express themselves in these terms to make it fairly evident that the so-called
"isolation of the American artist" of which our friends in Europe
are so fond of talking is an isolation quite as much by choice as
by necessity. The "political art" of the Thirties is as unpopular
in American artistic circles as it is among the politicians. And it
is unpopular not for political but for aesthetic reasons. It is not
that its artist was then a Communist or a Social Credit man or a
clerical Fascist or a New Dealer; it is simply that he proved himself aesthetically unreliable. He violated the American mystique,
or what has since become the American mystique. He was not a
pure artist. He was a political man.

The isolation of the American artist, which looms as a political
phenomenon in Rome, appears in America, in other words, in
different colors. The political and social and economic factors of
course exist. American materialism is as real as anyone in Italy
ever thought it was. But there is another factor also which must
be known and judged before the Republic is indicted as a country

on the way to materialistic suffocation, and that other factor is one only American artists and writers can speak of with conviction, for only American artists and writers, and the critics who surround them, know that it is there. That other factor is the current American aesthetic.

What the dogmas of this aesthetic are is not perhaps as certain as it might be. None of the numerous critics who accept them have spelled them out in detail. But the fundamental position is nevertheless reasonably clear. The American aesthetic rests, as so many modern aesthetics have rested before it, on the old dichotomy between life and art. It does not go as far as the London aesthetic of the Nineties which made of art, in the angry phrase with which Yeats turned his back on it, a "terrible goddess" to whom life must be sacrificed, but it goes far enough to make of art a minor divinity which must have no traffic with one entire aspect of life.

One of its explicators, for example, informed his hearers on a most solemn occasion that the temptation most dangerous to the artist — the temptation the artist most should fear — is the temptation of public duty. Another, the editor of one of the principal organs of the American aesthetic, explained patiently to the Negro author of a brilliant first novel about American Negro life that a novel about American Negro life written by an American Negro cannot be a work of art because it must necessarily be a novel of "protest." Nor did he shrink from the logical conclusion that American Negroes are thus foreclosed from writing novels that can be works of art at all.

The dogmas behind these various pronouncements may be vague, but what they add up to in the way of aesthetic doctrine is clear enough. What they add up to is a rejection, in the name of aesthetic value, of the old human dream of a possible reconciliation between the outward world of event and the inward world of conception through the act of art; the old dream that art may interpret the inward world to the outward and eventually *make* the outward world habitable for the creature within; the dream which every statue of the great age of Greece expressed and which some of them may, in their now unknown originals, have realized. It is not an admirable or very impressive doctrine. To declare, as the American aesthetic seems to do, that the effort to act upon the external world in the making of a work of art is a betrayal of the work of art is a misconception of the nature of art. The nature of art is action, and there is no part of human experience, public or private, on which it cannot act or should not.

But though this latest attempt to divide the practice of art from the political struggle in which the destiny of our time shapes itself is neither courageous nor noble, it has, nevertheless, its relevance. It puts the isolation of the American artist into a proper perspective. If more American writers and artists went abroad to work and talk, whether they were men who believed in the American aesthetic or men who didn't, the truth of their situation would become more visible across the water than it is. It would then appear that though the increasing materialism of their country is an affliction to them all, their "isolation" in American life is quite as much a matter of the turning of their own backs on the age as of the age's turning of its back on them. It would appear, that is to say, that American materialism is not yet the materialism of the Soviets and, with a bit more courage in its writers and its artists, need never be.

As for Wilder, I hope his vow of silence may wear thin and break. There is no man in America who knows the truth of the

American writer's dilemma better than he and no man whose words will carry farther round the earth. America may be the most magnificently industrialized nation in the world and the most powerful, but she desperately needs defenders who can use the weapons of the spirit, for it is there that she is vulnerable.

Why Can't They Say
What They Mean?

1955

THEY being, of course, the poets. Or rather, the contemporary
poets — those who are now around. "Why can't they put it in
so many words?" "Why can't they just come out with it?"
There are various forms of the question and various tones of
voice to ask it in — the indignant tone of the letter to the editor
of the literary review; the contemptuous tone of the full-page
institutional ad in the New York *Times* which bellows (lie quiet,
ghosts of Avon and Weimar and Florence!) that the prime characteristic of a great work of art is to be easily understood; the
earnest tone of the manifesto of the local poetry society; the outraged tone of the student who can't sit there silent any longer.
But whatever the form and whatever the tone the intention is
the same: "Why can't they say what they *mean?*" "Doesn't a
poet need to be read?" demanded a student of mine in the blazing
first paragraph of a paper on Pound's *Hugh Selwyn Mauberley*.
"If not, what is the purpose of poetry? Art must be amazed at
what some people do to attain her!"

No humane man can be indifferent to such a cry as that even
when it leaves him with a lecture to write over. At least *I*
cannot be indifferent, for its anguish takes me where I live. Not

only am I a practitioner of the art of poetry and contemporary to the extent of being still alive: I am also, in a sense, a teacher of the art. That is to say that I spend a considerable part of my time attempting to teach young men and young women, not how to write poetry — no one, I think, would seriously undertake to do that — but how to read it. The angrily held conviction, therefore, that one of the most characteristic of contemporary poems is not only unreadable but not seriously to be read is, to me, a matter of concern. When I reflect, as I must, that this conviction is not peculiar to one student in one college but may be held by many students in many institutions, the concern becomes an active anxiety.

And an anxiety of a rather disturbing kind. I am not anxious only for the intelligence of the rebellious student — he happened, as a matter of fact, to be one of the most intelligent members of his class. Neither am I fearful for the reputations of my contemporaries among American and English poets: they have done quite well in spite of the remonstrance and it is at least arguable that some of them have flourished because of it. What disturbs me is the relation of all this to what can only be called the health of our civilization. A civilization without a poetry of its own is a contradiction in terms, and a civilization which rejects the poetry it has itself produced is sick: it is an Oedipus civilization stabbing at its own eyes. We may not like the kind of poetry we have produced in the West in this century. We may wish it were some other kind of poetry. But the fact is that this poetry exists and that it is ours. And the further fact is that if we lose contact with it we shall lose an essential contact with ourselves. Only *this* poetry can give us to see the aspect of our lives which poetry in any generation makes visible. When the poetry

produced by a particular kind of sensibility is obscure to those
to whom the sensibility belongs, the sensibility is obscure also —
and the life out of which that sensibility has developed.

If this seems to imply that obscurity in poetry is, at bottom, a
reader's problem rather than a writer's, I should have to agree
that it means just that. Where the obscurity complained of is obscurity in an achieved work it is the reader, not the writer, who
must deal with it. Gide's observation that "obscurity is something the true poet should neither seek nor fear" carries the necessary corollary that obscurity is something the true reader must
neither evade nor avoid: he cannot reject the poem merely because he finds it obscure without failing in his reader's duty to the
art.

This does not mean, of course, that there are not forms of obscurity which justify the rejection of a poem. Gide makes it
plain that his remark applies to "true poets" only. The poet who
is obscure because he is incapable of accomplishing understanding, or who is obscure because he is afraid of being understood,
is not a true poet and should be judged accordingly. If a man
cannot write clean English, or if he affects, by calculated du-
bieties, meanings of which his intelligence is incapable, he deserves no one's serious consideration. There is, however, all the
difference in the world between the writer who deliberately con-
trives ambiguities in the hope of hoisting himself into significance,
not by his own petard but by the chances of the dictionary, and
the true poet who is obscure, or seems so, because of the con-
trolled and achieved and intended implications of his work. With
the true poet, obscurity, where it exists, is the condition of the
poem and must be accepted by the reader in that sense. If the
accomplished poem of the true poet is worth reading it is worth
reading with its density upon it, for its density is part of what it is.

But to say so much is not, of course, to dispose of the problem. The obscurity, if there is obscurity, remains — and all the darker because the reader must stand before it alone. What is he to do about it? The answer depends, of course, on what his difficulty is and only he himself can tell us that. Let us therefore put the question to ourselves. What *is* this contemporary obscurity of which we so persistently complain when we speak of our own poets? Is it something more than mere difficulty of interpretation? If so, what? When the student rages or the respectable lady in the correspondence column spits, is it merely because the reading of this poetry is hard, or is it something else the protestants have in mind? Take Yeats for example. Is Yeats "obscure" within our contemporary usage of that word? Certainly "Byzantium" is as difficult as it is great, which means very difficult indeed. I have spent months over its reading in the past and I have no doubt I shall spend further months before I die. But is "Byzantium" *obscure*? Are any of Yeats's geratest poems *obscure*?

Not, I think, if one means by the word an obduracy which will not yield to ordinary intelligence and perceptiveness. One of Yeats's less important poems, a lyric from *Words For Music Perhaps* which has discouraged many readers, may serve us here:

HIS CONFIDENCE

Undying love to buy
I wrote upon
The corners of this eye
All wrongs done.
What payment were enough
For undying love?

I broke my heart in two
So hard I struck.

What matter? for I know
That out of rock,
Out of a desolate source
Love leaps upon its course.

There is not a single word here which is not readily readable
nor is the syntax in any way complicated. What troubles those
readers who experience trouble is apparently the images and the
implications. Writing "all wrongs done" upon "the corners of
this eye" strikes them as meaningless. But the meaning, however
dark it may be to the intellect, is perfectly available to the image-
reading imagination, is it not? The imagination knows that it is
in the corner of the eye that the wrinkles of suffering are written. Once that is perceived the first stanza reads itself. I suffered wrongs willingly to buy what I hoped would be undying
love for which no payment would be too great.

What then of the second stanza? Here again the only problem
is that of the image and here again the image presents itself to
the eye that can see. The heart is struck so hard that it breaks
as one might strike and break a rock — as Moses struck the rock
from which water gushed forth in that wilderness. Only here
what gushes forth from the rock of the heart — from that desolate source — is love: love that leaps upon its course.

How then does the second stanza relate to the first? There is
no syntactical connection, but the connection of emotional relationship is obvious enough. I had hoped to buy love *for* myself
— undying love — by suffering: I did not succeed but by this
suffering I broke my heart, and from my broken heart — that
desolate source — poured forth *my* love. It is a small poem but a
poem profoundly and unforgettably true, not only of Yeats

and his unhappy love, out of which came so much else that leaped upon its course — poetry — insight, but of many, many others also: indeed, in some measure, of all of us.

The difficulty in reading "His Confidence," in other words, is in no way to be distinguished from the difficulty of reading a sonnet by Shakespeare or one of the Odes of John Keats. And the same thing is true of Yeats's greatest poems also. Indeed Yeats differs from his comparable predecessors in two ways only: in his use of particular symbols and metaphors provided by his personal philosophic system, and in the special character of the critical apparatus which has grown up around his poems. The symbols and metaphors, however, create philosophical rather than poetic problems: they are *poetically* comprehensible in their own right and the philosophic significances can usually be ignored for reading purposes. As for the critical apparatus, it need not interfere unduly with the pleasure of reading Yeats. It is true of Yeats's work as of the work of many of his contemporaries that interpreters have sometimes increased the poetic difficulties in order to increase the academic triumphs, but the general reader is under no obligation to accept professional estimates of the hardships and adversities. Yeats's poems are poems, not puzzles, and the academic tendency to make riddles of them should not delude nor discourage the reader who comes to them as works of art. He should remember that "difficult" poets, or poets who can be made to seem so, are godsends to the unpoetical instructor — which is why so many courses, miscalled courses in modern poetry, are devoted to their work: the instructor can teach the difficulties, not the poems — a far easier task. With Yeats, as with all true artists, it is the poems which matter.

And Yeats's poems are, to an unusual degree, whole and complete within themselves, requiring nothing of their readers — if we may call it nothing — but the power to see and hear and feel and smell and taste and, above all, think. Misinterpretation comes when it does come, not from ignorance of the glosses but from a failure to understand the syntax (which, in Yeats, is as powerful as it is subtle), or from a failure to be *present* sensuously and imaginatively at the scene, or from a failure to exercise the full power of the intelligence in relating the experience of the poem to one's own experience of the world. None of these things are easy to do in a poem like "Byzantium" or "Vacillation" or "Among School Children" or "The Statues," but the difficulties in the way are not difficulties which anyone, I think, could properly call obscurities. A work of art is not *obscure*, as I understand the usage of the word, if it demands of its readers or listeners or observers that they come to it fully awake and in the possession of all their faculties. It is obscure only if it demands of them what their faculties at their best and liveliest cannot provide.

No, what the assailants of contemporary poetry have in mind is not the difficulty of inward meaning one finds in Yeats. At least it is not Yeats they mention. Their principal target is and has been for many years Ezra Pound, and if there is one thing more than another which is patently true of Ezra Pound it is the fact that the meanings of *his* meanings are not in doubt. His diagnosis of his time and of all previous times in his *Cantos* comes down to the simplest of propositions — that usury is the mother of all ill. His ideas about literature — and they are numerous — are as definite and precise, and as fruitful, as ideas could well be. And his emotions, at least the emotions his poetry expresses, are as plain as they are few:

Tard, trés tard, je t'ai connue, la Tristesse,
I have been hard as youth sixty years.

J'ai eu pitié des autres
probablement pas assez, and at moments that suited my conven-
ience.

It is accurately said. Love of dead men and women you will find
in Pound, but for the living — including, at the last, himself —
little but exasperation or contempt or rage. It is not, therefore,
because his intentions are dark that Pound can be charged with
obscurity. It is for a different reason — a reason which may go
some way to elucidate the nature of the whole complaint about
contemporary poetry.

What brings the charge of obscurity down upon Ezra Pound
is the *character of the references* to persons and to events out of
which he constructs the fabric of his more important work. The
beginning of the Sixth Canto will serve as an example:

What have you done, Odysseus,
We know what you have done. . . .
And that Guillaume sold out his ground rents
(Seventh of Poitiers, Ninth of Aquitain).
"Tant les fotei com auzirets
Cen e quatre vingt e veit vetz"
The stone is alive in my hands, the crops will be thick in my
death year.

Who, says the indignant reader, is this William? And what was
seventh of Poitiers and ninth of Aquitaine? And why ground
rents? And what is this Provençal couplet about making love to
somebody a hundred and eighty-four times? And in whose hand
is the stone alive? And what stone? And what is the relation

between the live stone and the thick crops and the death year? And who am "I" who suddenly appear at the end? And why — a thousand times why — go at it in this way anyhow?

Well, the answers to the first seven questions can be quite accurately supplied if anyone is willing to take the trouble. A Mr. Carne-Ross was, with the following results: William is William IX of Aquitaine (d. 1127), crusader and troubadour, who sold his lands to tenants instead of hiring them out and thus living by "usury," and the couplet is from one of William's poems in which he boasts of having spent eight days incognito with two noble ladies who believed he was dumb and wouldn't be able to tell anybody (with the frequent consequences aforesaid), and the thick crops refer to the fruitful results throughout the kingdom of so much royal potency, and the stone alive in the hand, orchidaceous pun aside, refers to the fact that the arts of the stonecutter and the builder, like all the rest of the arts, flourish under a potent father-king as distinguished from an impotent usurer-king. All of which, of course, makes complete sense as well as establishing the fundamental truth in view: that everything does well, including, presumably the two noble ladies, where money isn't hired. The last question however still remains. Why go at it this way? Why not say it in so many words? Why, in any event, not put it all down so that it can be understood without the assistance of such scholars and interpreters as the ingenious Mr. Carne-Ross?

But here again our guide has gone before us. The fault, says Mr. Carne-Ross, is in ourselves, not in Mr. Pound. Mr. Pound should not be denounced because we can't take his broad hints and reconstruct an entire corner of history out of a man's name and a tag of Provençal verse. The trouble is that we have lost the common heritage of myth and legend to which earlier and more fortunate writers could appeal and have become incompetent readers. No one is to blame but the generations which broke the tradition and the only remedy, if we wish to read again, is to shore up the shattered columns and rebuild the city.

It is not, I think you will agree, a very comforting or a very persuasive answer. It is quite true that Milton made copious use of curious names and events which his readers were able to identify only because they and he had read the same books and studied the same languages. It is true also that all those elder poets who constructed their poetic world out of classic mythology or ancient history or the tales of Boccaccio found ready readers only because their generation knew Boccaccio and the myths as well as they. But are Guillaume and his couplet really of that order? Was there ever a time when an English poet could expect to be generally understood in such terms? And Pound — let there be no mistake about that — does wish to be understood: ". . . in discourse," he says in his Seventy-ninth Canto, "what matters is/to get it across e poi basta." Indeed the aim of writing, as his Eightieth Canto sees it, is "to bring your g.r. to the nutriment/ gentle reader to the gist of the discourse."

The problem is thus more complicated and more interesting than Mr. Carne-Ross makes it seem. Pound's references in his *Cantos* are drawn from the poetry and art and politics of a dozen languages and countries and there has never been a "common heritage of myth and legend" in English, or, I think, in any other tongue, which contained anything like that body of public knowledge. Nor has any "common heritage of myth and legend" in any country ever contained the *kind* of recondite or purely personal or purely scholarly allusion to which Pound is prone. Take, for example, the First Canto with its magnificently cadenced account of the voyage of Odysseus from Circe's island to that beach in Hell: the strong pull of the rhythm when the wind takes hold of the ship and the leveling off after, like the leveling off of the vibrations of a climbing plane, when the sail truly fills and the ship runs in the open sea. Toward the end of this Canto, after an extended passage which would be wholly intelligible to anyone who knew Homer, and readable enough whether one knew Homer or not, there suddenly appears a character named Divus (patently no Greek) who is commanded to lie quiet, and, beside him, a "Cretan" of whom nothing is said but that an unspecified "phrase" is his. Their position in the Canto indicates that they are persons of importance but nothing in the Canto itself identifies them, nor is there anything in the common heritage of the English-speaking peoples either now or at any previous time which would enable a reader to discover who they are or why they are there. As a matter of fact, only Pound himself, or a sedulous student who had read Pound's other writings, or, conceivably, a specialist in late Latin texts, should such a man take to reading contemporary poetry, could very well know the answer. For Andreas Divus was a scholar who lived early in the sixteenth century and wrote a Latin translation of the *Odyssey*, "little more than a trot or a pony," which Pound, as he tells us in an essay of 1918, had picked up in a Paris bookstall about 1908 or 1910 in an edition of the early 1800's which contained also the *Hymni Deorum* of a certain Cretan named Georgius Dartona, the second of which (to Aphrodite) contained, in turn, the phrase here suggested. And why is Divus to lie quiet? Because the preceding matter is largely a translation, or rather a magnificent transubstantiation, of his text.

Now this, you may very well think, is a special and understandable case: an ingenious method of at once confessing and concealing plagiarism. It is, I assure you, no such thing. To begin with,
Divus, not Pound, is the beneficiary of this traffic as the great
translator — for Pound is surely one of the greatest in the history
of our tongue — very well knew. Again, and more important,
Divus and the Cretan are not isolated instances. They are two
among multitudes in the *Cantos* and elsewhere. The Second
Canto, the most lyrical of the lot, contains, for example, in the
midst of such a Mediterranean scene as no other modern poet
has accomplished, "the voice of Schoeney's daughters." You find
there Sordello, whom even an age which has forgotten Browning
remembers; you find Eleanor of Aquitaine — no problem surely;
you find Homer — "Ear, ear for the sea-surge, murmur of old
men's voices"; you find Helen; you find Tyro whom any classical dictionary will identify as the beautiful daughter of the King
of Elis who was seduced by Neptune as she walked by the river
bank —

> *And the blue-grey glass of the wave tents them,*
> *Glare azure of water, cold-welter, close cover . . .*

you have the Mediterranean full of light and dazzle with
[Pound's phrases] the quiet sun-tawny sand-stretch and the
gulls broading out their wings in the sun and the snipe coming
for their bath, spreading wet wings to the sun film; you have evening and that tower like a one-eyed great goose craning up out of
the olives "And the frogs singing against the fauns/in the half
light"; — you have all this, and in the middle of it you have the
voice of Schoeney's daughters. And who are Schoeney's daughters? How can a man discover them? Only by reading Gold-

ing's translation of Ovid, which few have read and none can now buy, where it is written:

> *Atlant, a goodlie lady, one*
> *of Schoeney's daughters.*

Atlanta and her sisters stand alone in their private darkness amidst all that light, but not so the rest of the masked figures of Pound's poems. As you read on into the later *Cantos* the masks crowd around you until, in the Pisan group, the naked face is the exception. Only a reader who was himself present in the Disciplinary Barracks of the American Army at Pisa during the months of Pound's incarceration there could possibly identify the greater part of the shadowy figures of that Inferno: could possibly know, for example, that the roster of Presidents of the United States refers to a list of Negro prisoners, or that the Steele of "Steele that is one awful name" identifies the officer in command of the stockade. The references here are not only outside any common cultural heritage: they are outside the possibilities of common knowledge of any kind. Only with the aid of commentators and interpreters — very special commentators and interpreters — can they be read at all and some references have thus far mystified even the most devoted of the glossarists. The world still waits, I believe, for the identification of a certain nobleman with dirty lace cuffs who pops up out of nowhere in the Café Dante in Verona.

Now, the cumulative effect of all this is, without doubt, infuriating. Even so wise and gentle a man as that fine Greek poet, George Seferis, betrays irritation when he thinks back over his experience of the *Cantos:* "The reader turning the pages becomes dizzy noting the successive insertions of foreign texts; of incidents or of conversations, very often in a foreign language; of persons known from history or entirely unknown, whose unexpected presence he cannot explain . . ." The irritation is understandable. But is irritation or even rage an adequate answer to the puzzle? Is it really enough to say, as a very considerable number of our contemporaries do say, that you "can't read" Pound — or "can't read" contemporary poetry in general because of Pound; that its obscurities are unnecessary; that they could easily be dispensed with; that the whole thing is a fraud? Here is a man whose position as "true poet" is not open to question: Eliot gave it as his opinion some years ago that Pound was then the most important poet writing in English. Here, furthermore, is a man whose declared purpose as a poet is to communicate: a man to whom the first law of discourse is to communicate *e poi basta*. Is it possible to dismiss the work of such a man as deliberately dark or intentionally obscure or merely incompetent? Is it conceivable that a writer of this stature and these beliefs would devote his life and his art to frustration or could, without adequate reason, construct so curious a monument to himself?

And yet what reason can there be for the use by any writer, no matter what his position or his convictions, of a vocabulary of reference which no one but himself or his coterie or some desperate candidate for the Ph.D. can ever be expected to unravel? How can Pound feel obliged to represent essential parts of what he has to say not by common but by proper nouns, unknown as well as known; by fragments of quotations in numerous tongues, including tongues neither the writer nor his readers speak; by fragments of history as it was or as it might have been, either in his own country or in some other; by bits of conversation between unrecognized conversationalists; by the dry feathers and

old tags of the gossip of the art studios? Why doesn't he come
straight out with it in comprehensive and comprehensible words?
Why, in brief, doesn't he say what he means?

The question with which we started has, you see, somewhat
altered its character. What began as an irritable complaint about
the habits and practices of contemporary poets as a group has become a disturbed and rather disturbing inquiry into the reasons
for the behavior of one of them. Unless we are prepared to assert, as no intelligent man could, that Pound's principal poems are a vast and foolish hoax, we must consider that their
method has a purpose. But what purpose?

A specific example, taken from Pound's finest poem, *Hugh Selwyn Mauberley*, may perhaps make the question more precise.
In the first section of *Mauberley*, the *Ode* which sums up the
dilemma of the literary young man whose literary fate is to be
the subject of the sequence, there occurs the line

His true Penelope was Flaubert.

Here, of five words, two are proper nouns, but proper nouns in
this case with which any intelligent reader will be familiar. Penelope is of course the beloved to whom through thick or thin a
wanderer returns. Flaubert is a novelist whose theories of style
and whose handling of experience altered the course not only of
the novel but of the art of letters generally. What is being said,
then, to the reader who understands these references, is that a
certain literary style and attitude were the end and object of
someone's searchings — in this case Hugh Selwyn Mauberley's.
But this is being said not in several dozen words but in five, and
with a gain, not a loss, of allusiveness and precision. Pound's line

is far more meaningful than my paraphrase, as well as being briefer, handsomer, and more memorable. And the same thing is true, it will be found, throughout this poem. Very little of *Mauberley* is *about* its subject: the greater part of it *is* its subject. The poem is less a poem, in the ordinary sense, than a detailed tapestry made up of proper names and the figures they evoke; made up of moments of past time, of gods, of mottoes, of landscapes. Where a literary generalization would have been possible, there is Flaubert *tout court*. Where Mauberley's frenzied pride is in issue there, instead of the appropriate epithet, is Capaneus on the walls of Thebes. Where it is Mauberley's gullibility which is to be exposed there is no adjective, there is only the image of the trout and its factitious bait. The figure takes the place of the abstraction.

But what then is this figured writing? How, except in its own terms, is it to be described? In an age in which every other book is a book about symbolism, are we to call these figures symbols? Not certainly in any sense but Suzanne Langer's, to whom everything that means is so defined. These are rather *signs* than symbols. They stand, not, as Yeats's symbols do, for the invisible essence which only this particular visible form can express, but for general ideas or conceptions which general terms could also have communicated. The particular is chosen *instead* of the general: the figure *in place* of the abstraction.

What we have, in other words, as a number of recent writers on Pound have helpfully pointed out, is a kind of picture writing. The common coinage of familiar discursive writing in which the same word may serve a multitude of different uses, designating now one particular event and now another, is rejected wherever possible in favor of a series of unique and specific words designating unique and specific situations. As in the case of picture writing, the number of signs is limitlessly increased, but each sign belongs much more clearly to its thing than in the case of signs made out of the interchangeable terms of the generalizing dictionary. One critic of Pound's work has referred to his figures as pictograms or ideograms, but they are much more specific than that. Ideograms have also, in their way and within their limits, exchangeable meanings: Pound's figures have not. The figure of the line "His true Penelope was Flaubert" is not pictogram Flaubert set down beside pictogram Penelope in associated conjunction. The figure is Flaubert *and* Penelope; Flaubert *in the context of* Penelope; Flaubert, if you will, in Penelope's dress.

We could multiply instances throughout *Mauberley* and the *Cantos*, but the situation is, I think, clear. *The obscurity of which complaint is made in Pound is an obscurity of the specific.* His meanings are dark because he composes in pictures and because his pictures are sometimes, like private photographs, too peculiarly unique; because the particular figure does not signify to all, or, in extreme cases, to any of Pound's readers. Here is somebody in *Mauberley* whom an expert on the generals of the Franco-German War might recognize as one of them — though even he might well be wrong. Here in the *Cantos* is what may be a Chinese god or a Chinese girl or even a Chinese philosopher: only a Taoist would know, and not many Taoists read Pound. Here is "Poor Jenny" whom no one but the Pre-Raphaelites would recall — and the Pre-Raphaelites are dead. The figures are meaningful enough — specifically and wonderfully meaningful — when they are identified, but until we can place these ambiguous figures they are so many faces in a heap of faces signifying nothing, and our question repeats itself with point and passion: Why not *say* it in general and generally comprehensible terms? Why hand us the private photographs to figure out if we can?

Pound, if we asked him — if we looked back through his theories and his theorizing — would tell us something by way of answer but not enough. For years in his younger days he went about London attacking English poets of renown as fabricators of a mere "vehicle for transmitting thoughts" and demanding the substitution of what he called "specific rendering." Now "rendering" is a Symbolist word of the Nineties and we may look to Symbolist doctrine to define its meaning. To the Symbolists the poet's business was with his experience, and particularly with the experience of his consciousness, and every moment of that experience was unique. It was therefore the poet's task to invent a particular language appropriate to his particular life. What was basic to Symbolist doctrine, in other words, was the diversity of experience, and what Pound was doing in his early days in London was to carry Symbolist doctrine to its logical conclusion: the conclusion that diversity of experience must be expressed in diversity of terms. If you can't generalize experience neither can you generalize *about* experience. All you can do is "render" it "explicitly" in its inherent explicitness, placing your reader where you yourself have been — naked among the minute particulars. Literature to Pound, as every fortunate school boy has now been taught, is language "charged with meaning" to the greatest possible extent, and the greatest possible extent is the extent made possible by "explicit rendering."

That is the theory. But face to face with a poem we cannot read because the explicitness of the rendering is explicit in terms of someone or something we can't identify, the theory does not help us very much. It does not resolve the obscurity. If anything the obscurity resolves *it*. The poem stands there meaningless for all the talk, and we are suddenly given to see that the theory is merely what literary theories so often are — an excuse and a self-justification. Pound has made a virtue, as the Symbolists before him made a virtue, of rejecting the generalization, the least common denominator, and presenting the unique and diverse and fragmented experience in equivalents of itself. But in so doing he has quite obviously been driven, as the virtue-makers commonly are, by something other than literary choice — by an unnamed literary necessity. "Explicit rendering" is not inevitably and always a good thing in itself. It may produce marvelously precise and moving effects when its explicit equivalents are legible, but when they are not legible it may produce no effects at all. And it is quite obvious that they must often be illegible. There are simply not enough publicly recognizable photographs in any man's bureau drawer to enable him to present an extensive or complicated experience by this means.

The theory therefore fails to justify the obscurity of which we complain: we must go beyond the choice to the necessity. We must go to the reasons which produced the theory. We must ask why, granted that "explicit rendering" is not always and under all circumstances a better way of writing poetry, Pound was obliged to persuade himself and others that it was? Why was it impossible for him to employ those readier means of communication which had been open to poets, including the greatest poets, in the past? When anything happened to Goethe, as Gide once remarked, he turned it into a generality. Why could not Pound?

The answer — and it is an answer which has much to say

about the whole question of obscurity of reference in contemporary poetry — is, I think, this: *Neither Pound nor his contemporaries have been able to turn the particular into the general as Goethe did because the general is not available to them as it was a hundred years before.* Goethe's was a time in which the particular found its place in the general naturally and easily and was best observed in that context. Ours is a time of a very different character. The "general order," if there is one, is no longer open to serious writers in prose or verse, and the particular is so overwhelming in its particularity that it can only be understood, when it can be understood at all, in its character as itself. The consequence is that our literature has of necessity become a literature of particularity. In prose we have been forced toward that particularity of the external world which we call "realism," or toward that other inward particularity which attempts to present the moments of the individual consciousness in their ungeneralized and ungeneralizable diversities. Poetry, moved by the same influences, has been driven in the same direction. But because the end and purpose of poetry is not merely to represent or to comprehend experience but to *possess* it, "realism" of whichever kind has not served as the poetic means. Poetry has been driven not merely to *designate* the particulars but, in some way, to *contain* them. The labor is not new in kind. Thousands of years before our epoch it was praticed by Chinese poets in their attempts to possess isolated moments of experience. What is new with us is the application of the method. Ours are the first poets in the history of the art to attempt to use the poetry of specific equivalents for such extended renderings of public experience as Eliot's vision of the modern world in *The Waste Land* or Pound's view of universal history in *The Cantos*.

The essential point, however, so far as their obscurity goes, is not that our poets have made the attempt. The essential point is that the attempt has been forced upon them. Lacking a "general order" to contain the great sequences of time and space and to provide metaphors for their expression, our contemporaries have had no alternative, if they wished to handle those sequences, but to represent them in their specific equivalents. The obscurity of reference in contemporary poetry, in other words, is truly an obscurity of necessity rather than of choice. If it is not, for that reason, less obscure, it is, or should be, less offensive. A reader who feels that difficulties have been deliberately thrown in his way in accordance with some aesthetic doctrine or other, has occasion to feel indignant: a reader who understands that the difficulties he faces are difficulties inherent in the approach to the experience he is attempting to possess, has none. If labor is demanded of him it is labor imposed not by the whim of the poet but by the necessities of the poet's task.

This is not to argue that all the difficulties of reference in modern poetry are inescapable. The greatest of modern poets, Yeats, succeeded in forcing the most characteristic of all contemporary experiences to express itself in terms and images which a reader with the least awareness of himself and of his world can comprehend. There can hardly be a student in any American college worthy of the name to whom "The Second Coming" is not a meaningful statement. But the fact that other contemporary poets have not achieved Yeats's mastery of the experience of the age does not mean that their work is not essential to an understanding of the sensibility of our time, or, what is perhaps more important, to its expression. Those readers who have come to see that poetry is an instrument of knowledge, and that the knowledge it can convey is a knowledge of their own lives, and that their own lives must be lived in the age into which they have been born, will not willingly be excluded from the poetry of their own time by those difficulties of communication which are a characteristic of the time and a condition of its experience.

V

Teaching
and Harvard

Why Do We
Teach Poetry?

1956

It is a relief to come upon someone who feels no defensiveness whatever about the teaching of poetry, someone who is perfectly certain that poetry ought to be taught now as at any other time and who is perfectly certain also that he knows why. The paragon I have in mind is a young friend of mine, a devoted teacher, who was recently made headmaster of one of the leading American preparatory schools, and who has been taking stock, for some time past, of his curriculum and his faculty. Poetry, as he sees it, ought to be taught "as a most essential form of human expression as well as a carrier throughout the ages of some of the most important values in our heritage." What troubles him is that few teachers, at least in the schools he knows, seem to share his conviction. He is not too sure that teachers themselves have "an abiding and missionary faith in poetry" which would lead them to see it as a great clarifier — a "human language" capable of competing with the languages of mathematics and science.

But though teachers lack the necessary faith, the fault, as my young friend sees it, is not wholly theirs. The fault is the fault of modern criticism, which has turned poetry into something he calls "poetry itself" — meaning, I suppose, poetry for poetry's sake. "Poetry itself" turns out to be poetry with its meanings distilled away, and poetry with its meanings distilled away is difficult if not impossible to teach in a secondary school — at least *his* secondary school. The result is that secondary school teachers have gone back, as to the lesser of two evils, to those historical and anecdotal practices sanctified by American graduate schools in generations past. They teach "poets and not poetry." With the result that "students become acquainted with poets from Homer to MacLeish" (quite a distance no matter how you measure it!) "but the experience doesn't necessarily leave them with increased confidence in what poetry has to offer." I can well believe it.

The reason why modern criticism has this disastrous effect, the reason why it produces "an almost morbid apathy toward 'content' or 'statement of idea,'" is its excessive "preoccupation with aesthetic values." Modern criticism insists that poems are primarily works of art; and when you insist that poems are primarily works of art you cannot, in my friend's view, teach them as carriers "throughout the ages of some of the most important values in our heritage." What is important about Homer and Shakespeare and the authors of the Bible is that they were "realists with great vision . . . whose work contains immensely valuable constructions of the meaning of life"; and if you talk too much about them as artists, those constructions of the meaning of life get lost.

Now this, you will observe, is not merely another walloping of the old horse which was once called the New Criticism. It goes a great deal farther. It is a frontal attack upon a general position maintained by many who never accepted the New Crit-

icism or even heard of it. It is an attack upon those who believe
— as most poets, I think, have believed — that a poem *is* primarily a work of art and must be read as a work of art if it is to be
read at all. It is a high-minded and disinterested attack but an
attack notwithstanding. What it contends is that an approach to
poetry which insists that a poem is a work of art blocks off what
the poem has to say, whereas what the poem has to say is the
principal reason for teaching it.

I can understand this argument and can respect the reasons for making it. Far too many of those who define poetry in
exclusively artistic terms use their definition as a limiting and
protective statement which relieves them of all obligation to
drive the poem's meaning beyond the meanings of the poem: beyond the mere translation of the symbols and metaphors and
the classical or other references — the whole apparatus of *explication du texte*. Far too many, indeed, of those who have to do
with literature generally in our time, and particularly with modern literature, consider that meanings in any but a literary
(which includes a Freudian) sense are not only outside, but
beneath, their proper concern — that the intrusion of questions
of morality and religion into the world of art is a kind of trespass
and that works of literary art not only should but *can* be studied
in a moral vacuum.

But although I can understand this argument, and although I
can respect its reasons, and although I believe it raises a true issue
and an important issue, I cannot accept it; for it rests, or seems
to me to rest, on two quite dubious assumptions. The first is the
assumption, familiar in one form or another to all of us, that
the "idea" of a work of art is somehow separable from the work
of art itself. The most recent — and most egregious — expres-

sion of this persistent notion comes from a Dean of Humanities in a great institution of learning who is reported by the New York *Times* to have argued in a scholarly gathering that "the idea which the reader derives from Ernest Hemingway's *The Old Man and The Sea* comes after the reader has absorbed some 60,000 words. This takes at least an hour. . . . A similar understanding could come after a few minutes' study of a painting by a skillful artist." Precisely, one imagines, as the Doré illustrations gave one the "idea" of the *Inferno* in a few easy looks!

It is the second assumption, however, which divides me most emphatically from my young friend. For the second assumption seems to be that "art" and "knowledge" are somehow opposite and irreconcilable conceptions so that if you teach a poem as work of art you cannot teach it as instrument of perception. This too, of course, is a fairly familiar notion in our world: it is a commonplace with us that knowledge is the exclusive domain of science and that poetry has nothing to do with it. "Whatever," says Bertrand Russell, "can be known can be known by means of science." But because the notion is generally accepted does not necessarily mean that it is true. For the fact is that poetry also is capable of knowledge; that poetry, indeed, is capable of a kind of knowledge of which science is not capable; that it is capable of that knowledge *as poetry*; and that the teaching of poetry as poetry, the teaching of poem as work of art, is not only not incompatible with the teaching of poetry as knowledge but is, indeed, the only possible way of teaching poetry as knowledge.

To most of us, brought up as we have been in the world of abstractions which science has prepared for us, and in the kind of school which that world produces — schools in which almost all teaching is teaching of abstractions — the notion of poetry as knowledge, the notion of art as knowlege, is a fanciful notion. Knowledge by abstraction we understand. Science can abstract ideas about apple from apple. It can organize those ideas into knowledge about apple. It can then introduce that knowledge into our heads — possibly because our heads are abstractions also. But poetry, we know, does not abstract. Poetry presents. Poetry presents the thing as the thing. And that it should be possible to *know* the thing *as the thing it is* — to *know* apple *as* apple — this we do not understand; this, the true child of the time will assure you, cannot be done. To the true child of abstraction you can't know apple as apple. You can't know tree as tree. You can't know man as man. All you can *know* is a world dissolved by analyzing intellect into abstraction — not a world composed by imaginative intellect into itself. And the result, for the generations of abstraction, is that neither poetry nor art can be a means to knowledge. To inspiration, yes: poetry can undoubtedly lead to that — whatever it is. To revelation, perhaps: there may certainly be moments of revelation in poetry. But to knowledge, no. The only connection between poetry and knowledge we can see is the burden of used abstractions — adages and old saws — which poetry, some poetry, seems to like to carry — adages most of which we knew before and some of which aren't even true.

But if all this is so, what then is the "experience of art" — the "experience of poetry" — which all of us who think about these things at all have known? What is the experience of *realization* which comes over us with those apples on a dish of Cézanne's or those three pine trees? What is the experience of realization which comes over us with Debussy's *Nuages?* What is the experience of realization which comes over us when Coleridge's robin sits and sings

> *Betwixt the tufts of snow on the bare branch*
> *Of mossy apple-tree, while the nigh thatch*
> *Smokes in the sun thaw; . . .*

or when his eave-drops fall

> *Heard only in the trances of the blast,*
> *Or if the secret ministry of frost*
> *Shall hang them up in silent icicles,*
> *Quietly shining to the quiet Moon.*

And if all this is so, why does one of the most effective of modern definitions of poetry (Arnold's in his letter to Maurice de Guérin) assign to that art the peculiar "power of so dealing with *things* as to awaken in us a wonderfully full, and new and intimate sense of them and of our relation with them"?

The answer is, of course, that the children of abstraction are wrong — and are impoverished by their error, as our entire time is impoverished by it. They are wrong on both heads. They are wrong when they think they *can* know the world through its abstractions: nothing can be known through an abstraction but the abstraction itself. They are wrong also when they think they *cannot* know the world as the world: the whole achievement of art is a demonstration to the contrary. And the reason they are wrong on both heads is the reason given, quite unintentionally, by Matthew Arnold. They are wrong because they do not realize that all true knowledge is a matter of relation: that we *really* know a thing only when we are filled with "a wonderfully full, new and intimate sense of it" and, above all, of "our relation with" it. This sense — this *knowledge* in the truest meaning of the word knowledge — art can give but abstraction cannot.

There are as many proofs as there are successful works of art. Take, for obvious example, that unseen mysterious phenomenon, the wind. Take any attempt, by the familiar process of abstraction, to "know" the wind. Put beside it those two familiar lines of George Meredith:

> *Mark where the pressing wind shoots javelin-like*
> *Its skeleton shadow on the broad-back'd wave!*

What will be the essential difference between the two? Will it not be that the first, the analytical, statement is or attempts to be a wholly objective statement made without reference to an observer (true everywhere and always), whereas an observer — *one's self* as observer! — is involved in the second? And will not the consequential difference be that a relation involving one's self is created by the second but not by the first? And will not the end difference be that the second, but not the first, will enable us to know the thing itself — to know what the thing is *like?*

It would be quite possible, I suppose, to semanticize this difference between knowledge by poetry and knowledge by abstraction out of existence by demonstrating that the word, know, is being used in two different senses in the two instances, but the triumph would be merely verbal, for the difference is real. It is indeed the realest of all differences, for what it touches is the means by which we come at reality. How are we to find the knowledge of reality in the world without, or in the shifting, flowing, fluid world within? Is all this a task for the techniques of abstraction — for science as it may be or as it is? Is it through abstraction alone that we are to find what is real in our experience of our lives — and so, conceivably, what is real in ourselves? Or do we need another and a different way of knowing — a way of knowing which will make that world out there, this world in here, available to us, not by translating them into something else — into abstractions of quantity and measure — but by bringing us ourselves to confront them as they are — man and tree face to face in the shock of recognition, man and love face to face?

The question, I beg you to see, is not what we *ought* to do. There is no ought. A man can "live" on abstractions all his life if he has the stomach for them, and many of us have — not the scientists only, but great numbers of the rest of us in this contemporary world, men whose days are a web of statistics and names, and business deals, held together by the parentheses of a pair of commuting trains with three Martinis at the close. The question is not what we ought to do. The question is what we have the choice of doing — what alternatives are open to us. And it is here and in these terms that the issue presents itself to the teacher of poetry.

Colleges and universities do not exist to impose duties but to reveal choices. In a civilization like ours in which one choice has all but overwhelmed the other, a civilization dominated by abstraction, in which men are less and less able to deal with their experience of the world or of themselves unless experience and self have first been translated into abstract terms — a civilization like a foreign language — in such a civilization the need for an understanding of the alternative is urgent. What must be put before the generation of the young is the possibility of a knowledge of experience *as* experience, of self *a*s self; and that possibility only the work of art, only the poem, can reveal. That it is so rarely, or so timidly, presented in our schools is one of the greatest failures of our educational system. Young men and young women graduate from American schools and colleges by the hundreds of thousands every year to whom science is the only road to knowledge, and to whom poetry is little more than a subdivision of something called "literature" — a kind of writing printed in columns instead of straight across the page and primarily intended to be deciphered by girls, who don't read it either.

This sort of thing has consequences. Abstractions are wonderfully clever tools for taking things apart and for arranging things in patterns but they are very little use in putting things together and no use at all when it comes to determining what things are *for*. Furthermore abstractions have a limiting, a dehumanizing, a dehydrating effect on the relation to things of the man who must live with them. The result is that we are more and more left, in our scientific society, without the means of knowledge of ourselves as we truly are or of our experience as it actually is. We have the tools, all the tools — we are suffocating in tools — but we cannot find the actual wood to work or even the actual hand to work it. We begin with one abstraction (something we think of as ourselves) and a mess of other abstractions (standing for the world) and we arrange and rearrange the counters, but who we are and what we are doing we simply do not know — above all what we are doing. With the inevitable consequence that we do not know either what our purpose is or our

end. So that when the latest discoveries of the cyclotron are reported we hail them with the cry that we will now be able to
control nature better than ever before — but we never go on
to say for what purpose, to what end, we will control her. To
destroy a city? To remake a world?

It was something of this kind, I imagine, that Adlai Stevenson had in mind when he startled a Smith Commencement by
warning his newly graduated audience of prospective wives that
the "typical Western man — or typical Western husband —
operates well in the realm of means, as the Roman did before him.
But outside his specialty, in the realm of ends he is apt to operate
poorly or not at all. . . . The neglect of the cultivation of
more mature values," Mr. Stevenson went on, "can only mean
that his life, and the life of the society he determines, will lack
valid purpose, however busy and even profitable it may be."

As he had so often done before, Mr. Stevenson there found
words for an uneasiness which has been endemic but inarticulate
in the American mind for many years — the sense that we are
getting nowhere far too fast and that, if something doesn't happen soon, we may arrive. But when he came to spell out the
causes for "the neglect of the cultivation of more mature values"
Mr. Stevenson failed, or so it seems to me, to identify the actual
villain. The contemporary environment in America, he told his
young listeners, is "an environment in which 'facts,' the data of
the senses, are glorified and value judgments are assigned inferior staus as 'mere matters of opinion.' It is an environment in
which art is often regarded as an adornment of civilization rather
than a vital element of it, while philosophy is not only neglected
but deemed faintly disreputable because 'it never gets you anywhere.' " It is true that philosophy is neglected, and even truer

that art is regarded in this country generally as it seems to be regarded by the automobile manufacturers of Detroit: as so much enamel paint and chromium to be applied for allegedly decorative purposes to the outside of a car which would run better without it. But the explanation is not, I think, that we set facts — even facts in quotation marks — above values, or that we glorify the data of the senses, unless one means by that latter phrase not what the senses tell us of the world we live in but what the statistics that can be compiled out of the data of the senses would tell us if we were ever in touch with our senses.

In few civilizations have the senses been less alive than they are with us. Look at the cities we build and occupy — but look at them! — the houses we live in, the way we hold ourselves and move; listen to the speaking voices of the greater part of our women. And in no civilization, at least in recorded time, have human beings been farther from the *facts* if we mean by that word, facets of reality. Our indifference to ends is the result of our obsession with abstractions rather than facts: with the ideas of things rather than with things. For there can be no concern for ends without a hunger for reality. And there can be no hunger for reality without a sense of the real. And there can be no sense of the real in the world which abstraction creates, for abstraction is incapable of the real: it can neither lay hold of the real itself nor show us where to find it. It cannot, that is to say, create the *relation* between reality and ourselves which makes *knowledge* of reality possible, for neither reality nor ourselves exist in abstraction. Everything in the world of abstraction is object. And, as George Buttrick pointedly says, *we* are not objects: we are subjects.

But all this is a negative way of saying what a defender of

poetry should not be afraid of saying positively. We have lost
our concern with ends because we have lost our touch with
reality and we have lost our touch with reality because we are
estranged from the means to reality which is the poem — the
work of art. To most members of our generation this would
seem an extravagant statement but it is not extravagant in fact
and would not have seemed so in another time. In ancient China
the place of poetry in men's lives was assumed as matter of
course; indeed, the polity was based on it. The three hundred
and five odes or songs which make up the Song-word Scripture
survived to the fourth century B.C., when Confucius is said to
have collected them, because they were part of the government
records preserved in the Imperial Archive. For thousands of
years the examinations for the Chinese civil service were examinations in poetry, and there is no record that the results were more
disappointing to the throne than examinations of a different character might have been.

It was not for nothing Confucius told his disciples that the
three hundred and five songs of the Song-word Scripture could
be boiled down to the commandment: "Have no twisty
thoughts." One can see, not only in the three hundred and five
songs, but in Chinese poetry of other periods, what Confucius
meant. Consider two Chinese poems of the second century B.C.
and the sixth of our era, both written by Emperors. The first is a
poem of grief — of the sense of loss of someone loved: a poem
therefore of that inward world of feeling, of emotion, which
seems to us most nearly ourselves and which, because it is always
in flux, always shifting and changing and flowing away, is, of all
parts of our experience of our lives, most difficult to know. We
cannot know it through science. We cannot know it by knowing

things *about* it — even the shrewdest and most intelligent things. We cannot know it either by merely feeling it — by uttering its passing urgencies. How then can we know it?

The Emperor Wu-ti wrote (this is Arthur Waley's beautiful translation):

> *The sound of her silk skirt has stopped.*
> *On the marble pavement dust grows.*
> *Her empty room is cold and still.*
> *Fallen leaves are piled against the doors.*
>
> *Longing for that lovely lady*
> *How can I bring my aching heart to rest?*

Four images, one of sound, two of sight, one of feeling, each like a note plucked on a stringed instrument. Then a question like the chord the four would make together. And all at once we *know*. We know this grief which no word could have described, which any abstraction the mind is capable of would have destroyed. But we know more than this grief: we know our own — or will when it shall visit us — and so know something of ourselves.

The second is a poem of delight: youth and delight — the morning of the world — the emotion, of all emotions, most difficult to stop, to hold, to see. "Joy whose hand is ever at his lips bidding adieu." How would you *know* delight in yourself and therefore yourself delighting? Will the psychiatrists tell you? Is there a definition somewhere in the folios of abstraction which will capture it for you? The Emperor Ch'ien Wen-ti (again Waley's translation) knew that there is only one mirror which will hold that vanishing smile: the mirror of art, the mirror of the poem.

A beautiful place is the town of Lo-yang:
The big streets are full of spring light.
The lads go driving out with harps in their hands:
The mulberry girls go out to the fields with their baskets.
Golden whips glint at the horses' flanks,
Gauze sleeves brush the green boughs.
Racing dawn the carriages come home —
And the girls with their high baskets full of fruit.

In this world within, you see, this world which is ourselves, there is no possibility of knowing by abstracting the meaning out — or what we hope will be the meaning. There we must know things *as* themselves and it must be *we* who know them. Only art, only poetry, can bring about that confrontation.

Why do we teach poetry in this scientific age? To present the great alternative, not to science but to that knowledge by abstraction which science has imposed. And what is this great alternative? Not the "messages" of poems, their interpreted "meanings," for these are abstractions also — abstractions far inferior to those of science. Not the explications of poetic texts, for the explication of a poetic text which goes no farther ends only in abstraction.

No, the great alternative is the poem as itself, the poem as a poem, the poem as a work of art — which is to say, the poem in the context in which alone the work of art exists: the context of the world, of the man and of the thing, of the infinite relationship which is our lives. To present the great alternative is to present the poem not as a message in a bottle, and not as an object in an uninhabited landscape, but as an action in the world, an action in which we ourselves are actors and our lives are known.

On the Teaching
of Writing

1959

EVERYBODY KNOWS by now that "creative writing" can't be taught. Nevertheless thousands of professors in hundreds of colleges go on teaching it. Which is absurd but not as absurd as it sounds.

Everybody knows, too, that you can't teach a horse to race, but Kentucky is full of racing stables with neat oval tracks and miles of expensive, white-washed fencing which costs as much to maintain as a presentable professor. Even more.

There is one diffence, of course. In Kentucky they begin with the horse's sire and dam whereas the professor of writing rarely breeds his own students and wouldn't know where to begin if he tried. Who would have picked that pair from the livery stable to beget and bear John Keats?

But otherwise the situation in Cambridge is much like the situation in Kentucky. You have to have a horse that can race before you can teach it racing. You have to have a writer who can write before you can teach him how.

Which means, of course, that you aren't really teaching in Cambridge. To teach you have to have a subject: Elementary German or Physics A or The Novel Since Henry James. But there is no subject in "creative writing": there is merely an object: that boy (that horse). I say *that* boy because there isn't apt to be more than one in a year or maybe in five or even ten. Indeed a man would be spectacularly lucky, even by Kentucky standards, to have one distinct and distinguishable writer of real power in a professorial lifetime.

There are those, I know, who have tried to concoct a subject for "creative writing" courses by combining the best elements of the best writers in a kind of appetizer paste, a *mélange adultère de tous*, which their students are expected to consume. The young critics who make up the majority of any college writing course — the lads who have mistaken an interest in writing for writing itself — will thrive on such a diet but the young writers, if there are any, will gag on the surfeit. They know instinctively that there is no such thing as Best Writing. There are merely a number of different writers writing well and the successes of one would be the failures of another. You can't borrow and you can't mix. If anyone had tried to solve D. H. Lawrence's writing problems by teaching him Flaubert's solutions there would have been a suicide in the family attic — or more likely a murder in the local school. Exposition has rules and can be taught, as generations of British state papers demonstrate. The "art of writing" has graces and can be taught as armies of belletrists prove. But writing *as* an art cannot be taught because writing as an art is the unique achievement of *an* artist. Which is to say, of one unique and different man solving his unique and different problems for himself. When a student tells me that I haven't taught him *how*, I take it as a compliment — but not to him.

I am not saying, of course, that a young writer should not read.

He should, quite literally, read his head off. But he should do his reading for himself, following the leads that are meaningful for him, not for someone else, and least of all for an older professor-writer who did his own essential reading a generation ago and by a different light. To do an older writer's reading over again in a time like ours is to submit to that process, already so destructive in our fashion-following super-civilization, by which everything is turned into a vogue — even art which should be the great destroyer of all fashions, not their pimp. Everyone reads James. Then everyone reads Joyce. Then everyone switches to Eliot, to Proust, to Kafka — to the Communists in one decade — to the homosexuals in another — until the new writing begins to sound like the advertising patter in the smart magazines which echoes the changing chatter of the chic. It sometimes seems as though only Robert Frost were old enough and cantankerous enough and magnificent enough to be himself and remain himself and thus be disrespectfully and entirely new in this age of stylish novelties.

A real writer learns from earlier writers the way a boy learns from an apple orchard —by stealing what he has a taste for and can carry off. He will imitate his elders as every good writer has since the world began — even an original, even a Rimbaud — but the hunger and the pants pocket will be his own. Some of his apples will make him sick, but it will be *his* sickness. Others will shape his hand for life — because *he* picked them. When I set myself, after college and after law school, to try to find my way to a place where I could begin, I taught myself Italian enough to read *The Divine Comedy* because Tom Eliot had read it to his great profit and because I was — as I remain — his devoted admirer. It did me, I am sure, no harm. But neither did it do me Eliot's good, for it was not my need that took me to it.

The truth is that the whole situation in a writing course is a reversal of the usual academic pattern. Not only is there no subject, there is no content either. Or, more precisely, the content is the work produced by students in the course. And the relation of the teacher to his students is thus the opposite of the relation one would expect to find. Ordinarily it is the teacher who knows, the student who learns. Here it is the student who knows, or should, and the teacher who learns or tries to. The student writes. The teacher reads. And the object of the teacher's reading is to learn if he can how closely the knowing of the words approximates the knowing of their writer. It may be less. It may be far, far more, for such is the nature of the struggle between a writer and the obdurate material of words in which he works. But whether less or more, the only question the man who undertakes to teach can ask is the question of the adequacy of the writing to its own intent. As a writer himself he may call it "good" or "bad." As a man he may have his human opinion of the mind which conceived it. But as a teacher of writing it is not his task to tell his students what they should try to write or to judge their work by the standards he would apply to his own or his betters'.

A student's poem does not fail because it is not Yeats's "Byzantium" or even "Sailing to . . ." It fails only if it is not itself. And the labor of the reader who calls himself teacher is the difficult labor of discerning, if he can, what "itself" would be. For only then can he bring his own experience and skill to bear upon it. Only then can he say to the student across the corner of his desk: "Well, if *I* had tried to write this poem . . ."

The real relationship, in other words — the only relationship in which anything in this paradoxical undertaking can be accomplished — is a relationship between two writers. Which is why it is essential that at least one writer should enroll in a writing course if it is to get anywhere. The problems which arise, young as the students are, are problems all writers face, whatever their age or experience. They are problems which cannot be discussed in a class, any more than in a bar in Paris, without a text to relate them to, and a writer's human experience to give them perspective. And they involve, as such problems always do involve, a writer's conception of the world: a conception different in every way from a critic's or a scholar's because a writer never gets *outside*. He works as Tolstoy works in *Anna Karenina* — at Levin's heart and Kitty's and Anna's. Techniques without works are as empty to a practicing writer as faith without works to a practicing clergyman: only amateurs would waste time talking about them.

But difficult as it is to describe the relationships of a writing course, it is even more difficult to justify one, either from the point of view of the student who takes it or from the point of view of the college which pays for it. (I defer, for a moment, the point of view of the poor devil of a poet or a novelist who tries to do the teaching.) Why, if all there is is a couple of writers, should any young writer send himself to a college writing course instead of to a park bench in Washington Square or a jazz session in San Francisco or any other spot where he might find an older writer willing to help him to help himself? And why, even with academic salaries what they are, should a college pay for the ten or twelve necessary hours of a professor's time every week if only one student a year or one student every five is going to profit?

I don't know the answer to the second question. You could

probably justify a course in commercial fiction from the purely budgetary point of view if enough of its graduates sold stories to magazines with commercial prestige, but there is no way of adding up the justifications of a course devoted to the art of writing. Undoubtedly it is helpful to a college to be able to list a respectable number of writers as graduates but the trouble is that not all the proven writers come out of the writing courses. Harvard's poets from Robinson through Frost and Stevens to Aiken and Eliot and Cummings constitute an unequaled galaxy but I have never heard it said that any of them got their start in a writing course.

What justification there is must be academic rather than economic and there too one runs into trouble. One can argue that it is desirable to dilute the critical and scholarly atmosphere of a college community with a few artists but you won't get all the critics and scholars to agree. And if you remark that a good writing course will at least prevent English from becoming a dead language you might as well eat your lunches somewhere else than the faculty club. The plain truth is that these courses are eleemosynary enterprises so far as the college budget is concerned — opportunities provided to a small minority of students to investigate their artistic possibilities at the college's expense. The students who take them should be grateful. Sometimes, improbably enough, they are.

As for the first question, however, the answer is obvious. The young writer who graduates straight from high school into San Francisco, or wherever the people who used to congregate in Paris now hang out, in the innocent hope that he will thus combine his initiation into art with his initiation into life, is deluding himself. If we are to judge by its works there can scarcely be a worse place to get admitted to life than San Francisco. In comparison a great university or even a competent college is liveliness itself. There are more people of more kinds in a college than in a cult — particularly a cult in which Bohemianism itself is stereotyped and you can't even be a bum without bad liquor, boring sexuality, and the regulation beard. Indeed the American university — the American university I know best in any case — is almost the only place left in America where the infinite variety of the kind of life a writer wants to live can still be found.

In addition to which there is the highly pertinent fact that universities and colleges have books. Life is not all on the sidewalks or even in the bedrooms. The nine-tenths of it a writer needs under him to keep the rest afloat is in the books in which other men have put their living down. And there is one other consideration which bears upon those long conversations with older and sympathetic writers of which the young so understandably dream: most of the older writers are now employed by universities and colleges and the rest put limits on the number of young strangers they will entertain. Also the rest aren't as constantly available as the prisoners of the academic offices. They have a way of traveling to Africa or Spain.

As for the point of view of the poor devil who does the teaching, it can be given as briefly and simply as the annals of the poor. The rewards depend on the students. If they are uninteresting he will be bored to death. If they are exciting there will not be hours enough in the week. But it is not as simple as that, either. For if the students are dull the fault is his whereas if they are good *they* get the credit.

Mine have been good more often than I deserved.

Education and
the *Work* of Art

1954

IT OUGHT to be obvious but isn't that an education which ignores the *working* of the arts is defective, however it may devote itself to their works. The college graduate who has read all the significant poems and novels, and looked at all the significant pictures and statues, and listened to all the significant quartets and symphonies, and can unerringly arrange the lot according to the best canons of taste and the best theories of historical scholarship, but has no comprehension of the *experience* of art by which they came to be, is not an educated man for he has not related all these riches to his life. He carries them around in the pocket of his memory like coins. He knows, because he has been told, that they are valuable but he does not know why they exist because he does not know how they exist. And not knowing why or how they exist he can only possess them: he cannot make them his.

What has been left out of his education is the discovery of the relation between the work of art as it stands there on the page or hangs there on the wall and himself as a living, sentient being. And that discovery has been lost to him because its counterpart in the *creation* of the work of art has not been discovered to him.

He has been shown the work of art as an end product: as a completed masterpiece which he is to admire or "criticize" as such. He has not been shown that the work of art is not only end product but continuing action, and that what it acts upon is the artist's experience of a world which is also his. To see a poem as a piece of literature is to see it passively as something requiring only to be accepted or rejected. To see a poem as a creative action in time and space is to see it in the context of human life, as something demanding collaboration or resistance — something present and alive and real: beneficent or dangerous.

This gap in education is not one, as we have reason to know, which historical scholarship can supply. It is no good telling a student that Shelley had a high voice or Baudelaire a mulatto mistress. It's no good supplying the autobiographical details about Blake. The only consequence will be to put two obstacles instead of one between the reader and the experience of the poem: first, the poem as artifact; second, the poet as man. The educational gap must be filled, if it is to be filled at all, from the other side. The reader must be helped to go through the text of the poem to the context in which the poem exists — the artistic context not the biographical. He must see for himself, in the poem and through the poem, the nature of the action he is observing. And he must come to understand the relation of that action to his *own* life and to himself.

Above all, he must come to understand that though there may be the most immeasurable distance in degree between the action of the poem and certain actions of which he is himself capable, there is no difference in kind — at least in *human* kind. He may be wholly incapable of artistic creation, but between the labor of artistic creation — between *this* labor of artistic creation — and the continuing labor of being man, which he has performed from the beginning of his life and must still perform, there is, he must discover, no gulf fixed. He also, like the rest of mankind, like the poet of this poem, is and has been from the beginning a shaper and orderer of his experience of the world. His perceptions of the world are not, as he has so long imagined, automatic products imprinted by the sensible universe on his brain as though his brain were so many feet of Kodak film. Though acting for the most part unconsciously, he, like every one of us, has constructed out of his own struggle with the chaos of experience a picture of the world: a picture of the world which is a kind of mirror image of himself.

And this poem before him, though immeasurably more subtle and more articulate and more precise, is also such an image and such a picture. For art, considered from this point of view, is only the continuation into infinitely more effective, more expressive, terms of the common human labor — the labor common to us all as men. What distinguishes us all from the animals, as Suzanne Langer puts it, is our power to use symbols: not the professional symbol-makers alone, not the poets, the sculptors, but all of us. We all select. We all synthesize. We all invent. We have to, to live as conscious beings, as men, in a world which consciousness can inhabit. And the poet, the artist, is merely a man who is driven by the compulsions of his deepest nature to carry this labor on out to those regions at the frontiers of common experience where it is necessary to do more than select or synthesize: where it is necessary truly to create. Such a symbol as Coleridge's albatross is a symbol which opens to human migration a whole ice-cap of experience never viable before, but it differs only in power, not in kind, from the symbols we all put together for ourselves in order to find our way around in our own little familiar cellar ways and orchards.

This fact is a key not only to education in the arts but to education itself — true education — education for the human experience of life. For education, if it means anything, means training in the process by which men become men, and it is in great works of art, seen not as artifacts but as actions, that that process is most revealingly observed. We cannot discover the process in ourselves for the simple reason that "ourselves" are undiscoverable to us. We can stumble across places where "ourselves" have been and we can examine the objects, the images, the abstractions, "ourselves" have collected — the coins, jack-knives, ends of string and old photographs in the school-boy drawer — but "ourselves" in action as shapers and orderers we never see from one end of our lives to the other. So little indeed, do we see them that we are astonished to be told that the shaping and ordering goes on. Only in the lives of others, and only when those others are conscious shapers, conscious orderers — only in the lives, that is, of artists, and the work of artists — can we begin to perceive why and what we are. And only then if we see the work of shaping and ordering — the work of art — *as action*. When Virginia Woolf, wondering in her *Diary* why a certain good novel is not a great book, asks herself what qualities it lacks, she replies: "That it adds nothing to one's vision of life, perhaps." Which is of course the final judgment. A great work of art is great because it adds to the vision of life of which humanity is capable. It adds to the vision of life because it brings more of life into the focus of vision. And it brings more of life into the focus of vision because it acts upon life: because it acts upon life for its author and goes on acting upon life for its readers

(Which incidentally, is why even the greatest work of art can die: it can die when there are no longer readers for whom the action it performs is necessary or real.)

But if great works of art are great because they enhance the human vision of life, then it follows, by the most elementary reasoning, that it is in their power of enhancement, which is to say, in their characteristic relation to the experience of life, that great works of art are significant to us. They are significant because they are capable of enlarging the area in which we can live; because they are able to carry farther *for us* the experience of being men; because they leave us, as the common but truthful saying goes, more alive. To read Yeats is to multiply one's being. And this enhancement results not from any refining of our aesthetic faculties through what is called — unhappy word — "appreciation," but far more directly, far more sensibly, from our witnessing of the action of the poem on the world: from our participation as readers *in* that action. It is not by any ideas it may communicate, however lofty, that a great work of art compels us, in Rilke's phrase, to change our lives. It is not by that removed aesthetic experience which philosophers of art have tried so often and so unsuccessfully to define. It is by the increased awareness of self and world, of world and self in it, which the work of art, perceived as *act*, evokes.

The *Archaïscher Torso Apollos* says it in the only way it can be said — in the saying of art. A rough paraphrase of the poem would read, in English, like this:

> The legendary head of the broken statue in which the eyeballs ripened is gone — unknown to us. Nevertheless the torso still glows with its own gaze like a candelabrum in which the light is only turned down, turned low. If this were not so the curve

of the breast could not blind you nor could a smile cross the slight turn of the loins toward that middle part which carried the power of procreation. If this were not so, this stone would be deformed, mutilated — would be standing maimed and too short under the plunge of its shoulders — would not have that shimmer it has of the fell of a beast of prey nor break out of all its contours like a star . . .

For *there is no place that does not see you* . . . no place upon the marble eyeless skin of this maimed and headless statue that does not *see* you. And so?

Du musst dein Leben ändern — You must make your life over.

Why? You must make your life over because this stone figure *exists* to a degree which puts to shame your half-alive life, your half-sleeping body — because the sight of this unseeing stone suffuses its being, whereas you? . . . you have only eyes! A student of mine at Harvard put it this way: "The reality and intensity of the work of art thrusts the sham of our existence in our faces." He meant just that.

Increased awareness of that strangest of all phenomena, the human situation in the universe, the human position under the innumerable stars, is the consequence of the artistic act of creation. Indeed it is, in a sense, precisely this increased awareness which the act of art creates. And unless the act of art plays its part in education — unless education is aware, not only of the hermetic objects made of stone and sound and signs and color in which the creative act can lie concealed, but of the creative act itself — life is impoverished. A nation educated in ignorance of the *work* of art is a nation educated in ignorance of the possibilities of life, and no amount of so-called cultural instruction in the naming and identifying and describing and arranging of books, pictures, symphonies and marble shapes will turn that ignorance into knowledge. Something more and, above all, different is required of those of us who undertake to teach.

Granting, as I freely do, that we cannot produce creative artists by the processes of education, and that it is not in this way that education and artistic creativity are related, we have nevertheless, as I see it, other obligations to the *work* of art, as distinguished from the works, which we cannot avoid or evade. First and foremost we have the obligation to acknowledge to ourselves that art exists in the context of life; that art is an action on the scene of life; that art is a means of perceiving life; of ordering life; of making life intelligible; and thus also of changing it. For to confess these things is to found one's self on the consciousness of the creativity of art. To deny them, to assert that art has no consequences, that art never makes anything happen, is to deny, in the same breath, the creativity of art, for if art does not create in terms of life it does not create at all.

That, as I see it, is the first obligation, the inward obligation. The second is the obligation to teach in terms of this conviction: to place the work of art in the context not of its historical associations, or its biographical associations, or the associations summoned up by textual criticism but in the context of its creative associations — the experience of human life which it organizes, or is capable of organizing, for those who approach it. I realize, of course, that this is a difficult duty to fulfill — the most difficult, perhaps, a teacher can set himself. To place the poem in the context of the human experience to which it relates, so that its creative action upon that experience may accomplish itself once again, is only less difficult than the original creation of the poem. And yet, unless this labor is performed, what has been performed? Has the poem done its work *as poem* when it is

caught in a web of dates and names? — when the reactions of
others, even the most distinguished others, have been quoted? —
when the biographical facts have been recited and the testimo-
nials read?

And finally there is, as I see it, a third obligation: the obligation to achieve this recreation of the creative act of art through
the collaboration of those who are being taught. It is not through
listening to a lecture — even the most inspired lecture — that
a man comes to an understanding of "the creative process." It
is only by establishing the relationship between the poem
and the experience of life *as he knows the experience of
life,* that any human being reaches an understanding of what is
happening before his eyes: happening to *him* now and here, no
matter when or where the work was done. Unless, as reader of
this poem, he is able to make *his* way back through this movement
of images upon a pattern of music, into a context of meaning
which is real for him, which is alive for him, which is human for
him, he will not have shared with the poet the creative experience
which the poem is; he will not have shared in the creative act.

And to me, it is by sharing in the creative act of art that education in humanity advances.

The Knowable
and the Known

1965

THIRTY YEARS AGO, when Mr. Roosevelt informed me of my
desire to be Librarian of Congress, I thought I knew what a library was: it was the last place a writer ought to be found until
he was stone cold on the page in print. I used to think of John
Donne as I heard the early morning janitors carting the jangling
brass spittoons across the marble floors on their double-decker
dollies to be flushed and buffed for yet another learned day.
Never ask for whom the bell tolls — you may find out.

But things have happened to the world in the last thirty years
and not least to the world's libraries — particularly the great
libraries and more particularly still the great libraries which serve
the work of science. They have been swept from their respectable positions on the periphery of things, where they once sat back
behind their Carnegie marble fronts waiting to receive the cus-
tomers if and when they came. They have been swept away to
find themselves at the crossroads of the time.

Ours, as we all know and constantly remind ourselves, is a
revolutionary epoch. But it is not a revolutionary epoch in the
political sense only, or the economic or even the technological.
The turmoil with us goes far deeper — goes indeed to the roots

of our human lives — to what is most human in our human lives — to the process of human knowledge, of human knowing itself. And it is there, of course, that the libraries are involved. For the ultimate question now is not the question whether this political order or that will prevail, or when technology will take us to the moon, or how cancer is to be conquered. The ultimate question is whether we can *know* the knowledge we have now accumulated.

Man has become at last what our remote forefathers dreamed he might become: the thief of fire. He has gone farther into the darkness than the boldest of his ancestors ever dared to hope that he might go. And what he has found, what he has brought back again, is what Prometheus found: not only the precious ember glowing in its secret pith but a destiny also — the challenge to the gods which is a challenge to himself: the challenge of knowledge. If we can inflict death as the gods in their immense catastrophes inflict it (and we already have) — if we can create life from acids and from sunlight as the gods create it (and there are those who think we may) — then the question will present itself whether we can also know as the gods know . . .

And, if we can, if we can stand it.

It may not be in the great scientific libraries that this question will be answered — the question whether mankind can bear to know *as knowledge* what hitherto we have known only as faith — but it is almost certainly there or thereabouts that a beginning will be made at the answering of that other earlier question: not whether we can bear to know this new knowledge of ours in all its frightening implications but whether we can know it in its entirety at all.

Pierre Auger's calculation that 90 per cent of all the scientists who ever lived are alive today is sometimes taken as a tribute to progress, a compliment to the generation. Actually it has a different sense. It measures the immeasurable rapidity with which the flood of scientific discovery has inundated our age. Most of the revolutionary advances which have changed the world — or changed, at least, our human relation to the world — have taken place within the memories of men now living.

And within that same time, science itself has changed, grown, proliferated, multiplied. What was once a single discipline or family of disciplines — Physics, Biology, Chemistry, Geology — has become a society of nations speaking as many different tongues as there are territories in which to use them. A few years ago Sir Charles Snow set the academic world to arguing about the two cultures, by which he apparently meant the two languages of the humanities and the natural sciences. But as time passed and the debate went on it became clearer and clearer that there were not two languages but many more than two and that the scientists had quite as much trouble understanding each other as the rest of us had in understanding them. "Learned societies," said Lord Ritchie-Calder of Edinburgh University, "themselves splinter groups of natural philosophy, have sub-groups within groups and sub-sections within sections" to such a point that "it is questionable whether anyone or any body has ever made a complete list of all the so-called branches of science," and the consequence, he goes on, is that we have "narrower and narrower briefings in the fluorescent glare of seminar and colloquia where, in their private jargon, the scientists discuss last week's meson, the latest amino-acid synthesis or a hair on the whisker of the banana fly."

What Lord Ritchie-Calder was talking about was the effect

of all this on science: the burgeoning babel, the increasing fragmentation. But there is another consequence far more serious: the effect on human knowledge itself — on the techniques for making that knowledge available, making it *known* at the time and place where it is needed. Prior to the beginnning of the great proliferation, when those techniques were in process of development in the principal libraries of the world, human knowledge was a common human possession, the common inheritance of educated men. Few, perhaps, were masters of it all but from no part or province was any educated mind excluded. The Royal Society can be traced back to Comenius' proposal of an international college where the wise of the world were to meet to examine together and make universally known the whole body of natural knowledge, and it was still possible at the beginning of the nineteenth century for learned societies to hear famous engineers arguing music with professional astronomers and chemists debating political philosophy with biologists while obstetricians lectured judges on the caesura not in the female abdomen but in a line of verse.

The knowable, at that point, differed from the known only in terms of time and labor — the time and labor required for reference and reading — and the function of the librarian was merely to provide the tools and facilities which would make the search brief and the reading comfortable. But now, within a century or less, all this has changed. It is no longer true, if we are to believe the scientists themselves, that knowledge is whole — that what is known to one mind is necessarily knowable to another and therefore part and parcel of a common knowledge. Robert Oppenheimer is reported to have dismissed the Snow complaint about the failure of humanists to study physics with the remark that it didn't really matter whether they did or not since no one but the modern physicist can understand modern physics anyway. And the same thing can apparently be said, whether it has been or not, of the rest of the modern sciences, or, in any case, of the languages in which they express themselves. The commonly known, or, more precisely, the commonly knowable, no longer includes the growing edge of science, the new frontiers of experiment and discovery where the future of mankind is being made. That is specialists' country which one man or a dozen can enter but not more — not the rest of us — not the ordinary educated man.

What this has done to the universities is a familiar story. No longer able to assume that a disciplined mind will enable a man to travel anywhere, the makers of curricula have invented courses, commonly called courses in General Education, which take account of the intellectual fragmentation of our world. Apprentice physicists are led back into the old heart-land of the humanities for a tour of the more memorable sites while apprentice scholars or lawyers or businessmen or writers are taken up upon a temporary mountain from which they can just make out the distant, unplowed, scientific country where the dust begins. It is a pleasant journey in both directions but not always a productive one. The apprentice scholars still remain apprentice scholars with a vague and uncomfortable memory of something glimpsed they have no wish to glimpse again and the apprentice scientists, though they may loaf among the olives for a while, can hardly wait to head their horses west.

But what creates difficulties for the teachers creates impossibilities for the librarians. The mere existence of a library collection, as distinguished from a warehouse full of printed pages,

presupposes the intellectual coherence of the materials collected. Books can be brought together according to an organization, a classification of one kind or another, only if what they
contain composes an organization — composes, that is to say,
a whole of which no part is foreign to any other part. All, it
must be assumed, have come from the human mind and all are
therefore parts of human knowledge, and human knowledge, by
hypothesis, is one — one because the human mind can hold it.

When that hypothesis breaks down, when human knowledge
is no longer one because the human mind can no longer hold it,
when there are parts — essential parts — of human knowledge
which are not knowable at all to the vast majority of human
minds, the library is in trouble. It can no longer perform its
function of making the knowable known at the time and place
where it is needed by merely possessing classified and catalogued
collections and providing space for their use. It must intervene
actively in the increasingly difficult process of knowing, prepar-
ing itself when necessary to mediate between the human mind
and those who have — or think they have — outdistanced it;
undertaking, if not to translate the untranslatable knowledge of
those scientists Oppenheimer had in mind, at least to place it in
its spectrum, so that what we cannot *know*, we can know *of*.

The significance — the historic significance — of the dedication of the new library of the Harvard Medical School is precisely that this is such a library. The library of the Harvard
Medical School will combine two of the best medical collections
in the world to form a total collection of about three quarters of
a million volumes rich with rare and irreplaceable books — the
Streeter bequest and many others. It will be housed in a handsome and efficient building designed specifically to meet its needs.

It will be associated with the other great medical libraries of the area in a communications net which will make the resources of all available for the needs of any one. But none of this is as important, either for the library itself or for the society in which it exists, as the fact that this new library proposes to use its human and intellectual resources, which include the human and intellectual resources of the greatest medical school in the Republic and those of the university to which that school belongs, to perform a positive function in what its librarian calls 'the handling and communication of scientific *information*.' No longer will this library limit itself to the great custodial and reference tasks which have occupied librarians in the past: keeping the collection up and in order, perfecting the catalogues, leading the readers to the books. In addition it will play an active part in the process of the dissemination of information, attempting to develop means to carry the new knowledge in the sciences related to medicine directly to the working doctors throughout the area who need it.

If the effort succeeds — and who can doubt that it will — the library of the Medical School will have done something more than improve the practice of medicine in these parts, something more than enlarge the function of the scholarly library. It will have connected the republic of common knowledge with parts at least of that revolutionary frontier which so often seems to turn its back, like all frontiers, on the peopled lands behind it.

And this will be no accidental or unintended consequence. In the new library there is to be a room of a kind not ordinarily found in scientific libraries — a room without a scientific book on its shelves but poetry instead, music, history, art. This room will be called the Aesculapian Room, dedicated thus to the god of medicine and healing. Why is it this room which is so called? Why not the others with their shelves full of physiology and anatomy and biochemistry and the rest? Because the library recognizes, as Harvard herself, I think, has always recognized, that there is no such thing as knowledge by itself but only knowledge *to* the knower, and that the knower is never anything but man, man in his old condition as man, man with his wonder on him, his poetry, his music. Because the library recognizes, as Harvard recognizes, that the god is in the question, not the answer. Because the library recognizes, as the university recognizes, that it is only when the answer is responsive to the question, when the science has been mastered by the man, that civilization is possible.

What Is English?

1961

I DO not put this question to be impertinent. I put it because I should like to know. I have been — officially at least — a teacher of English for the past twelve years and I have yet to hear myself defined. I will go further than that: I have yet to be told precisely what I'm doing.

The trouble in my case may be Harvard. Certainly the trouble at the beginning was Harvard. When I was notified in the early summer of 1949 that the Board of Overseers of that University had approved my appointment to the Boylston Professorship of Rhetoric and Oratory I decided to drive down to Cambridge to find out what I was supposed to teach. It seemed like a good idea at the time: my last ten years or so had been in Washington and the years before that in journalism and my real profession throughout had been the writing of verse. I had never occupied a professorial chair before.

I say it seemed like a good idea. It didn't turn out that way. My first call, logically, was at the Department of English since it was a Committee of the Department of English which had approached me — "approach" in the technical sense — the year before. It was an agreeable call but brief. Chairmen of Harvard departments, I was informed, do not tell their colleagues what to do: they merely circulate the memoranda. I was back on the wooden porch of Warren House in something under five minutes with the impression that Harvard would be an attractive place if one could get into it.

My second call was on the only member of the English Department I knew at all well, a displaced Yale man like myself. He listened, looked at the ceiling, and replied that I could teach his course in Shakespeare if I wanted. I left with the impression, later verified, that he was not entirely enthusiastic about my presence in Cambridge.

There remained the Provost of the University, the President being in Washington in those months. (By "the President" I mean, of course, the President of Harvard.) The Provost, when I found his office, was engaged but, being desperate, I decided to sit him out and that fetched him. He popped out of his office, listened mildly while I stated my business, and popped back in again with the remark, delivered over his shoulder as the door closed, that when Harvard appointed a man to a full professorship, to say nothing of the Boylston Professorship, it expected him to *know* what he wanted to teach.

It was an enlightening afternoon. I had been told in three different ways that freedom to teach at Harvard is literally freedom — with all the penalties attached. But it was not an *instructive* afternoon. I knew no more about my duties on the way back to the Franklin County Hills than I had known on the way down, and twelve years later I still know little more than I knew then. I have taught the advanced writing course which all Boylston Professors since Barrett Wendell have offered and I have invented and annually reinvented a course in the nature of poetry; but though I take, or sometimes take, a proprietary satisfaction in both of them I am not at all sure that either is the course I should have taught or would have taught had I known what "English" is. It is not always English that turns up in the novels and poems and plays of the advanced writing course, nor does the course in poetry confine itself to poems in the English tongue. It can't very well since poetry recognizes no such limitation.

In those early days — my young days as a teacher of English when I was still in my late fifties — I used to assume that I was the only member of the profession who did not know what he was doing, but as time has passed I have begun to wonder. We have, at Harvard, an institution called the Visiting Committee, one to each department, which descends annually upon the appropriate classrooms to observe the progress of education. Our particular Visiting Committee in the Department of English ends its investigations, or always did when John Marquand was chairman, by offering a dinner to the permanent appointments. And the dinner always includes, or always included, a question which seems to stir the Departmental subconscious: Why are the graduates of Harvard University incapable of composing simple declarative sentences? Under ordinary circumstances a question such as this might be expected to serve as the gambit to a lively exchange involving, among other things, the truth of the fact asserted, but under the circumstances of our dinner, when the questioner is a distinguished alumnus who is also a member of the Committee to Visit the English Department, and when the effectiveness of the English Department in performing its duties is the subject of the Visitation, the innocent words take on a different aspect. They become charged with meanings, the most challenging of which is the implication that if graduates of

Harvard University are incapable of composing simple declarative sentences the Department of English is to blame. Which, in turn, implies that the teaching of English and the teaching of the composition of simple declarative sentences are one and the same thing. It is that last implication which spills the coffee on the tablecloth. Chairs are pushed back. Throats are cleared. And a strained voice, laboring under an emotion which an ignorant observer might think disproportionate to the cause, protests that teachers of English have better things to do than instruct the young in the composition of simple declarative sentences. Silence falls. Time passes. Someone suggests another drink all around. And there the issue reposes for another year. No member of the annual Visitation has ever yet been rude enough to ask: What better things? And no member of the Department within my memory has ever volunteered to say.

I suppose the reason for the persistence on one side and the passion on the other is historical. What our Visitors are remembering, consciously or not, is the importance of simple declarative sentences in the early days of the Republic, and the part played by Harvard College in the shaping of the minds of those who used them best. What my colleagues almost certainly have in mind is the importance to the growth of Harvard College of the liberation of their predecessors from precisely such concerns. It was because the two Adamses and their contemporaries in Massachusetts and Virginia and Connecticut and Pennsylvania could write meaningful English that the American Revolution was not merely a defeat of England but a victory for human liberty. But it is also true that it was not until that famous sail-maker's son, Francis J. Child, was relieved of his responsibility for the teaching of freshman composition that the Department of English at Harvard became an educational influence in the larger sense of that term.

It is, I think, this latter fact that explains the difficulty of defining "English" even today and even among those whose lives are devoted to its teaching, for the emancipation of Stubby Child took place less than a century ago. There was little "English," as we use the word, prior to 1876 — at least in Cambridge. When letters were first taught in the Colonial colleges they were taught in Latin with Latin manuals and Latin and Greek examples. The teaching of composition in the vulgar tongue had begun, it is true, before the Revolution, but the extraordinary debate which preceded and accompanied that event was conducted with the classical modes and models in mind. Harvard's historian, Samuel Eliot Morison, puts it with his usual pithiness: "The classical pseudonyms with which our Harvard signers of the great Declaration signed their early communications to the press were not pen-names chosen by chance, but represented a very definite point of view that every educated man recognized." And the same thing seems to have been true thirty years after the Revolution when the first chair in letters was established. John Quincy Adams, the first Boylston Professor, signalized his installation by delivering an inaugural address in which the word "English" never once occurs. It was not London to him, nor Stratford, from which the great tradition flowed but Athens and Rome. "Novelty," he told his audience, "will not be expected; nor is it perhaps to be desired. A subject which has exhausted the genius of Aristotle, Cicero, and Quintilian can neither require nor admit much additional illustration. . . ."

He was thinking, of course, of rhetoric and oratory, the two subjects attached by statute to his chair. *English* literature, in the year 1806, was something a gentleman read on his own time and for his own entertainment if he read it at all. Even a quarter of a century later instruction in this area seems to have been informal — and correspondingly pleasant. Mr. Morison quotes a member of the Harvard class of 1832 as remembering "our evenings with Chaucer and Spenser" in the study of John Quincy Adams's successor, Edward Tyrell Channing. The account hardly evokes the meeting of a course as we understand such things: "How his genial face shone in the light of the winter's fire and threw new meaning upon the rare gems of thought and humor and imagination of those kings of ancient song." It is a charming scene and one its author obviously relishes but even so he does not forget the serious business of his association with Professor Channing. It was not for those rare gems that he sat at the great man's feet. It was to learn to write. "Who of us," he reminds himself, "does not bless him every day that we write an English sentence for his pure taste and admirable simplicity!"

All of which would seem to support the conclusion that it was not until well along in Mr. Eliot's administration that "English" began at Harvard with the beginning of those laborious studies of Francis Child's in Anglo-Saxon and Middle English and Chaucer and Shakespeare and Dryden on which our modern literary scholarship is founded. But if this is so — if "English" is as new as this — then the difficulty of discussing it with members of Visiting Committees becomes understandable. Eighty years is a short time in which to fix the character and limits of a discipline. One can learn in so brief a time what "English" isn't — as, for example, that it isn't the thing it rebelled against at its beginnings. It isn't, that is to say, the "mere" teaching of the use of the English language. But one cannot learn so quickly what "English" *is*.

Literature? The teaching of literature in English? It sounds reasonable: if "English" isn't the teaching of the writing of the language it may well be the teaching of the reading of the language — the reading of what has already been written that deserves to be read again. But what do we mean by reading? Do we mean the reading of the words as words, the recognition of the structure, the interpretation of the references — in brief, the explication, as we put it, of the text? Or do we mean the reading of the substance of the words, what the words in their combination and their structure, their sounds and their significance, are *about?* But if we mean the latter, where does "English" end? The substance of the literature of our tongue is the whole substance of human experience as that experience has presented itself to the mind, the imagination, and the sensitivity of the most gifted users of that tongue. Nothing is foreign to it. Nothing is excluded. Everything has been touched, turned over, nuzzled, chewed, and much has been mastered, much has been perceived. If "English" has to do with the substance of English literature, where will we find faculties qualified to teach it? And how, if we found them, could they fit themselves into the academic order? What would be left for the other faculties — for the departments of philosophy and theology and biology and history and psychology — above all for the departments of psychology?

Obviously "English" cannot claim so vast an empire. But what lesser kingdom is there then? The texts as texts? It was the teaching of the texts as texts that destroyed the classics in American education. When *The Odyssey* was assigned in the last century as so much Greek — so many lines a day and so many days in the year, leaving the poem to take care of itself — *The Odyssey* began to die and Greek with it. And when, later, the magnificent scholarship of Kittredge attached itself to English texts as texts, a generation of graduate students was produced which itched to teach anything else — biographies of poets, economic and sociological interpretations of novels, literary history — anything but the texts themselves. Whereupon this revolution, in its turn, produced the counterrevolution of our own time. Back-to-the-text was the word with us — and the word became flesh in an army of brave new critics who carried everything before them only to leave us, when the counterrevolution subsided, where we are today: betwixt and between. We are agreed that it was a mistake to teach the poems of Shelley by way of the bonfire on the beach but we are not yet entirely persuaded that *explication de texte* has told the truth about poetry either. "English," we think today, is something more than the teaching of the reading of words as words but something less also, surely less, than the teaching of the private life the words came out of.

Less and more — but how much less and how much more? That is the question we do not answer for our newly chosen colleagues knocking at our doors to ask us what they ought to teach. Can it be answered? I think for myself, over boldly perhaps, that it can. It can, that is, if we will look for the answer where answers are to be found in such cases: not in the theory but in the practice. Percy Bridgman once remarked of the language of physics that you can tell the meaning of a term far better by seeing what is done *with* it than by hearing what is said *about* it. The same thing is true of the language of education. The theoretical fences will all blow down, give them time enough and wind, but the actions will stand. A colleague working in an ungrateful corner of the curriculum brings the dust to air, raises the too long familiar from its accustomedness, calls Dr. Johnson from his sepulchre and makes him walk the College Yard. This is the teaching of "English," but what has this colleague taught? Or a lecturer somewhere else, struggling with an exhausted theme, renews a poem which had lost its voice and makes it cry like the first bird in Eden. This too is "English" — but what then is it?

Take the lecturer. Take Robert Penn Warren teaching "The Rime of the Ancient Mariner" in a lecture which has been widely published and much read: a lecture which gives voice to the poem. What *happens* in this lecture? The poem is "read," yes, but is it the "reading" that happens? There have been better "readings" — "readings" which place the poem more perfectly in its dramatic setting and better reveal the necessity that drives it. What truly happens here is something else. What happens is that the relation between the poem and the world of life in which the poem exists is discovered — discovered by a stroke as brief and brilliant as the blast of light which sometimes ties the earth and sky together. Every man, says Mr. Warren quietly, kills his own albatross . . . and there, with those words, the bird, the scene, the poem all come true — come real. The metaphysical talk about symbols and symbolism which usually fogs discussions of "The Rime" — is the albatross a symbol? Isn't it? But *is* it? — chokes on its own inanity and what is left is *meaning*, the only kind of meaning that truly means, personal meaning, immediate meaning. That world of ice and snow becomes the world of vision we all have glimpsed — we also. The murder of the bird becomes the murder of which we also are guilty, all of us: the diminishment of life, the denial of love. The horror of thirst and windlessness, motionlessness, becomes the horror of stagnation we too have sensed when our rejection of love, of life, has stilled the winds of vision that should drive us. The salvation by wonder and pity becomes a salvation we could recognize if it came. Even the little precept at the end, those lines the overeducated read with titters of embarrassment, takes power to move our hearts:

> *He prayeth best who loveth best*
> *All things both great and small.*

One sees, looking back, what has happened. This myth of the poetic imagination which students in colleges are called on to admire as literature has become a myth of myself which I — student, teacher, man, woman, whoever — am called on to live as life. And one sees how this miracle has been accomplished. It has been accomplished not by squeezing the pips of the text but by a perception which has one foot in the text and the other in the world so that the two, text and world, are made to march together.

But is this what the teaching of "English," *in its actions,* is? Is this what happens in W. J. Bate's lectures on Johnson and in all the rest of the great achievements in the discipline? I think it is. I think "English" always stands with a foot in the text and a foot in the world, and that what it undertakes to teach is neither the one nor the other but the relation between them. The greatest poem, removed from the ground of our being, is an irrelevance. The ground of our being without the poem is a desert. "English," I think, is the teaching which attempts to minister between.

A Retiring View
of Harvard

1963

An address to the Department of English in that University

UNLIKE HOWARD JONES who retires as a famous scholar and teacher enriched over half a century by his colleagues' professional regard, I go out as I was when I came in — a Michelmas swallow, a man-who-came-to-dinner, an inveterate amateur who was carried in on a Chair and out on a Statute. But I have nevertheless and notwithstanding, my recollections — above all my recollections of men — men in abundance and overflowing. At an age — late fifties — sixties — when almost no one finds new friends, I found a whole new world of friendship. Or, rather, a whole new admiration of a world — that particular admiration on which an old man's friendships can be built. In those earlier years when one *expects* to make new friends — when one is miserable if one does not make them — the grounds of friendship are mutual liking, an instinctive compatibility. But in one's seventh decade it takes more than liking to crack the hardening shell of self-preoccupation. One must be moved by passion then — which means, the passions being what they are, by intellectual passion. And I was: unexpectedly — and without warning — was. I can demonstrate, I think, *how* unexpectedly.

A few years before my brief incumbency began I came up to

Cambridge from Washington where I had spent the years of the war and the years before and the years after — came up to see a few old friends of my Nieman year — Perry Miller and Kenneth Murdock in particular. But war-time Washington had not prepared me for the impressive changes I found in them and in their conversation, and when I got back to my Franklin County farm and fell exhausted into a hot bath, a little defensive jingle began beating its way through my defeated brains. It called itself "The Learned Men" — the learned men

> *Whose minds like horse or ox,*
> *Dispassionate in the stall,*
> *Grow great in girth and wax*
> *Beyond the animal,*
>
> *While mine, like country hog,*
> *Grows leaner as I age,*
> *Chivvied by flea and dog,*
> *Baited by love and rage . . .*

I was already, as you can see, intimidated: brain-washed for the panic which was to follow when, against every cautionary instinct and in the face of President Conant's natural skepticism about the entire project, I found myself a member of this Department.

But the panic, with Perry Miller's encouragement and Harry Levin's skillful guidance, eventually passed to be replaced by a sense of pride in the mere fact of association — a pride unlike any pride I had felt before. To be part, not of a personal relationship, but of an intellectual passion fed by such fires as Ivor Richards fanned and Douglas Bush (to name one is to mean all) was quite literally in the Rilkean sense, to "change one's life."

And to change one's life at that age was to begin again. And to begin again was to find a whole new world of friendship which included not only old friends new-made like Perry and Harry and Kenneth but young friends made old like Bill Alfred, twice my student, and Dave Perkins and John Bullitt.

I do not speak of all this to embarrass or to pay debts of friendship: those of you I most mean know what I have in mind whether I name your names or not. I speak of it because I think we should admit to ourselves once or twice in a decade, Harvard indifference or no Harvard indifference, that we are bound to each other by something more than common duties and the accidents of time and place. I think, for most particular instance, that we should, on occasion, acknowledge to ourselves and to each other what we really think of this Mozart of ours, this master of the emotions of the mind, this Jack, this Bate, to whom we owe the warmth and brilliance of these warm and brilliant years.

Which brings me to my second recollection — the Department to which we belong — the Department of English, or, more explicitly, *The* Department. Of the Department I have one thing to say which is also, I fear, a little hortatory. Here too, it seems to me, we should perhaps acknowledge, more explicitly than we usually have, what it is we *do*.

Teach literature? But what is literature? "The writings," says the Oxford dictionary, "of a country or a period, or of the world. . . ." But what are the writings of a country, or of a period, or of the world? The record of man: a long and intimate letter perpetually written and rewritten by men of one age for men of another to read; an account of life in this place; a report by those who have been here; an endless tale of who we are and where we have been and what we have said and done and felt and why (insofar as we know) and what we looked like saying it, doing it — in brief, an image of ourselves as it is given the best and most observant of us to perceive that image, a reflection in the purest, stillest pool.

What we teach is literature, yes. But to teach literature is inevitably and inescapably to teach what literature is about. And what literature is about is man. Whether we acknowledge it to ourselves or not, what we *teach* is man. And we bear, therefore, the responsibility. We bear it all the more because, in this as in most contemporary universities, we bear it alone. Philosophy has surrendered to science its Himalayan frontier — its frontier upon the unknown which is man's other country. Psychology concerns itself not with who we are but what — and that's another question. History, when it is not literature itself, is not history either. And as for the social sciences (which are never literature) a remark of Robert Frost's will define the difference: politics, said Robert, is about the grievances — poetry about the griefs.

We teach the griefs and should and can't escape it. For only in literature — in the arts — in poetry which contains the arts — only in poetry does *man* appear, man as he really is in his sordidness and his nobility. Elsewhere in the University man is a clinical specimen, or an intellectual abstraction, or a member of a mathematical equation, or a fixed point in a final dogma. Only with us is he himself — himself as Swift smelled him and as Keats saw him — himself in all his unimaginable — unimaginable if literature had not perceived them — possibilities.

But to return to the university is to arrive at the end of my recollections. The end, because I find I cannot say what I should like to say about it. A university is an institution, and how can a man feel about an institution as we feel about Harvard — most of us — all of us, perhaps? How, to put it plainly, can a man fall in love with an institution? Did anyone ever hear of a man falling in love with General Motors or the Prudential Insurance Company or Cravath, de Gersdorff, Swain & Wood? Men give their lives to such institutions as those and are well rewarded for it . . . but love?

And the answer is not that Harvard is an educational institution and therefore a nurturer of youth and thus to be distinguished from the others. Not all of those who feel most strongly about her went to Harvard as students. And not all universities are esteemed, even by their students, as Harvard is.

Nor is the answer that Harvard is rich or that she is old or famous. It is not her wealth we think of when we think of Harvard nor her fame in others' minds — and as for her antiquity, the university we mean goes back a hundred years at most.

Neither is it beauty that holds us — beauty in any ordinary sense. It would be difficult to find a less lovely city than Cambridge as it looks today.

And yet the emotion is real — realer than one guesses until one goes.

Why?

I can offer only hints and clues from my dozen years here. It sometimes happens, driving through a particular countryside — New England say — that some accident of the scene, a man going home across frozen furrows in a late, cold light, shows you the meaning. I remember two such moments at Harvard.

One was in Sanders Theater late on a wet afternoon with a few professors on the wooden benches and a new President of the University on the stage with the retiring Provost beside him and the Senior Fellow and the Dean of the Law School and a few more. There was no formality; no ceremony. Members of the Faculty had drawn up resolutions which they wished to present and did present — resolutions commending the courage of the University administration in standing, wholly alone and without measurable public support, against the most vicious menace to intellectual freedom in the history of Harvard — which means, in the history of the country. The resolutions had no authority but the authority of the names signed to them — professors' names. The event had no public recognition: no reporter was there or would have found anything to report if he had been. But in that almost empty room and in that failing light was the presence of the thing we mean.

The other was last year in the Memorial Church when a service was held for Percy Bridgman. There too there was no ceremony. Five men spoke of his life and of his death and the University, though no one summoned it, was there. One felt the passage of time and the passage of life, and the meaning of the passage of life and time in this place: the high commitment, the intellectual passion, the pure integrity. It was almost as though the life of the mind had been made palpable and one were *in* it.

And perhaps that is the answer after all. Perhaps the reason why grown men, mature men, give themselves to this place with such wholeness of heart is precisely that here the life of the mind, which is a metaphor in ordinary speaking, is a presence, a reality. And that here the free society of which we talk is truly free.

An Hellenic Center
in Washington

1963

IF ONE thinks of education (as the Greeks thought of it) in its relation to the conditions of the public world, the political world, what some of us call the "actual" world, then the striking fact about the establishment of a Harvard center for Hellenic studies in the city of Washington is not the fact that the new center is to be part of Harvard but the fact that it is to be part of the capital of the American Republic. For the implication of this choice of site is obvious: that someone in Washington, or someone at Harvard, or someone, conceivably, in both, has decided that a Greek Revival is what this country chiefly needs.

It is an unusual idea but not, for that reason, necessarily a bad one. There have been Greek Revivals in the Republic before this, and the city of Washington has felt their influence. As a matter of fact, the city of Washington owes its existence to one of them. If Thucydides had never lived or the fathers of the Republic read him, the Potomac might still flow silently and sluggishly to the sea with nothing to watch it but the fertilizer plants in Alexandria. Readers of John Adams's account of the goings-on in the committee appointed by the First Continental Congress to "state the rights of the Colonies" will know what I mean. Everyone in Philadelphia knew that the rights of the Colonies had been violated: that was why the Congress had been called. But *what* rights, and whence derived, was another matter. Were they Mr. Locke's "natural rights of man" deriving from the natural law of nature? But Mr. Locke was a philosopher and therefore a dubious legal authority. Were they rights derived from the British Constitution? But the British Constitution, according to Sir William Blackstone, was whatever Parliament said it was, and it was precisely Parliament which was now passing the Townsend Acts and all the rest of the abominations.

Fallen thus between philosophers and lawyers, the American cause might have withered, as it very nearly did, for lack of reasons, had not the Greeks supplied them. John Adams recommended to his fellow citizens that they look to "the great examples of Greece and Rome" for the origin of the rights which, as he put it, "the King, his ministry, and Parliament will not endure to hear the Americans talk of," and Abigail, as she wrote to John, found that she had "taken a great fondness for reading Rollin's *Ancient History*": she had even set her seven-year-old son, John Quincy, to reading it aloud.

Abigail, as usual, was right. Precedents are better than principles in any ideological struggle, and Greek precedents, in the American Colonies of the Seventeen Seventies, had more authority than most, for the Sons of Liberty were better Hellenists than the grandsons. They knew Thucydides' simple, matter-of-fact, and overwhelming statement that "in Athens there was no interference with the personal life of any man." They knew that the word Herodotus used for liberty, when he wished to say that the Athenians, once their liberty was gained, were braver than other men, was the word meaning freedom of speech.

They knew that freedom of speech, to Euripides, was "the one great thing." And they founded themselves on that knowledge. The rights they demanded were the rights men ought to have because men *had* had them.

I do not wish to claim too much for Greece. There might have been — there would surely have been — American independence without the Greeks: the ministers of George the Third would have seen to that. But the founding of the city of Washington is another matter, for the city of Washington assumes a *United* States, a united Republic, a union; and there would have been no union, as Lincoln reminded his contemporaries at Independence Hall, without Thomas Jefferson's Declaration. Which means that there would have been no union, without the example of Athens. Jefferson's language in the Declaration may be the language of Locke, but his precedent is the precedent of Pericles, and Jefferson was no man to send a new nation to sea in a philosopher's cockle without a precedent to row with. What is philosophically true of "all men" in Jefferson's preamble had been historically true of every man — or at least of every citizen — in Pericles' Athens. The citizens of Athens were not subjects of the state: they were men inviolable in their quality as men. And so, in Jefferson's Declaration, should the Americans be. Their government should exist to secure their unalienable rights, deriving its just powers from the consent of the governed. If glory had come of true freedom once, it would again. And it did. It won a war, and it founded a nation.

But will it again *now?* That, I suppose, is our question here today. Whoever decided to open a new Hellenic Center in Washington at this particular moment in American history could not have done so for antiquarian reasons, or merely to remind the world by a dramatic conjunction, a symbolic paradox, that the foundations of this enormous city were laid in the Cerameicus at Athens. Consequences must have been expected. But — and this, I repeat, is the question here — are Hellenic consequences still expectable today?

Not, certainly, practical Hellenic consequences — consequences such as John and Abigail Adams hoped for — and got. We have come a long way from the Age of Pericles in this American generation, and even farther, it sometimes seems, from that morning of the world in which John Adams lived. Pericles' description of his city, in the great oration, would read, to the subscribers of *Time*, like the classic definition of what that magazine and our generation calls a shallow liberalism — as of course it is. And that solemnly immutable organization, ironically called The Daughters of the American Revolution, would draw from Thucydides only the lesson that Athens lost the Peloponnesian War — doubtless because there was not, in the entire Ecclesia, a single Unathenian Committee to investigate and expose the private thoughts of the citizens. One recalls that even after the Athenian democracy fell, Socrates had to accuse himself.

But practical consequences are not the only consequences to be derived from a study of the Greeks. There are deeper findings, profounder lessons, and the deepest of all is a lesson which might be useful even in a time like ours — particularly, perhaps, in a time like ours. I mean the lesson of the conception of man which underlies the Athenian practices.

Every historical age, every "civilization" as we put it, has its characteristic notion of what a human being is: indeed it is precisely that notion which distinguishes an age, makes a civilization. But in most ages, as in ours, the notion is fuddled, confused, too near or too far off to focus. It was the great glory of the Greeks that they, almost alone among human societies, achieved a sharply human perspective and thus the perfectly focused clarity which we can recognize even now in fragments at Olympia and bronzes at Athens and the lines of Aeschylus and Homer. The consequence was that the whole world knew what a man was to the Greeks: what beauty he had, what balance on the wheeling earth, what dignity in the labyrinth of his inexplicable fate, what courage under the vulture's beak, what ultimate grace. And the further consequence, the further consequence at least in Europe, was that the world — the world down to *our* world in any case — accepted the Greek image. Europe, says Yeats, became Europe when the Athenian sculptors "gave women dreams and dreams their looking glass."

Unhappily, the importance of that looking glass to us today is the fact that we have broken it. We first, as we would tell the story, have freed ourselves from the humanistic delusions of the Greeks. And how have we freed ourselves? By courage. And where have we found the courage? In the new insights of the social sciences, in the new honesty of the arts. We are the first to look at man as he truly is and to dare to see him. A lover of freedom? Everywhere we turn, the free fear freedom; and new peoples, newly freed, rush to forge themselves old chains. A lover of life and of virtue and of love? Scientific surveys inform us that the human race is fascinated not with love, which is a personal commitment, but with sex, which is a faceless commerce. Antagonist of death? We see a whole world preoccupied, not with death itself, which is an individual action, but with a totality of death — a massacre of death — which is a statistical event.

And facing these facts thus honestly, and many others —
many private and secret observations — many statistical conclusions and equations — we begin, little by little, in a work of letters here, in a labor of philosophy beyond, to shape *our*
concept of a man — a concept very different from the Greek.
The figure we begin to see is not the figure of the hero, even the
defeated hero — Prometheus on the bloody stone — but something else: the victim. And the victim, not of fate — nothing so
grand as that — but of "predicament"; man's human, sad, half-
comical predicament as anguished, mortal creature in an absurd
world. It is this our courage and our honesty have given us the
eyes to see.

I do not mean to mock the courage. It is true that this new
courage of ours is sometimes, as in Kierkegaard, a courage rancid
with self-pity, and sometimes, as in Sartre, a courage bitter with
a brutal spite, but it is courage notwithstanding. Rilke needed
something more than a superb prose style to face that hospital in
Paris in *The Notebooks,* and so did Camus in his myth of Sisyphus turned upside down — that myth in which the toiler at
the endless task *chooses* his failure, elects to love his muddy
stone, and so accomplishes the only triumph possible to man.

No, our fault is not lack of courage. But there *is* a fault. And
a reexamination of the Greeks might help us to discover what it
is. Our fault is to think that this new courage of ours is peculiar
to our time; that we first in the long history of mankind have
dared to look our human condition in the face; that the Greeks
were ignorant of the tragic facts we now confront, or at least
ignored them.

Certainly, if ever a human consciousness faced the facts of
its condition it was the Greek. What is Socrates facing but these
same facts — or Euripides, or Sophocles? How did Pericles

comfort the families of the Athenian dead in the first year of the Peloponnesian War? By telling them their sons still lived? The Greeks had no such solace. By changing their deaths into rhetoric adorned with verbal wreaths? No, by telling them the truth. You know what he said: how he reminded his hearers of the realities of their lives — how he reminded them "that life is full of vicissitudes and that it may well be that the greatest good is an honorable death like that of your sons or an honorable grief like yours. I know how hard it is to make you feel this . . . Some of you, of course, are of an age when you may hope to have other children and these should bear their sorrow better . . . But some of you have passed the prime of life. To these I say, Congratulate yourselves that you have been happy during the greater part of your days; remember that your sorrow will not last long, and be comforted by the glory of those you have lost. Honor is the delight of men when they are old and useless."

Cold comfort? Colder than that of our own philosophers. But delusion? Is there delusion here? Or in the epitaphs? "I weep not for thee for thou knewest many fair things, and then again God dealt thee thy lot of ill." Even the women of Greece, and even in that confrontation which is most difficult for any woman, looked their lives in the face. "O friend," reads a fragment of Sappho's,

> *O friend, the singer of shrill lyres*
> *All flesh old age already . . .*
> *And the hairs have become white from black . . .*
> *And the knees do not carry . . .*

It is Sappho too who says of the finality of the passage of time what no other woman perhaps has ever dared put into words:

The moon is down and the Pleiades.
It is the middle of the night
And time passes, time passes,
And I lie alone . . .

No, we are not the first to find the courage to see what we are. Nor do we see more clearly than others have. Nor, finally, is it our only error to think we do. Our deepest self-deception is to believe, as a great part of contemporary literature and contemporary philosophy seems to believe, that it takes more courage to write life off as a brutal absurdity than to love it in spite of itself. But the contrary is assuredly the case. It takes more courage to know what Sappho knew and to say nevertheless

> *But I love delicacy,*
> *And the bright and the beautiful belong for me*
> *To the desire of the sunlight . . .*

than to know what Dostoevski knew and to write *Notes from Underground*.

Which offers, perhaps, a clue of sorts. What a Center of Hellenic Studies might do for the modern capital of a great democracy which has lost a part of its faith in freedom because it has lost a part of its belief in man, is to remind it that a people at least as candid and courageous as ourselves once held a view of man much nobler than the view we hold, and that this view carried a little city in a narrow land to the brightest height humanity has ever reached.

VI

People

Eleanor Roosevelt

1962

I SUPPOSE Mrs. Roosevelt was known — known, that is, to be recognized and remembered — by more human beings than any woman in history.

For one thing, she went everywhere and went always as herself, a woman concerned with a woman's things — which means with human things. Even when her husband was President she was never a public figure, a symbol, a representative of one kind or another. Wherever she was, she was there in her own right, her own person.

And then again, wherever she was she was distinct, distinguishable — her height, her fine carriage, her face: a plain face which could be beautiful as merely handsome faces never are. She was a great lady and therefore a woman first and a lady afterward, her exquisite manners a means always of reaching others, not of putting them off, holding them at a distance.

There have been famous women known the world over for their profiles on coins or their images in light. The world knew Eleanor Roosevelt by heart.

Why was she famous? For herself. What she did was useful and generous and good, but what she was will be remembered longer. In a starved and hungry time haunted by intellectual abstractions and scientific divinations, she remained a woman. Others might identify themselves by their dogmas, as we all are expected to do in this century — Communist or anti-Communist or Nationalist or Pacifist or whatever. Others might think in terms of their slot in the census, as white or black or Jew or gentile, or judge themselves by their status in the statistics. Mrs. Roosevelt identified herself by herself and judged herself as herself and did her own thinking. She belonged to herself in the old American way of belonging to one's self and thus belonged to everyone as a human being always does who reminds the rest what human beings ought to be.

It was not what she said in her columns or in her speeches or anywhere else. It was her response to her time. Where the rest of us increasingly respond in formulas dictated by the place we live or the paper we read or the income we earn, so that a man's opinions can be predicted the moment you know he comes from the North Shore of Chicago, Mrs. Roosevelt always responded in her human person. No problem was big enough to become abstract to her — not even the problem of a world full of underfed children or exploited women. And no conviction, no matter how firmly she held it, ever made her doctrinaire. She felt what she thought. And she made others feel it. Not by eloquence, for she was not eloquent. Not by mere persistence: she was far too busy to waste time. By candor. By the unanswerable honesty of her own commitment.

And by the reality, the humanity, of her world. To most of us, the world — what we continue to call "the world" — has become an abstraction of one kind or another: an economic mechanism such as the Marxists still believe they have discovered;

the Absurdity which contemporary literary fashion plays with; the hard-headed Reality which only Republicans can ever know; the ultimate Equation which science will someday write. To Mrs. Roosevelt the world was never an abstraction. It was human.

This, I think, was the key to her hold upon the imagination of her time. Because the world was human to her, people, in her presence, took themselves upon her terms. They talked like human beings — were even unashamed to feel like human beings. With her there on the platform, or in a chair by the window, or merely passing on the street, things took on their old human proportion again and the slogans somehow withered and went away — even those enormous outdoor slogans of American suburbia, and those prestige-building, inside slogans of American intellectualia and the sky-high slogans of the various cults and creeds. Things got simpler where she was. Good became good again, and nonsense nonsense, and evil evil, and a man could love again and even pity.

It was for this reason, of course, that the doctrinaires of all the doctrines railed against her or patronized her with their silence. She left them nowhere at all to stand. And it was for this reason too, I suppose, that she never answered them. It was not that she ignored them. She knew what they said and some of it — the worst of it — must have hurt her. But what she meant and what they meant were so far apart that there were no words left in which to meet them. Doctrine is what life leaves behind like a skim of ice above a run of water: her thought was for the water.

Or not perhaps her thought: her being. For it was her being that counted. What renewed the feel of things where she passed was not what she thought or said but what she was. It was Eleanor Roosevelt, a great lady in a great tradition, who was also a woman and who saw the world as women see it and who gave it life. That, perhaps, is the word one needs: that she gave our time her life. All of it. Not just the end of it, the death, but all of it — the whole, full life.

Mrs. Roosevelt
An Anniversary
1963

DEATH IS NOT an automatic confirmer of fame: more often than not it opens questions life had seemed to close, dissolving indestructible reputations in an ironic silence. Only rarely does a great name grow greater when its owner leaves it, as Mrs. Roosevelt's unquestionably has. A year ago she was admired and loved by human beings of all sorts and kinds in every corner of the earth — but admired and loved not as an historic figure but as a remarkably brave and warm and persistent woman who had given herself to her time as no one else had done before her. Few doubted Mrs. Roosevelt's greatness as a person but fewer still, even among her most devoted followers, thought of her fame as an impersonal force which might go on to influence a time beyond her own. Sophisticated people allowed themselves to be impressed as well as amused by her indefatigable energy. Politicians regarded her as an embarrassing friend even while they twisted and dodged to avoid the appearance of opposing her. Intellectuals patronized her opinions while acknowledging, with more or less grace, that her opinions had a vitality others lacked. But all these were human reactions, personal reactions. The notion that Mrs. Roosevelt might be one of those infrequent human beings who somehow create, not only lives for themselves, but *conceptions* of those lives, *ideas* of those lives, capable of living on beyond them, was not often met with.

It is met with now. When Mrs. Roosevelt died a good deal was said, and rightly, about her breeding — about the fact that she was, as the phrase went, a "great lady." She was a great lady. But she was also, as we are now beginning to see, something more important to us: she was a great American lady. Which is to say that she belonged to that remarkable line of American women, of whom Abigail Adams was perhaps the first, who were born and bred into a natural and easy relationship with the American tradition of feeling and thinking.

It is not and never has been an easy tradition for strangers to understand, particularly strangers from parts of the Old World where the immemorial traditions of church and state are authoritarian. Take, for example, the word, conservative. To be a conservative in the eighteenth century in most of Europe was to believe in keeping things as they were, opposing change. In the American Republic, however — a republic which began not only with a revolution but with the most revolutionary statement of political principle in history (including modern history) — the opposite was true: to be a conservative in America was to believe in the conservation of American revolution, which meant, necessarily, the conservation of that freedom of change by which, and by which alone, revolutionary principles can be realized. Men do not achieve the inalienable right to life, liberty and the pursuit of happiness — to say nothing of the equality of opportunity which is fundamental to everything else — by keeping things the way they are.

This paradoxical American truth which so many contemporary

Americans have never understood — Southern "conservatives" whose "conservatism" consists in keeping things the way they were under slavery — right-wing "conservatives" whose "conservatism" means keeping things the way they were with Joe McCarthy — this paradoxical American truth was born and bred into Eleanor Roosevelt as it was born and bred into Abigail Adams. It would be difficult to think of two women farther apart in the political spectrum. Abigail Adams, if she had lived in Mrs. Roosevelt's time, would have been a Republican. Mrs. Roosevelt, if she had lived in the Seventeen Nineties, would have been an Anti-Federalist, which is to say a Jeffersonian. But when it came to American principles, Abigail Adams, who could contain her philosophical enthusiasm for John Locke, came out precisely where Mrs. Roosevelt would have come out.

"Neighbor Faxon" who called on Mrs. Adams in February of 1797 to complain about a little Negro boy she had sent to the Quincy school found out quickly enough what American Conservatism was. If the boy persisted in coming, Mr. Faxon said, the school would break up because the rest of the students wouldn't attend. "But, Mr. Faxon," she replied, "this is attacking the principle of liberty and equality upon the only grounds upon which it ought to be supported, an equality of rights." Men might not be as equal in Federalist Quincy as Mr. Jefferson thought they were in Monticello but when it came to the *future* and one's right to inherit it, every man in America was as equal as every other — including every Negro boy. How but by instruction, she asked the unhappy Mr. Faxon, was this lad to make a future living? To which she added, looking a little farther ahead, "Tell them, Mr. Faxon . . . I hope we shall all go to Heaven together."

Abigail Adams's voice was doubtless very different from Mrs.

Roosevelt's (which was unlike any voice I, for one, have ever heard) but the laugh at the end of that little interview belongs to them both. And so does the ease, the confidence, the lack of pretension in the use of American terms, the American vocabulary. Mrs. Adams could talk about "an equality of rights" as naturally as she could talk about her hope of Heaven because her husband — and she with him — had lived through the hammering out of the phrase and knew its meaning in terms not only of declarations but of human beings. Mrs. Roosevelt had the same assurance and the same simplicity. She could speak of "the revolution of equality" as naturally as though she had passed it on the street which, of course, she had: it was "the concept on which our life is based . . ." and she knew "our life" because she had lived it.

The trouble with most of the rest of us is that the American terms have become abstractions to play with as the Marxists play with their "scientific" propositions until the human meaning blurs like a President's face on an old bill. We believe in "liberty," yes — but not in the liberty Jefferson had in mind or John Adams believed in: a way of life for a new people, an enlargement, a hope. More and more, liberty becomes with us nothing more than the right to be left alone, meaning the right to be left alone to go on doing whatever it was we were doing before. With the result that segregationists can use the word to justify the denial of liberty to Negroes because the denial of liberty to Negroes is what segregationists have always done — their "heritage."

And with the further result that we are rapidly becoming the timidest people on earth. Liberty to be left alone by others inevitably turns into liberty to be left alone by life, and liberty to be left alone by life sooner or later turns into fear of the future —

fear of the Russians in the future — fear of the Chinese in the future — fear even of what America may become in the future. Indeed, what passes for political conservatism in our day is very largely nothing but just such fear, with anti-Communism replacing freedom as a national purpose and a whole list of hatreds and prejudices and denials as ultimate objectives.

Mrs. Roosevelt, like Mrs. Adams, was not afraid — and least of all afraid of the future. She saw what the timid never see — that life in a living time like ours and in a living country like ours is necessarily a continuing revolution and must be faced as such. Why have we not faced it? "The chief reason," she said at the end of her life, and at an age when most of us leave courage to somebody else, "is fear. Change means the unknown. . . . It means, too many people cry, insecurity. Nonsense! No one from the beginning of time has had security. . . ."

That too is American idiom. It has an honorable ancestry which goes a long way back. But when we think of that kind of talk today our thoughts are obliged to return to Mrs. Roosevelt. And it is because they are obliged to return to her that her stature has increased and her authority grown since she died. Not because she was the only American of her time to believe what she believed, or even to practice it — she was not — but because the whole inherited vocabulary of the American mind was as natural in her mouth as its convictions were native to her spirit. She renewed our trust in ourselves by *being* what we trusted — and being it so easily, so honorably, so humanly that no one, not even her bitterest adversaries, ever doubted her good faith.

If democracy had saints — and no other cause demands a greater selflessness, a greater devotion — Mrs. Roosevelt would be one. She proved her faith in action as saints do. And her memory may restore a measure of it to her country.

F. F.

1965

THE WISEST of the Greeks is said to have warned his fellow mortals to "call no man happy till he dies." Justice Frankfurter, whose impetuous Viennese parents ignored that injunction, was known to innumerable friends throughout a long life as Felix. And yet his history, if one rightly considers what old Solon meant, makes no exception to the rule. It was not until Felix Frankfurter died — not till his life could be seen as a completed thing, safe from its own vicissitudes — that any of us understood how truly happy it had been.

I do not mean, of course, that it was only happy, or always happy, or happy in all its accidents and chances. The Justice had his disappointments like other men, and, like other men, his failures. His death was difficult and its sufferings — the long inhibition of movement and of speech — were precisely the sufferings he was least prepared by temperament to endure . . . though he endured them. I mean simply that the distinction of his life, the quality above all others which distinguished it, was its happiness: not its good fortune, not its extraordinary success, its offices, its honors, but its happiness.

It is not, I know, a quality much considered in this generation.

We regard ourselves as sadder, wiser men (in the contemporary world increasing wisdom is always increasing sadness) who have learned at last that life is inescapably tragic and that those in other ages who counted happiness its crown were immature or ignorant or both. Even our own American ancestors with their eloquent talk of the pursuit of happiness as the ultimate end and aim of man's existence, leave us uncomfortable and cold. We have seen too much of the world's realities, have looked too deeply into science and men's minds. Happiness, we tell ourselves — happiness in an age like ours — is an incongruity to be left to children; or not, perhaps, to children even, but to that innocuous universe of television and of advertisement where all the words are wishes and only photographs come true.

But the fact is, notwithstanding, that it was precisely in an age like ours, because it *was* our age, that Felix Frankfurter's life was lived. And the fact is, further, that his life was happy in that age in the old, high, noble, classic sense. Which means, in the deliberate sense, in the conscious sense: a happiness well aware of the risks of happiness; the happiness of

> *such men as come*
> *Proud, open-eyed and laughing to the tomb.*

When an insensitive man, a thoughtless man, an unthinking man, lives happily through blundering wars, through the destruction of civilizations, through a worldwide psychological collapse which opens cisterns of human depravity long closed, long forgotten, his happiness is an affront, a deformity, which condemns himself and the society which produced him. But when an intelligent man, a man of more than ordinary intelligence, more than ordinary sensitivity and perception, lives through such a time knowing what it is he lives through, facing its dreadful revelations not in his mind alone but on his nerves, himself an intended victim of its most terrifying inhumanity, when such a man can live through such a time believing in life, believing in human kind, delighting still in his work, his world, his friends, his country, that man's happiness is not deformity or defect. It is not complacency. It is greatness.

Felix Frankfurter's greatness — and we are only beginning now to see how great it was — was of this kind. He was one of the few — one of the very few — who kept the belief in man alive in a generation which had more reason than any other in three hundred years to lose it. No one, I think, will ever know how many of his contemporaries in positions of high and difficult responsibility thought of him as Landor thought of that fire at which he warmed his hands. And as for the young, as for the intellectual leaders and begetters of the generation which followed his own, the generation which grew up from one world war to another through the years of social and psychological disintegration which were once regarded as nothing more than an economic depression — as for the young, not even the members themselves of that generation knew what they owed to Felix Frankfurter. The greatest gifts, the spiritual gifts, the gifts of courage and belief and hope, can no more be measured than the sunlight. Like the sunlight they are taken as they come — received.

But if the Justice's influence, certainly one of the most remarkable influences in the history of any country, cannot be counted or contained, it can be talked of. Most men who profoundly influence the minds of others reach them as writers or as

speakers: as political orators or as university lecturers or as judges
of high courts with a gift like that of Oliver Wendell Holmes for
making the interpretation of a nation's laws interpret its nature;
even as novelists and poets — a Herman Melville who can make
us struggle with the great white whale — a Robert Frost
who puts words in our mouths whether we like them or not.
Felix Frankfurter, however, was not one of these.

Or, rather, he was all of them — all, that is, but novelist and
poet — and yet his influence on his time was something else.
He was a persuasive writer and an articulate speaker — one of
the most articulate speakers, certainly, any of us can recall.
He was a famous dialectician in the classrooms of the Harvard Law School where Socrates was once the local divinity.
He was a brilliant journalist: his editorials for the Republican
Boston *Herald* were surpassed only by his editorials for the
liberal *New Republic*, and his *Atlantic* piece on the trials of
Sacco and Vanzetti is as unanswerable today as it was when it
stung the conscience of the Boston Bar. He was a Justice of
the Supreme Court of the United States — how distinguished a
Justice it is not for me to say, though I may, perhaps, be permitted the observation that few men who ever sat there were more
sedulously watched by friend and foe — particularly friend —
and that few opinions were more widely read than his, or more
widely (and variously) interpreted. He was all these things —
judge, journalist, teacher, even, on occasion, the tongue, though
not the voice, of political authority.

But nevertheless, and in spite of his achievements in all these
numerous capacities, it was neither as one nor the other that his
extraordinary impress on his time was made. To understand that
paradox, one must look more closely at the central mystery, the

man himself. And there the Justice's friend, Sir Isaiah Berlin of All Souls College in Oxford, may bear witness for us all. In a collection of reminiscences published a year or two ago Professor Berlin describes his second meeting with the Justice at All Souls in 1934 when Frankfurter was visiting professor at Oxford and the great and near great had come up from London to cultivate him "as a man of influence in Washington, an intimate friend and adviser of the President of the United States." The usual after-dinner ritual was observed: the port, the polished mahogany, the old men at the table, the young men back behind, the ceremonial interrogation, the attentive pause, the answer. Mr Frankfurter, as Professor Berlin remembers it, "responded to this treatment with the greatest naturalness and lack of self-consciousness . . . He did not display the slightest sign of grandeur, did not pontificate . . . but talked copiously, with an overflowing gaiety and spontaneity which conveyed the impression of great natural sweetness." But he had his eye on his deliverance notwithstanding. Under cover of a sortie toward, but not to, the brandy bottle he "almost literally buttonholed a junior fellow who looked lively and sympathetic," refused to be detached from him by any number of solemn questions from the head of the table and ended the evening, or, rather, the better part of the night, in a corner of deafening talk with the younger dons. "So far as I and my friends were concerned," says Sir Isaiah, "his genius resided in the golden shower of intellectual and emotional generosity that was poured forth before his friends . . . Whenever I met him . . . he was the center, the life and soul, of a circle of eager and delighted human beings, exuberant, endlessly appreciative, delighting in every manifestation of intelligence, imagination and life."

It is so. of course, that we all remember him. And it was so that he touched our lives and the life of our generation and our country. What he gave his friends, even the greatest of them, was something more than counsel though his counsel was wise; something more than courage though his courage was unquestionable and never questioned; something more even than affection though affection flowed from him and love was the motive and the motion of his heart. What he gave his friends, and through them others than his friends, was their own lives. He had the power, which only those who love life ever have, of giving life, enlarging life, enhancing it: no man ever left him smaller than he came.

But the extraordinary thing was not Felix Frankfurter's possession of this power: it was his ability to exercise it not only in his relation with his personal friends but in his relation — that long and never lessening love affair — between his country and himself. Somehow he was able to pour his own proud, passionate belief in life, belief in man, belief in the possibilities of man, back into a national mentality in which these words were rapidly becoming only words. Because he was himself a highly intelligent and shrewdly skeptical human being, because he was aware, as few of his contemporaries were aware, of the actualities of his country and his time and because, for all his awareness, for all his skepticism and for all his intelligence, he still believed in the American adventure, the American hope, others believed in it. Faith is not taught by arguments. It is taught by lives. It was Felix Frankfurter's life which was the secret of his influence on his century and his republic — the life itself — the indescribable, inexhaustible, various, vehement, creative, understanding, generous man who had the courage to be whole and happy in a tragic time.

Adlai Stevenson

Remarks at the Memorial Ceremony in the General Assembly Hall
at the United Nations, July 19, 1965

WHEN ADLAI STEVENSON spoke at the memorial service
for Eleanor Roosevelt who had "come home to the Rose Garden
at Hyde Park for the last time," he told her friends that it was not
her life they had lost — she had lived that out to the full: it was
the thing she was . . . "and who can name it."

Who can name what *he* was? Not I certainly. But if there is
a room anywhere in which it can be spoken of, it is this room
built for the Assembly at the United Nations. Not because —
not only because — the United Nations was, for so many years,
the center of his life and of his concern, but for a different reason: because the organization itself, the nature of the organization, creates a perspective in which a life like Adlai Stevenson's
might perhaps be seen — in which it might assume the nobility,
the significance, which are its inward form.

In the ordinary context, the context to which our age is increasingly accustomed, a life like his becomes a puzzle, a contradiction, which even those who love him — and this room is
full of those who love him — cannot readily resolve. Our generation — and not in the United States alone — not only in the
United States — is obsessed by a view of human life which leaves

no room for any human greatness or magnificence but one. Power fascinates us, and the exercise of power, and we judge our public figures by the power they dispose of, by the offices they hold which give them access to the thrust of power. Adlai Stevenson cannot be measured by these measures: cannot be known or recognized by them or even named.

He had no taste for power, no desire for it. The remarkable speech in which he accepted the inevitability of his nomination for the presidency was a portrait of himself as ill-advised politically as it was personally honorable. And the two disastrous and superb campaigns which he conducted were proof that his reluctance at the start was not the reluctance of political calculation but of passionate belief. When he said, years afterward, that he would like to be remembered for those unsuccessful ventures, for those two defeats, he meant that there are some things in the life of a democracy more important than to come to power — more important ultimately than the possession of power.

And yet, as the last few days have demonstrated, it is in terms of power or of the failure to come to power that his life is still most commonly conceived. In the shock and sorrow of his sudden death, the minds of those who wrote and spoke of him went back again and again, over and over, with admiration and regret and more sometimes than admiration or regret, to what were called the contradictions and the paradoxes of his history. He was, we were reminded, a great political figure who had never held a great political office; a master of the art of government who had governed only in his own state; a public man unsuccessful somehow in public life — too fine for it perhaps; a Hamlet who thought too long too deeply, who doubted too scrupulously, who could never permit himself to be as sure as an American politician in the Fifties was supposed to be sure, that that voice beneath the battlements urging to violence and revenge was the king his father's voice.

Well, it was true in part of course — true that he thought long and deeply — true that he had the courage of his doubts — true too that he was skeptical of hatred and its prophets in a day when the great majority of his fellow citizens were listening to those prophets and believing them. But the conclusions most often drawn from these observations are not true. Hamlet dies to those heart-breaking words in which the pity overwhelms the grief: Good night, sweet Prince. In Adlai Stevenson's death there is no room for pity. Those of us who mourn him and will always mourn him, think of him not as a man defeated in his purpose but as a man fulfilled in it: not as a man whose life was a contradiction and a paradox but as a man whose life had a particular singleness, an unusual wholeness, its own law.

And it is here in this room, I think, that that wholeness is most certain to appear. For the United Nations, though it knows and suffers from our contemporary trust in power, is dedicated to another end: the subordination of power to the hope for peace — which is to say the hope for humanity. Those qualities in Adlai Stevenson which seemed, in other surroundings, to be traits of character, attributes of personality — his warmth, his charm, his considerateness, his intelligence, his humor, his devotion, his incisiveness, his eloquence — were fused here, in their employment in the noblest of all causes, to compose a complete man, a man so balanced, so harmonious as a human being, that his greatness passed almost unnoticed while he lived.

His effectiveness here, his services to this organization and to the country to which his life was given, others have spoken of and will speak. They were great services, greatly rendered. But the most important thing about them, or so it seems to me, was their humanity. It is not, in the long history of civilization, the accomplishment which counts but the manner of the accomplishment. Works of will are notoriously short-lived and even works of intellect can fail when the intelligence is cynical or dry. It is only when the end is reached through the human heart as well as through the human mind that the accomplishment is certain to endure. And it is for that reason that Adlai Stevenson seems certain of remembrance.

His great achievement was not political triumph or, indeed, triumph of any kind. His great achievement was the enrichment of his time by the nature of his relationships with his time. If his intelligence was remarkable it was remarkable, even more than for its clarity, for its modesty, its humor, its naturalness, its total lack of vanity or arrogance. If he was one of the great articulators of his time, one of the few, true voices, it was because the words he spoke were the words of his own thought, of his deepest and most personal conviction. It was himself he gave in word and thought and action, not to his friends alone but to his country, to his world. And the gift had consequences. It changed the tone and temper of political life in the United States for a generation. It humanized the quality of international dialogue throughout a great part of the world. It enlightened a dark time.

Which means, I suppose, that Adlai Stevenson's great achievement was himself. What we have lost as he said of his friend, Mrs. Roosevelt, is not his life. He lived that out, if not to the full, at least more fully than almost any other man. What we have lost is himself. And who can name the warmth and richness of it?

Elmer Davis

1954

If it weren't for Elmer Davis and a few more — but chiefly
Elmer Davis — an observant traveler might conclude that the
Americans were dying out. Like the moose in Newfoundland,
which are reported to be perishing of some obscure psychological
disorder — crashing half-blind into trees, mooning morosely
around swamps, unable or unwilling even to rid themselves of
their ticks.

A generation ago Americans were fairly common in this country. You could hear them blundering about in the bush at all
hours, sniffing at everything, snorting at what they didn't care
for, elbowing their way through any kind of trouble, respect-
ing themselves and intending to be respected by others, cautious
maybe but hard to intimidate and impossible to stampede. One
mark of an American was the way his neck would swell if you
tried to tell him what to think or where to line up. Another was
his courage, not always wise, and his humor, not always subtle,
and the way he got round by himself.

American conservatives, back in those days, were men who
believed in conserving America, including the American Constitution, including also the American Bill of Rights — men like

Charles Evan Hughes. American liberals were men who believed in the achievement of the American Revolution no matter
who was against it. And neither side ran in packs. And neither
side was herded by fear or by anything else. Where they have
gone to now, and why, is the great American mystery. With
the moose it is said to be the climate.

About all we can really be certain of is that the big single animals are disappearing and that their place is being taken by something very different — something that loves a herd — something
that reacts not to conviction but fear — something that has a
strange look against the background of our history. John Keats,
who took a wholly unreasoning dislike for Devonshire because
his brother Tom lay sick there, wrote his friend Bailey that "a
Devonshirer standing on his native hills is not a distinct object —
he does not show against the light. . . . Homer is fine, Achilles
is fine, Diomed is fine, Shakespeare is fine, Hamlet is fine, Lear
is fine, but dwindled Englishmen are not fine." Neither are
dwindled Americans. But what is least fine of all human objects
is the American so dwindled that he can only run in herds.

To such Americans the existence of a man like Elmer Davis is
a living reproach — which is perhaps why so many of them hate
him. But it is not the hatred of the dwindled which makes Elmer
Davis so particularly valuable. It is the reminder he gives us all
of what an American really is and therefore ought to be. People
talked about the courage with which he told the truth in a difficult time. But Elmer Davis, I feel quite sure, did not think of it
as courageous. He knew as well as anyone that he ran risks. But
unless I am very wrong, he would have regarded it as shameful
to his country and shameful to himself to dignify that danger by
facing it with anything but contempt. An American — what an

American once was and what Elmer Davis still is — cannot permit himself to believe that it takes courage to tell the truth in this republic. To believe that would be to believe that the enemies of American freedom have already destroyed it and that the herd now rules. Mr. Davis may have his sober doubts about the immediate future, as any sensible man must have, but I don't think he considers that the tradition of individual liberty and of the government of the people by *themselves* has yet been wrecked.

Robert Frost
and John F. Kennedy

Remarks at the breaking of ground for the Frost Library
at Amherst College, October 26, 1963

THIS is not the first time I have assisted a President of the
United States to start a library. The first occasion was some
twenty-odd years ago at Hyde Park in the state of New York,
where a building had been constructed to house the papers of
Franklin Delano Roosevelt; which was all very well except for
two facts: that I was Librarian of Congress at the time, having
just been appointed to that office by Mr. Roosevelt, and that the
Library of Congress, until the date of my appointment, had itself been the usual repository for presidential papers.

Mr. Roosevelt's invitation to me to speak at Hyde Park — if
"invitation" is the word I want — was, I daresay, kindly meant;
there was to be nothing personal about the affront. But it is one
thing for an invitation to be kindly meant and another thing altogether to accept it in kind, particularly when it involves a
speech by the director of the library to which invaluable papers
ought to have gone, celebrating the opening of the library to
which they are going. I made, I am told, a memorable impression.
Indeed, my friend and classmate Dean Acheson, on whose unfail-
ing candor I have always been able to rely, assured me on my return to Washington that no public servant in the history of the

Republic had ever appeared to better advantage with his pants firmly caught in the crack of the door.

There are differences, of course, between that day and this. I don't work for Mr. Kennedy; or if I do, it is from the private heart, not from public office. And as for the Library of Congress, it has long since grown accustomed to the alienation of hoped-for papers, some having been alienated as far west as Independence, Missouri. But whatever else is altered, the fact remains that a library, or the idea of a library, is here again in process of inauguration by a President of the United States and that I seem again to be part of the proceedings. If precedents mean anything in this revolving world, the probability must be very great indeed that no good will come of it.

No good, that is, to me. Amherst can be more hopeful. And so too can this October valley and the old, soft, lovely hills off to the west of it where I have lived for half a biblical lifetime. The people of this countryside may forget in ordinary human course what anyone says on this occasion, but they will remember for many, many years that a young and gallant President of the United States, with the weight of history heavy upon his shoulders, somehow found time to come to our small corner of the world to talk of books and men and learning.

I say "small corner," not in modesty but in *Yankee* modesty, which is a different thing. We may not be as conspicuous at this end of the Commonwealth, Mr. President, as some you must have heard of at the other, but we bear up. We remind ourselves that it was a citizen of this very town of Amherst who was once described by a famous daughter as "too intrinsic for renown," and we like to think that now, nearly a century after Edward Dickinson's death, there are still men in these valley villages and up along the Deerfield, Bardwell's Ferry way, and in the hills behind, who deserve the tribute of Emily's unfractured crystal of pure poetry, pure praise. But whether we are right or not — whether we and our neighbors are too intrinsic for renown or merely too remote for notoriety — we know an honor when we see one, and your presence here we take to be just that: an honor to this college and these counties and ourselves.

Not to mention Robert Frost. For Frost, of course, is another matter, as he always was. There is an old Gaelic tale of the West Highlands called "The Brown Bear of the Green Glen," which has a whiskey bottle in it so definitively full that not a drop can be added, and so fabulously copious that nothing is lost, no matter how you drink. Frost's fame is like that bottle: it can't be added to because it is full already, and it won't draw down however it is drunk. We may name a library for him. We may go further than that; we may give his name to the first general library ever to be called for a poet in America, which is what this library will be. We may pass even that superlative of honor; we may designate as his the first general library but one in the entire world to bear a poet's name — the one being the A. S. Pushkin State Library in farthest Kazakhstan in the U.S.S.R. We may do what we please. Nothing whatever will have happened to the bottle; it will merely continue to be full.

This, I suggest, is a phenomenon which might well concern us on this particular occasion — the secret of that bottle. Is it the mere bulk and body of the fame which keeps it so miraculously brimming — the fact that no poet of our age, with the single exception of Yeats himself, had as much fame in his lifetime as Frost had at the end of his? Is it the quantity of the reputation, the number of people who knew Frost's name or recognized him on the streets or crowded into those wonderful talkings which some called readings and lined up afterward for autographs they rarely got?

I doubt it, and so do you. We know a little in our time and country about fame in bulk and its effect on lasting fame. At least we know what happens when a whole new industry is established, dedicated to nothing but the manufacture, in larger and larger quantities and in shorter and shorter periods of time, of crude, bulk reputation; we have seen its fruits. If great actresses are in short supply, as they invariably are, two or three to a century being about all the natural processes can produce, the industry will assemble you a dozen assorted Greatest Actresses in a single season, inflate them with adjectives, and launch them like blimps to float about for a year or three or maybe five or longer. But then what happens to them? Or to the greatest novels, the greatest plays, detergents, sedatives, cigarettes, laxatives, which circle with them?

Or even to the greatest men? And even when they *are* great? For the industry processes everyone, true as well as false. Let the actual thing itself appear — Keats's seldom-appearing Socrates in fact and in the flesh — and the assembly line will multigraph him and pass him current by every mechanical means until nothing is left of the single, human fact of the man himself but his bubble reputation in as many million mouths as the new technology can activate. It takes an Einstein to survive it. And even Einstein had reason to be grateful for the isolation of his vast achievement out among the galaxies of space and mind where the copywriters couldn't follow.

Yet Frost too survived, and with no such adventitious aid. Everything about him — the seeming simplicity of his poems, the silver beauty of his head, his age, his Yankee tongue, his love of talk, his ease upon a lecture platform — everything combined to put him within easy reach — which still could not quite reach him. No one in my time upon this planet was so pursued by fame as Frost, so "publicized" in the specific sense and meaning of that word. But even now, a few months after his death, the "public image," as the industry would call it, has already begun to change like elms in autumn, leaving enormous branches black and clean against the sky.

Frost too, it seems, but in a different way, an opposite way, is "too intrinsic for renown," too intrinsic for renown to touch. Something in the fame resists the fame as burning maple logs — rock maple, anyway — resist the blaze. And what it is, I think we know. At least there is an evening, not many years ago or many blocks from here, an evening others in this room remember, which might tell us. It was his eightieth birthday. Frost had been in New York where every possible honor, including some not possible, had been paid him, and, returning here to Amherst and his friends, he fell to talking of what honor really was, or would be: to leave behind him, as he put it, "a few poems it would be hard to get rid of." It sounds a modest wish, but Frost knew, as his friends knew, that it wasn't. Poems are not monuments, shapes of stone to stand and stand. Poems are speaking voices. And a poem that is hard to get rid of is a voice that is hard to get rid of. And a voice that is hard to get rid of is a man. What Frost wanted for himself in the midst of all that praise was what Keats had wanted for himself in the midst of no praise at all: to be among the English poets at his death, the poets of the English tongue.

Which means something very different from being talked about or passed from mouth to mouth by reputation. Reputation — above all, literary reputation — is a poor thing. It rises and falls. Consideration leads to reconsideration, fashions change, and as for posterity, no one has ever heard its verdict because posterity has never come. Frost will be praised and then neglected and then praised again like all the others. It wasn't reputation he was thinking of that wintry evening; it was something else. To be among the English poets is to *be*, to go on being. Frost wanted to go on being. And he has.

It is this fact — this actual and not at all imaginary or pretended fact — I wish to speak of for a moment: the persistence of this man. It has a certain relevance to what we do here. On the surface of these proceedings Frost's part in them is purely passive: nothing is asked of him but to receive the honor we now pay him and to relinquish a great name he does not own, having bequeathed it to the future — three syllables to be carved above a doorway, Frost and stone to age together. In fact, however, if one includes among his facts the fact I speak of, these roles are quite reversed: like that of the citizens of Colonus at the death of Oedipus in Sophocles's great play, the passive part is ours. He gives; we take.

Not that Frost was Oedipus precisely, except, perhaps, in his constant readiness to talk back to sphinxes. But there is something in the ending of that myth that gives this myth of ours its meaning. You remember how it goes: the wretched, unhappy, humbled, hurt old king, badgered and abused by fate, gulled by every trick the gods can play on him, tangled in patricide and incest and in every guilt, snarled in a web of faithful falsehoods and affectionate deceptions and kind lies, exiled by his own proscription, blinded by his own hands, who, dying, has so great a gift to give that Thebes and Athens quarrel over which shall have him. You remember what the gift is too. "I am here," says Oedipus to Theseus, King of Athens, "to give you something, my

own beaten self, no feast for the eyes. . . ." And why is such a
gift worth having? Because Oedipus is about to die. But why
should death give value to a gift like that? Because of the place
where death will meet him:

> *I shall disclose to you, O son of Aegeus*
> *What is appointed for your city and for you —*
> *Something that time will never wear away.*
> *Presently now without a hand to guide me*
> *I shall lead you to the place where I must die!* *

And what is that place? The Furies' wood which no man dares
to enter, the frightening grove sacred to those implacable pursuers, ministers of guilt, who have hounded him across the world.

> *These things are mysteries, not to be explained,*
> *But you will understand when you have come there.*

The gift that Oedipus has to give is a great gift because
that beaten, suffering self, no feast for the eyes, will face the dark
pursuers at the end.

Frost, I said, was not Oedipus, and so he wasn't. But he too has
that gift to give. And I can imagine some future reader of his
poems in the library that will bear his name feeling, like
Theseus, that the beaten and triumphant self has somehow, and
mysteriously, been given *him* — a self not unlike the old The-
ban king's. Quarrelsome? Certainly, and not with men alone but
gods. Tangled in misery? More than most men. But despairing?
No. Defeated by the certainty of death? Never defeated.
Frightened of the dreadful wood? Not frightened, either. A
rebellious, brave, magnificent, far-wandering, unbowed old man,

---

* Adapted from Robert Fitzgerald's translation, Harcourt, Brace.

who made his finest music out of manhood and met the Furies on their own dark ground.

We do not live, I know, in Athens. We live now in an insignificant, remote, small suburb of the universe. Reality, if one can still speak of reality, is out beyond us in the light-years somewhere or farther inward than our eyes can see in the always redivisible divisibilities of matter that is only matter to eyes as dim and dull as ours. Homer's heroic world, where men could face their destinies and die, becomes to us, with our more comprehensive information, the absurd world of Sartre, where men can only die. And yet, though all our facts are changed, nothing has been changed in fact: we still live lives. And lives still lead to death. And those who live a life that leads to death still need the gift that Oedipus gave Athens, the gift of self, of beaten self, of wandering, defeated, exiled self that can survive, endure, turn upon the dark pursuers, face its unintelligible destiny with blinded eyes and make a meaning of it: self, above all else, without self-pity.

This is the self that Frost had, and has given, and will go on and on and on to give, and we should thank him for it.

Far in the pillared dark
Thrush music went —
Almost like a call to come in
To the dark and lament.

But no, I was out for stars:
I would not come in.
I meant not even if asked
And I hadn't been.

Ernest Hemingway

1961

I wrote a poem some years ago in which there was a question about Hemingway and an answer:

> . . . *the lad in the Rue de Notre Dame des Champs*
> *In the carpenter's loft on the left-hand side going down —*
> *The lad with the supple look like a sleepy panther —*
> *And what became of him? Fame became of him.*
> *Veteran out of the wars before he was twenty:*
> *Famous at twenty-five: thirty a master —*
> *Whittled a style for his time from a walnut stick*
> *In a carpenter's loft in a street of that April city.*

Now, with his death, the question asks itself again: what became of him?

How shall that question be answered now? By the fame still? I don't suppose any writer since Byron has been as famous as Hemingway was when he died, but fame is a young man's passion. It has little to say to the fact of death.

Or is the style the answer? The style remains as surely as the fame. It has been praised, imitated and derided for thirty years, but it endures: the one intrinsic style our language has produced in this century. And yet Hemingway was the last man to wish to be remembered as a stylist, and none of his critics, however much he has admired the style or detested it, has been able or willing to leave his judgment at that.

To answer one must go further back. It is not Hemingway's death or even the manner of his death which poses the question now: it is his life — the fact that his life is finished and demands to be looked at, to be measured. What makes the answer difficult is that Hemingway's life was a strange life for a writer as we think of writers in our time. Writers with us are supposed to be watchers: "God's spies" as John Keats put it once. They are supposed to spend themselves observing the world, watching history and mankind and themselves — particularly themselves: their unsaid thoughts, their secret deeds and dreads. Hemingway was not a watcher: he was an actor in his life. He took part. What he took part in was not the private history of Ernest Hemingway or the social history of Oak Park, Illinois, or the intellectual history of a generation of his fellow countrymen. What he took part in was a public — even a universal — history of wars and animals and gigantic fish. And he did take part. He could never go to a war — and he went to every war available to him — without engaging in it. He went to the First World War as an ambulance driver and got his knee smashed by a shell in a front-line trench where no one had sent him. He went to the war in Spain to write a scenario for a movie and learned how you washed the powder burns off your hands without water. He went to the last World War as a correspondent — and worried the high command by turning up with other tools than typewriters — mementos he called them. And between wars there were lions and elephants. And between elephants and lions there were marlin. Also bears.

Again, modern writers, if you can believe the novels, associate

with other writers or with other writers' wives or with the people who hang around writers. Hemingway preferred boxers and
bicycle racers in Paris, and Charlie Thompson and Old Bra in
Key West, and nightclub addicts in New York and matadors
in Spain and commercial fishermen and game-cock fighters in
Cuba. He had writer friends. Scott Fitzgerald was a good
friend,* and Dos Passos sometimes was and sometimes wasn't.
But writers as writers — writers disguised as writers — he didn't
fancy. He and I had lunch in the middle Twenties with Wynd-
ham Lewis, the painter who had set himself up briefly and locally
as a literary dictator in London. When the two of us walked off
home across the Seine, Hemingway astonished me by saying,
"Did you notice? He ate with his gloves on." He had too —
though there were no gloves.

Most modern writers are literary — more so than ever now
that the critical mind has completed its conquest — but Hemingway wasn't literary. He read as much as most English professors
and he remembered what he read, remembered it usefully and
in its relevance to himself — but he rarely talked about writing.
Ezra Pound, the greatest and most successful teacher of writing
in our time, gave him up. "The son of a bitch's *instincts* are
right," said Pound. But you can't converse about instincts. Even
Gide, the most articulate writer about writing in modern France,
was defeated by that hulking body and artless air and charming
smile. I had dragged Hemingway along to a French literary
afternoon where Gide and Jules Romains and others of that generation sat on stiff-backed chairs around a bookshop wall talking as though they had rehearsed all morning, but Hemingway,
whom all of them were watching, watched the floor. It was
too much for Gide. He dropped the topic, whatever it was, and

* *A Moveable Feast* to the contrary notwithstanding.

drew Hemingway aside to explain how he punished his cat. He
punished his cat, he said, by lifting him up by the scruff of his
neck and saying PHT! in his face. Whether Hemingway restrained a desire to hit him, I don't know. I was watching the
back of his head.

.

A strange life for a writer and a difficult life to judge at the end.
Indeed, a difficult life to judge before the end — which is perhaps why Hemingway attracted, alive, more critics of more
schools and opinions than most writers who have been dead for
centuries. Writers generally are judged by their work, but Hemingway's life kept threatening to get in the way of his work with
the result that his critics never found themselves in agreement.
Those who were drawn to him called him, as one of them actually did on the day of his death, "a man who lived it up to write
it down." Those who were repelled — and most of the hostile
critics seem to have been repelled emotionally as well as intellectually — called him in one form of words or another a phony: a
man who ran away from his real task to masquerade as a big
game hunter or a hero or a tough guy. What they will say now
I don't know — perhaps that he had run as far as he could and
that the truth caught up with him at seven-thirty on the morning of the second of July.

Both views are based on a misconception of the relation between a writer's task and a writer's life. Both conceive of life
and writing as different and even contradictory things. The deploring critic thinks of Hemingway's life as a betrayal of his obligation: you don't fight marlin by the hour and watch the kill-
ing of 1500 bulls if you are loyal to your craft. The admiring
critic thinks of the obligation as incidental to the life: you shoot

grizzlies and then you write about it. Neither understands the simple and primary fact that a writing — a true writing — is not the natural by-product of an isolated experience, nor the autonomous creation of an isolated man, but the consequence of a collision between the two. Neither realizes that the collision when it occurs, even when the experience is a lion in the gun sights or a German in a Normandy hedge, may provide, for the right writer, something more than a thrill and something very different from an escape. It may, indeed, provide a realization — precisely such a realization as the art of letters at its greatest is capable of providing: the realization of the meaning of a man. Danger is not the least revealing of the mirrors into which we look.

That this obvious fact was obvious to Hemingway is a matter of record. Long before he had money enough for a safari or time enough to compose a theory of aesthetics, had he ever wished to compose one, he had learned that lesson. Of the time in his twenties when he was learning to write, he said, "I found the greatest difficulty, aside from knowing truly what you really felt, rather than what you were supposed to feel . . . was to put down what really happened in action; what the actual things were which produced the emotion that you experienced." The problem, that is to say, was to master the collision of man and event, writer and experience in *both* its terms: the perception of the event as it really was and the recognition of the emotion that the event really excited. A later remark of his added another dimension to the task. In a letter to a young man who had sent him some imitative work he said, ". . . see the things you write about not through my eyes and my ears but through your own with your language." To see "with language," to see "what really happened in action" and to recognize "what you really felt, rather than what you were supposed to feel," *with language* was a writer's task as Hemingway saw it. Most writers I think would agree that the task was well seen and that accomplishment of the task so defined would be anything but a betrayal of the obligation which every writer assumes. To put together what "really" happened and what you "really" felt as you faced it is not only to see the lion but to understand the man. The writer who can do this, as Hemingway demonstrated that he could, is no less a poet of the human experience — God's spy — than the writer who spies upon nearer and more familiar worlds.

•

What became of Hemingway? Fame became of him, yes, but something more, I think, than fame. Art became of him — became of him in the truest and the largest sense. Rilke once said of the writing of a verse: it is not enough merely to feel; one must also see and touch and know. But it is not enough, either, to see and touch and know: one must have memories of love and pain and death. But not even these memories are enough: the memories must be "turned to blood within us" so that they are no longer distinguishable from ourselves. Experience, Rilke was declaring, must turn into man before a poem can be written. Experience, that is to say, must reach such an intensity that it contains our own being. When that happens — when experience and man *so* meet — the poem may be written and when the poem is written we may discover who we are.

Hemingway brought himself to face experience of this intensity not once, but more than once. And what became of him was that great triumph.

St. John Perse

1949

I AM no more capable of tasting and testing the work of St. John Perse in the usual fashion than Moses was of rinsing in his mouth the water from the dry rock. To me the living spring is a marvel to be praised and never praised enough; and the news that the next number of the *Cahiers de la Pleiade* is to be devoted to an "Hommage à Saint-John Perse" under the patronage of Gide and Claudel is the most natural news in the world. As for "Exil," if it is not Perse's finest poem, it has not been surpassed by him or any other living poet.

Perse's poems are difficult of course. But difficulty is only a fault in an artist when he intends it, or when he is not artist enough to overcome it. Perse's "difficulty," as Roger Caillois points out, is the result neither of ineptitude nor of willfulness but of the opposite of both: an extreme precision and richness of language and a vocabulary capable of extraordinary reverberations of intellectual and emotional meaning. Those who regard words as the mathematical equivalents of dictionary definitions may consider Perse "rhetorical," but his "rhetoric" is as precise as the language of the makers of sails and the navigators of planes, and its sonority is not in the thorax but the mind: ". . . *un lieu flagrant et nul comme l'ossuaire des saisons*" — which his translator, Mr. Devlin, does not convey with his "a place glaring and null as the bone-heap of the seasons . . ." "*Et la mer à la ronde roule son bruit de crânes sur les grèves* . . ." which Mr. Devlin gives somewhat more happily as, "And the rounding sea rolls her noise of skulls on the shore."

Perse is too much of an artist to accept the promptings of the subconscious as perfected poetry, and too intelligent a man to write private letters to himself for public distribution. His "difficulty," in other words, is not the difficulty usually associated with the word modern. But the fact is that only in the real — not the snobbish — sense of that ambiguous term can Perse be classified as a modern poet. He belongs to no clique and has never been a partisan in the literary wars. ("On the subject of literary doctrine," he once wrote, "I have nothing at all to state. I have never relished scientific cooking.") He affects none of the fashionable literary maladies of the time: not even the chronic malady of the mirror: not even the despair which that malady produces in poets as in foreign secretaries and unoccupied women.

Perse's modernism is a function of time, not of aesthetic theory. If he is one of the first of those who have brought new life to Western poetry — one of the half dozen great innovators and creators who have renewed the phoenix in an altered age — he owes his distinction, not to the acceptance of aesthetic formulas and fashions, but to the writing of poems which have pushed forward the sensibility of his generation as well as the frontiers of his art. Like the best work of Yeats and Rilke and Eliot and Pound, the best work of Perse is a Discovery of This Time. Unlike the others, however, Perse has pushed his discovery outward into the world of earth and men. The time in which he journeys is the time which passes over the generations of mankind, and the hero he seeks is the hero who inhabits, not the shadows of the mirror, but the eternal earth. Of Perse's contemporaries, only Sandburg, whose male and vigorous art has wholly different purposes, faces the same quarter of the sky, and only Pound, in his first few, long-deserted Cantos, has inhabited even briefly the same ground.

It is this difference in the orientation of the compass which underlies the peculiar quality of Perse's work. Perse almost alone among the major poets of this generation is capable of the act of praise — the ceremony of the love of earth and men — the celebration of the sea and of the herb and of the dry bone and the living bone. From the beginning of his work, through the years of his greatest personal happiness, and through the years of an unhappiness such as few contemporary writers have been obliged to endure, the love and praise of the beauty of the world have commanded his mind. "Eloges" was the title of his first book, and the refrain which ran through the poems of that collection was the phrase *"Oh, j'ai lieu de louer."* But praise and the occasion of praise were not merely the passion of his youth. They are still, to this day, the law of his art and the charter of his life. Even now, his public career destroyed by the Nazis, his closest human relationships broken off by a long and painful exile, his property confiscated, his books and manuscripts lost or burned, Perse can say that he is "sworn, in defiance of our time, to take nothing from it but joy, free and freely given."

From another man, from a closeted intelligence ignorant of the true nature of this time, from a literary poet occupied with the imitation of academic models rather than the discovery of a great and tragic age, such words might well be suspect. From

Perse they have an indelible accent of candor: an unbearable simplicity. For Perse knows this time of ours. He is, of course, the poetic alter ego of Alexis St. Léger Léger, for many years the permanent secretary of the French Foreign Office — a man who knew Europe through the Twenties and Thirties as few others did or could. Perse knows this time. And what he finds in it to praise, he finds not by sentiment or delusion but with a seeing eye, a poet's eye, an eye that dares to see and to believe.

To see and to believe even here in this other country, the Quai d'Orsay exchanged for a modest cubicle in the Library of Congress in Washington, *l'Europe aux anciens parapets* traded for Francis Biddle's beach at Harvey Cedars on the New Jersey coast. For though Perse's world now is the world of exile his new poems are not — "Exil" itself included — poems of estrangement from life. The exile of which Perse writes is, in poignant part, his own physical exile from the France he loves, and in part the spiritual exile from certain aspects of his time ("the threshold of Lloyd's where your word has no currency"), of the poet ("precarious guest"), and of all those others on all the shores of the world who must *"porte à l'oreille du Ponant une conque sans mémoire."*

But the poem "Exil" — and this I think is its supreme achievement — is something more and different. It is a poem *about* the poet and about his relation to that companion of his exile, his art, which goes closer to the nerve of truth than any but the very greatest poetry can go. Perse was not only exiled from political France: he was also confronted in his exile, after many years of silence, with the demands of the art he had put aside.

"Que voulez-vous encore de moi, ô souffle originel? Et vous, que pensez-vous encore tierer de ma lèvre vivante. . . ."

When Perse, at the beginning of his exile, came to the Library he told me there was no thought, no possibility, of poetry again. But there was poetry. And he faced its demand upon him, if I do not misread this poem, on the New Jersey beach, facing east across the Atlantic, in those winter months.

There was poetry indeed. Read in "Exil" the catalogue of the Princes of Exile — of the most intense moments of man's experience as man — of those occupations and actions of man which are most himself and show him most himself — and you will find three things. You will find the portrait of a poet. You will find the portrait of *the* poet. And you will find poetry itself.

No one more than Perse detests the literary ritual. No one more than he despises the comparison of incomparable beings. Nevertheless it is impossible to put down this book without asking oneself where among living men — in what nation or what tongue — a poet equal to this poet may be found.

A Memoir of Muir

1 9 6 2

FAME, in any generation, is a better guide to the generation than to its poets — which is why the reputation of Edwin Muir is not commensurate with his accomplishment. Readers of poetry in Muir's generation thought of themselves as sophisticated people, the first English readers since Chaucer's time to understand that poetry is literature, that literature is art, that art is European, and that the grandfather of excellence is therefore Dante, with the line of descent falling through Provence and Paris to reach the Channel belatedly about the time of the First World War. They were uncomfortable in the presence of that other, older poetry which is at once less and more than literature and less and more than European, and they regretted its survival into sophisticated, modern times. Frost, for example, was never one of *the* poets of that generation. And Edwin Muir, though loved by his friends and respected by everybody, was famous rather as the translator, with his wife Willa, of the novels of Kafka than as one of the authentic poets of the half century: the only poet of the period in whom the crystal eye of poetry was also the limpid eye of innocence.

That curious double vision with its uniquely penetrating

power he owed to the happy circumstances of his childhood and the tragedy of his adolescent years. Muir had the poignant fortune, good and bad, of living his first twenty years in two worlds so far apart in historic time that his own life seems almost to recapitulate the history of the social change and industrial revolution which produced the world we live in. The result of that strange fortune was that he brought to the confrontation with chaos, which is the lot of the contemporary mind, a consciousness, a sensibility, which saw farther into his time than any of his contemporaries with the exception of Yeats.

Muir was born into a world as old as Greece and older, a world of farmers who also followed the sea and of fishermen who also farmed. The Orkney Islands off the northeast coast of Scotland were little changed in 1887 from what they had been a thousand years before when they were settled from Norway and Scotland. The language was a mixture of Norse and Scots and the life, as Muir says in his *Autobiography*, was still the ancient ordered life of the ship and the plow. "The farmers did not know ambition and the petty torments of ambition; they did not know what competition was, though they lived at the end of Queen Victoria's reign; they helped one another with their work when help was required, following the old usage; they had a culture made up of legend, folk-song, and the poetry and prose of the Bible . . ." And elsewhere in that extraordinary book he describes the economy of the farm on the little island of Wyre where he spent his childhood. It was an economy Odysseus would have understood:

Our life at the Bu was virtually self-supporting. The pig, after being slaughtered each year, was cut up and salted, and the pork

stored away in a barrel. I helped with the salting when I was
quite small, and got a sense of pleased importance from rubbing
the raw slices of meat on coarse salt strewn on a wooden board;
Those neat cubes did not seem to have any connection with
the butchered pig. We had fish almost as often as we wanted it,
and crabs when Sunderland went to lift his creels; and Aunt
Maggie was often down on the beach gathering whelks. The
oat bannocks and barley bannocks, the milk, butter, cheese and
eggs were our own produce. We sent part of the wool after
the sheep-shearing down to a Border town, and it came back
as blankets and cloth. We bought at the shop such things as
white bread, sugar, tea, treacle, currants and raisins, and paraffin
oil for the lamps.

And this life was not only self-supporting in economic terms:
it was self-supporting in spiritual terms also.

. . . at the heart of human civilization is the byre, the barn and
the midden. When my father led out the bull to serve a cow
brought by one of our neighbours it was a ritual act of the tradition in which we have lived for thousands of years, possessing
the obviousness of a long dream from which there is no awak-
ing. When a neighbour came to stick the pig it was a ceremony
as objective as the rising and setting of the sun.

The myth, in other words, was underneath the furrow and the
field in Orkney, and the limits of reality were not fixed, as they
are with us, by the limits of the probable.

The Orkney I was born into was a place where there was no
great distinction between the ordinary and the fabulous; the
lives of living men turned into legend. A man I knew once
sailed out in a boat to look for a mermaid, and claimed after-

wards that he had talked with her. . . . Fairies, or "fairicks"
as they were called, were encountered dancing on the sands . . .

What all this would do to the consciousness of a child one can
enviously imagine. Muir's *Autobiography* allows us to see what
it did to a child who was to become a poet. Writing of the relation of his childhood to his beginnings as a writer he recalls a
summer afternoon when a neighboring farmer gave him a lift
home from school in his cart. "He invited me to climb in the
back and I found myself beside a pale young man who smiled
at me and then stared at something which he alone seemed to see;
for he never looked at the fields . . ." This was the farmer's
son "home from Leith." Later that evening he heard his mother
tell his father that the boy had "come home to die." "The
words," says Muir, "were simple and yet strange, and dying became a sad and deliberate act which could be accomplished only
in its own place, and for which careful provision had to be
made . . ." And the account goes on:

A few weeks later, standing at the end of the house, I watched
the funeral procession moving along the distant road. There
were six men in front carrying the coffin on their shoulders,
and behind them a long line of men in black clothes. Presently
they reached the edge of a hill and one by one disappeared. But
I stood for a long time afterwards looking at the white empty
road, the hills and the sea, and what thoughts were in my mind
then I shall never know; they were certainly tinged with sadness, but at the same time suffused with wonder and a simple
acceptance of the wonder. The fields were empty out of respect to the dead. It was a calm bright summer day and the
hills and the sea hung suspended in light and peace.

At fourteen, by a tragic family miscalculation, that wonder and simple acceptance of wonder were brought face to face with the "modern" world as it revealed itself in the Glasgow of the year 1901. It would scarcely have been possible to take a longer journey. Glasgow, as I saw it a few years later when my father, who had been born there, took his children back, was the most repulsive city of my young experience — and I had started from Chicago. To a child born and brought up on an Orkney farm it should have been a vision of misery. And it was.

> I walked to and from my work each day through a slum, for there was no way of getting from the south side of Glasgow to the city except through slums. These journeys filled me with a sense of degradation: the crumbling houses, the twisted faces, the obscene words casually heard in passing, the ancient, haunting stench of pollution and decay, the arrogant women, the mean men, the terrible children, daunted me, and at last filled me with an immense, blind dejection.

These terrors and despairs were not imaginary. Within a few years Muir's father, his mother, his brother Willie and his brother Johnnie were dead — Johnnie of a brain tumor after a terrible illness — and the rest, his two sisters and his brother Jimmie and himself, scattered and lost.

And even then the tragedy was not played out. Muir had his apprenticeship to this industrial, "modern" world to serve and each task was worse than the task before. Underpaid as a clerk in a law office he became a chauffeur's assistant, then a bookkeeper in a beer-bottling plant and at last an office hand in a factory for the rendering of bones.

This was a place where fresh and decaying bones, gathered from all over Scotland, were flung into furnaces and reduced to charcoal. The charcoal was sold to refineries to purify sugar; the grease was filled into drums and dispatched for some purpose which I no longer remember. The bones, decorated with festoons of slowly writhing, fat yellow maggots, lay in the adjoining railway siding, and were shunted into the factory whenever the furnaces were ready for them. . . . Raw, they had a strong, sour penetrating smell. But it was nothing to the stench they gave off when they were shovelled, along with the maggots, into the furnaces. It was a gentle, clinging, sweet stench, suggesting dissolution and hospitals and slaughterhouses, the odour of drains and the rancid stink of bad roasting meat.

If Kafka had invented that rancid world he would have been credited with yet another triumph of the grotesque imagination, but not even Kafka could have invented the conjunction of bone factory and Edwin Muir, for Muir was beyond the reach of Kafka's genius.

And yet it was that conjunction which made the poet. "All that time," Muir wrote, "seemed to give no return, nothing but loss; it was like a heap of dismal rubbish in the middle of which, without rhyme or reason, were scattered four deaths." But there was more than rubbish: there was rubbish framed by the Orkney world — by the furrow and the sea. Fifteen years later when Glasgow was far behind him, and when he had met and married Willa Anderson, the marriage which made possible his life, and when he had served his second apprenticeship, a literary apprenticeship, in London, and when, at last, in Germany, he had begun to write poems, he discovered that the furrow and the sea were there — had always been there.

Verse was difficult for him. "I had no training; I was too old to submit myself to contemporary influences; and I had acquired in Scotland a deference toward ideas which made my entrance into poetry difficult." All he could do was blunder along "in baffling ignorance." And then all at once he felt an influence at play, something that moved to help him, and at last he discovered what it was: those years had "come alive after being forgotten so long." The years of his childhood had returned from beyond the rubbish heap and from beyond oblivion to give him what every poet needs, a world in which to hold the world: a stage, he called it — "a symbolical stage on which the drama of human life can play itself out." It was a great gift and he knew how to value it, for he knew that it was not a gift he could have chosen for himself: "I doubt," he said, "whether we have the liberty to choose it" — meaning that he doubted whether any poet is free to choose the world he invents. The stage must present *itself*. And it had. "The bare landscape of the little island became, without my knowing it, a universal landscape . . ."

It was that universal landscape which put the heap of rubbish in a right perspective, the perspective in which the heart can see. And it was that perspective which made Edwin Muir the poet he became. He found its metaphor in one of his most famous poems:

> *One foot in Eden still, I stand*
> *And look across the other land.*
> *The world's great day is growing late,*
> *Yet strange these fields that we have planted*
> *So long with crops of love and hate.*

Time's handiworks by time are haunted,
And nothing now can separate
The corn and tares compactly grown.
The armorial weed in stillness bound
About the stalk; these are our own.
Evil and good stand thick around
In the fields of charity and sin
Where we shall lead our harvest in.
Yet still from Eden springs the root
As clean as on the starting day.
Time takes the foliage and the fruit
And burns the archetypal leaf
To shapes of terror and of grief
Scattered along the winter way.
But famished field and blackened tree
Bear flowers in Eden never known.
Blossoms of grief and charity
Bloom in these darkened fields alone.
What had Eden ever to say
Of hope and faith and pity and love
Until was buried all its day
And memory found its treasure trove?
Strange blessings never in Paradise
Fall from these beclouded skies.

One foot in Eden, that "other land" takes on its meaning and its beauty. It is in those darkened fields that blossoms of grief and charity can bloom. Even Glasgow is forgiven.

In 1955, a few years before his death, Edwin Muir came to Harvard to give the Norton lectures. He was a quiet man with a gentle voice which almost defeated the public address systems and the engineers but he was still the lad Willa Anderson had seen for the first time almost forty years before, "blue flash in

his eyes, charming smile, Nietzsche sticking out of his pocket."
Nietzsche was gone by the time he came to us but the surprises
were not. American reviewers of his books had prepared the
Cambridge audience for a Celt and a mystic but to the aston-
ishment of everyone Muir devoted his six lectures to an effort
"to measure the gap between the public and the poet and to find
some explanation why it is so great." Mystics and Celts are not
supposed to care about the public or to know that it exists, but
here was Muir, taking issue with those of his contemporaries
who had resigned themselves to the defeated notion that poets
write only for other poets, and establishing his own position in
the great tradition of the Scottish ballads which had a whole nation for audience — not to say a world.

I know no other discussion of this nagging and persistent question as enlightening as Muir's or as courageous, for it takes courage to stand up to the mounted men: those who ride in the saddle
of the time. Muir however is uncompromising in defining the
terms of his dilemma. This "public" of ours, he says, is a new
thing under the sun, a faceless aggregation begotten by general
education on an artificial, industrial world in which sensibilities
have been numbed and imaginations corrupted by the proliferation of those "secondary objects," those machine-made goods,
which get between us and experience. When this "public" speaks
to us "it speaks indirectly, at intervals, in an ambiguous voice, in
newspapers." "It seems to be an impersonal something, a col-
lectivity which, if you break it up, does not reduce itself to a
single human being, but at best into chunks of itself, sections, per-
centages."

That is one side of the great gap. The other is the poet.
"What can he say to the public or the public to him"? The language of the public is the language of "the third party and the on-

looker" whereas the poet "is not concerned with life in its generality but in its immediacy and its individuality." His "first allegiance" is to "imaginative truth" and "if he is to serve mankind,
that is the only way he can do it." Thus "the idea of confront-
ing him with the public . . . appears strangely anomalous."
And it is made even more anomalous by a temptation which se-
duces the modern poet and which modern criticism urges on
him: "the temptation for poets to turn inward into poetry, to
lock themselves into a hygienic prison where they speak only to
one another and to the critic, their stern warder." "The great
danger" of the analytic criticism which dominates the time "is
that it shuts the poem in upon itself as an object, not of enjoy-
ment but of scrutiny, and cuts it off from the air it should breathe
and its spontaneous operation on those who are capable of receiving it."

Seen in this way the gap between the public and the poet becomes a gap which only the poet can close, and he only by rejecting the temptation of the time. "In the end a poet must create his audience and to do that he must turn outward." This
does not mean that he should attempt to become a popular
poet for that is no longer possible: "The attempt, if he tried,
would only degrade poetry, without being of any profit to the
public." But the alternative to popularity is not the academic
chrysalis. The alternative is the *audience* and this the poet must
himself create as Yeats, who knew that poetry without an audience is inconceivable, created his. But how is an audience to be
created? Not by thinking of the public — "its vastness and im-
personality would daunt anyone" — but by holding before one's
self "the variety of human life, for from that diversity the audience will be drawn."

This is heretical doctrine, as Muir well knew. Poets nowadays are not encouraged by their critics to think about audiences, and poems which find audiences of any size — particularly audiences outside the hygienic prison — are deprecated. But heresy did not bother Muir. He saw clearly that "the audience is part of the business" and he understood that "the smaller and more select the audience . . . the more the poet will be confined," which means conversely, that "the more wide-reaching the imaginative world of poetry . . . the greater will be the audience it wins." Great poetry, he reminds us, was once a general possession of mankind: "a fact which we should not forget — those who write poetry and those of us who criticize it."

It is a fact Edwin Muir never forgot. If anything in our time justifies his hope that "a great theme greatly treated might still put poetry back in its old place" it is his own work.

Mark Van Doren

Remarks at a meeting at Columbia University
in his honor in 1959

I DON'T KNOW why I am asked to speak of Mark Van Doren
if not because I am an outlander, an old man from over Tweed
who is allowed past the threshold of the tribe to declare that
the fame of greatness has crossed the Cheviot Hills and has spread
as far as the North Inch of Perth — which is even farther than
Harvard Square. But whatever the reason, I rejoice in raising
my alien yawp in this Columbia gathering. There ought to be
more such. "What should a man do but praise excellence . . ."

And yet I do find it difficult to imagine what I can add to the
praises of those who have been around the whole time and who
can address the subject and victim of our approbation in the
intimate vocabulary of events I never heard of. It's not that I
don't know Mark but that I don't know him *here* where all the
rest of you do and where the laurels are particular. *I* know him
only because he and I have shared a life in an unusually intimate
way — though for the greater part of the time we never knew
we were sharing it. We were born on the same prairie though
his part of Illinois was more like Illinois than mine by a couple
of counties. And we were born at about the same time though
there too he had the advantage of me, coming into the world a bit

younger than I — an advantage he has stubbornly maintained ever since. Furthermore we have made our later homes more or less in the same hills about as far from Illinois as we could get in a northeasterly direction; we have practiced, he for many years, I for a few, the same profession; and we have pursued, both of us, over our whole lives, the same art. So that when, after half a century of this, we finally fell in with each other, we recognized each other at once — realized (and not without a sense of loss) that we had been friends all our lives. I do not mention this because I think the experience was peculiar to me. It is surely an experience many others must have had at their meetings with Mark, though not perhaps to the same degree. I mention it only because it says as much about Mark Van Doren as a mere fact can. I can't imagine a human being of any sensibility at all, coming to know Mark Van Doren late in his life as I did, who would not regret the decades he had missed.

And there of course is the difficulty for all of us in talking about the man in his presence. You can't talk about Mark without talking about *him* and it's not easy in the presence of that face, in which benevolence has a watchful glint. If, as Mr. Lincoln is supposed to have said, a man's face is his own fault after forty, then *there's* a document to make hangdogs of us all. The only way out of the difficulty is to jump into the middle of it and let the embarrassments splash whom they may. And it's the right way too. The older I grow — or, rather, the more aware I become that I *am* growing older — the more important the human thing seems to me to be; and so even at those elevations which some of us try to raise above the level of the human. When I was young I put poems as far as possible in my mind from the mouths which had spoken them. I made a deliberate effort not to remember the words Severn says Keats spoke at the end of his suffering. Today, if a poem is *merely* a work of art it means nothing to me. I keep listening for the human speaking voice — for the voice humanly speaking — Yeats's voice in "The Wild Old Wicked Man." And I have no shame now in confessing that I have the life mask of Keats on my wall and on my desk the drawing Severn made of him in the candlelight with the round, black candle shadow there behind.

I have no shame in confessing it because I have learned, or imagine I have learned, that the art of poetry is not, as Mallarmé said and as so many of us, thinking or unthinking, still believe, an art of words, but an art of words *in a voice.* A poet is a man who lives, like the rest of us, between experience and understanding but who has a peculiar gift for both of them and who has also the mastery of a means by which they may be brought together. But the poet's means are not words, but words in a voice, as the means of the sculptor are not stone but stone under a hand. A poem is a poet's saying and his voice is in it or it is dead. The proof of that lies in the body of any poet's work — a cruel proof but a sure one. In the poet who is truly poet you will hear in each poem the identity of a voice however that identity may be worn and changed by time or distorted by emotion. Even in Rimbaud who felt nothing but disgust for the poems he wrote before that violence in the Paris barracks, and who commanded his friends to destroy them, the voice that speaks in "Les Effarés" is not a different voice from the speaker's in *Une Saison en Enfer.* But in the poet who is not a true poet, who is a poet by will or wit alone, there will be many voices or none at all. And so too when a poem is carried over from one language to another. Robert Frost, with that unironic irony of his, says that what is lost in translation is "the poetry." And he is right — but it is because the voice will not come over. The images of the poem are translatable, but no one has ever carried the speaking voice out of its own tongue. If the translator is a Chapman — or, in our time, a Dudley Fitts or a Robert Fitzgerald or an Ezra Pound — there will be a new voice. If he is a hack there will be no voice at all. But in either case the voice which was the other part of the poem itself has vanished.

All of which means that for me at least there is no awkwardness in coming at Mark's achievement as a poet through Mark himself as speaker in his poems — which is to say, as man. It is because Mark's voice is never in doubt that his work is never in doubt. When the few remembered poems from our time are put together there will be poems of Mark's among them because Mark is among the men who have spoken the time. He will be alive then precisely because he has been truly alive now.

Jorge Guillén

1961

THE ENGLISH IMAGINATION, says young Martin Green in his *Mirror for Anglo-Saxons*, "has been dominated by a feeling of death, decay and hopelessness." Others would extend that statement beyond Great Britain. We are no longer Anglo-Saxon in the United States, but the American imagination, according to those who make a profession of observing it, is wandering in the same dark wood, and so too, and by the same authority, is the French. Indeed, it is the current assumption of all accredited intellectuals that our entire generation in every country is afflicted by a common darkness of rejection and denial. *That*, they signify, is how posterity will see us — a generation which has learned at last that life is an absurdity, that the world is a gutter, that Godot never comes, that death is the only thing that really happens, and that not even death will happen when it's wanted.

But, unhappily, that is *not* the way in which posterity will remember us. I write with some assurance, not because I know more about posterity than the next man but because I am certain that posterity will not form its opinion of us on the evidence on which we form our opinions of ourselves. We are perhaps the most self-conscious generation which ever lived. We read our daily notices with the avidity of a company of touring actors. We know what the sociologists think of us, what the psychiatrists conclude, what the philosophers opine, what the critics judge. But posterity, it is reasonably certain, will not read the notices; it will read the works. And the works of our generation — those that have the look of surviving — will include some which will give a very different impression.

I am not contending with Mr. Green, who is the first new, fresh, and credible voice in a long time. Mr. Green's indictment may hold for the British Isles after Yeats withdrew from them. But posterity will not judge us by the works of our contemporaries in one nation only. If it interests itself in our time at all, it will interest itself in the whole of our time. And if it reads the principal works of our time as a whole, it will come upon works which will not fit our portrait of ourselves. One of our seeings and sayings which will almost certainly survive is a poem addressed to the age itself by St. John Perse — his *Chronique*, which ends: "*Grand âge, nous voici. Prenez mesure du coeur d'homme.*" And there are other lines of Perse — a poet who knew his time better than most because he was political man as well as poet, one of those who shaped the world he wrote in — there are other lines of Perse which would sound strange to a posterity which took Jean-Paul Sartre for our official witness:

> *Bitter! Have our living lips ever been bitter?*
>
> *I have seen, smiling in the fires offshore, the great holiday thing: the Sea festive with our dreams like a green-grass Easter and like a celebration one celebrates . . .*
>
> *The drums of nothingness surrender to the fifes of light.*

And Perse is not alone. There is another of our contemporaries whose work, if it survives, will contradict the oracles. Nikos Kazantzakis was a Greek who knew as much about suffering and absurdity as those who carve the literary totem poles which celebrate those deities, but Kazantzakis was not himself a worshiper of revulsion and the dark: "My prayer is not the whimpering of a beggar nor a confession of love. My prayer is not the trivial reckoning of a small tradesman: Give me and I shall give you. My prayer is the report of a soldier to his general. . . ."

And there are others still: there is the Spanish poet, Jorge Guillén. Jorge Guillén knows this time of ours as Perse knows it and as Kazantzakis knew it. He belongs to the generation of the two wars, and — because he is a Spaniard — of that horrible third war, too, which changed the first into the second. Like Perse, he has lived the life of exile which so many of our contemporaries lived and live. But though he is a man of this time in the historical sense — all the historical senses — he is not a man of the time so many of our critics and philosophers think they live in. He knows the dark, yes. "My certainty is founded in the dark." But the dark that Guillén knows is anything but the dark of hopelessness and despair: "That strong unknown thing by night will break through . . . whatever seals it and from the deep abyss draw up those finest splendors that are still so far from death." Dark to him is what a man awakes *from* into the wonder of the world:

I. Here. Now.
Wide awake. Existing here and now.
Once more, the marvelous adjustment.

And what awakes from night into that *ajuste prodigioso* is not a frightened and denying victim but a man who wishes, as the great end of life, to *be*.

> *I wish to be . . .*
> *To be. That suffices me —*
> *Absolute happiness.*

Guillén is a poet of this time — a great poet of this time. But he is a poet, nevertheless, who has devoted his whole life to the writing of a single book, which has grown slowly from seventy-five poems in 1928 to three hundred and thirty-four in 1950 — a single book, of which the title is *Cántico* and the theme praise. And what does he praise?

> *Joy of joys: the soul beneath the skin.*

Posterity, if it comes upon the great resounding Yes of *Cántico* among the tumbled fragments of our time, will not believe that No was all we had to answer to the world.

Jane Addams in Chicago

NOVEMBER 21, 1960

ROBERT FROST, who has, as all the world knows, a genius
for putting unsayable things in wry simplicities, found precisely
the word for our view of what lies ahead when he was asked, at
the dedication of the Seagram Building in New York, to talk
about the future. "I don't," said Mr. Frost, "*advocate* it." And
neither do the rest of us. When we look ahead we see nothing but
impossible alternatives — slavery of soul on the one hand, death
of body on the other. Nothing beckons us. Where there is not
malice there are lies, where there is not dogmatism of one kind
there is dogmatism of another, where Communism has not
eaten everything, anti-Communism has corroded everything,
where the mind is still free the heart is afraid. There is a shadow
across the whole prospect ahead which we call the shadow of
the bomb but which may well be the shadow of our own fear
or of our own failure. The old men are glad they will not have
to cross into that country while the young men shy away, double back, hunt for hatchways leading underground, and the rest
of us sleep-walk forward, our eyes and ears closed to everything
but the hum of the new deep freeze and the lilt of the singing
commercials. We don't blame ourselves for this — rather we

pity ourselves. And certainly we never compare ourselves to our disadvantage with that earlier and braver generation. Theirs, after all, we say, was a simpler time when it was easy to be brave — no bomb — no Communism — no worldwide religious war. Jane Addams's Chicago was the great, brawling, burly, bustling Chicago of Carl Sandburg's early poems — a city that was going somewhere in a country that was going somewhere in a world that was watching with envious awe. There was nothing to fight in those days but crooked politicians and goons and gangsters. The future was possible then — more than possible — a promise. You could walk toward the future as you walked toward the Lake. It was there.

But was it? To us that future is the past: we can afford to be confident about it. But how did it look to the men and women who saw it ahead of them? Were they as comfortable with Carl Sandburg's poems as we are who know them so well we take them for granted? It is true Jane Addams's generation had no ingenious suicidal invention to worry about but it had killers of its own — humbler in status and more modest in murderousness but no less lethal for that: filthy milk, foul sanitation, rotting garbage, miserable schools, all of them aided and abetted by political corruption and social indifference. And it is true too that Jane Addams's generation had no Communists — nothing but an occasional terrorist, a few harsh voices — but it had its social and political fanaticism notwithstanding: a fanaticism of a kind which, as McCarthy proved, can be far more dangerous to the United States within the United States than Communist dogma has yet become.

To look back now into the world of the Pullman Strike, of the Altgeld controversy, of the fight over factory legislation, of the invalidation by the state Supreme Court of the eight hour law for women, of the fight against clean milk legislation, is to look into a black night of American reaction which might well have seemed as hopeless to Jane Addams as the black night of Communist reaction looks to us.

Blacker perhaps, because she had so few beside her who thought it was black. We have friends in our darkness. The best minds of our generation are with us. A few, in France particularly, may have drifted across to the side of night but only to drift back again when they woke to where they were. But it was not so with Jane Addams. The decent and responsible opinion of her time was either against her or indifferent to the issue she raised. It was not a crank who said that Jane Addams ought to be hanged to the nearest lamp post: it was a solid citizen who, like other solid citizens, regarded any legislation aimed at the protection of children in factories as an attack on his right, as a citizen of a free country, to do as he pleased. And it was not an irresponsible newspaper which hounded her as a radical: it was a newspaper most of the responsible people of the city read.

I know, I think, what I am talking about. My father who came to Chicago as a Scots boy of eighteen in 1856 became one of the responsible men of the city. He was the founder, though not the owner, of one of the city's principal businesses. He was one of the founders of the University of Chicago and for many years vice-president of its board of trustees. He was one of the most respected men in his church. He was high-minded in the precise and literal sense of that term, scrupulous in his relations with others, generous even when he could not afford generosity — a just man and a fair man. Above all he was a man just and fair in his relations with his employees as he understood those relations.

And yet one of my earliest memories of my father is a memory of a burst of anger — they were rare for he had mastered his tongue — occasioned by the beginnings of trade union organization in Chicago. And he was not, of course, alone in that anger. On the contrary he was milder in it and certainly less vociferous than most of the employers of labor whom Jane Addams knew.

It does not require, I think, an unusual effort of imagination to realize that the future must have looked about as dark at the turn of the century to a woman who believed what Jane Addams believed as it looks now to men and women who believe what we believe. Nor does it require unusual powers of discrimination to perceive that one difference between Jane Addams's generation and ours was her unwillingness, and the unwillingness of her friends, to be frightened by that darkness. But that is not the sole difference between us. There is also another. Not only did Jane Addams and her friends *dare* the future: they dared it *themselves*. From the moment when Jane Addams, after her doubting and questioning in her own country and abroad, stumbled upon that auction of rotting vegetables in a London slum — from the moment when her "idea" crystallized at Toynbee Hall in Whitechapel — she saw her life ahead as something *she* must *do*. Hull House was not a house: it was an action — a young woman's action — a personal action undertaken on the basis of a personal experience and a personal decision. Anyone who does not understand that fact does not understand her history. On that first trip of hers to Europe Jane Addams wrote that "somewhere in the process of being educated" the "first generation of college women" to which she saw herself belonging "had lost that simple and almost automatic response to the human appeal — that old healthful reaction resulting in *activity* in the mere presence of suffering or of helplessness." *She* had not lost that response nor had those others who joined her at Polk and Halsted streets. They were not trained social workers: there were no trained social workers in our sense of the phrase in 1889. They were not even students, in any formal sense, of sociology. There was no department of sociology in any American university until one was established at Chicago in 1892. But unprepared and inexperienced as these women were they nevertheless set about to do *themselves* what they were persuaded had to be done. And it is there that they differ most dramatically from us.

We are so accustomed to have specialists of one kind or another live our lives for us that it rarely crosses our minds that we might at least *attempt* to live them for ourselves. We complain — particularly here within reach of the Voice from the Tribune Tower — about the "welfare state," but the last thing we would think of doing would be to accept responsibility for the public welfare in our personal capacities as Jane Addams did. We rage against the risk of idiotic war in a time in which war means suicide and worse. We repeat, until it is worn of meaning, the old adage about war being too serious a business to be left to the generals. But when it comes to actualities we leave war to the generals as it was never left to them before — and even go so far as to silence each other's protests by agreeing that in military matters criticism may be treason.

When a citizen in our time decides to intervene on his own behalf in the affairs of the world he does not buy a house in the heart of his problem and go live in it himself. He establishes a foundation and staffs it, not with ardent and ignorant amateurs, but with competent professionals directed by a board of experienced advisers. The result, as we all have reason to know, is far more intelligent and efficient public service or social service or educational service than Jane Addams's generation would have thought possible. But the result, for the same reason, is *not* Hull House. Jane Addams was not engaged in social service in this sense. She was not working *for* her immigrants and her poor: she was committing herself *with* them to the common life — that life our generation watches more and more as spectators, as though it were not common, as though it were a life for someone else. She was as explicit about that as a woman could be. She was not, she said, a reformer: she wanted to establish a place "in and around which a fuller life might grow for others *and for herself*." And having made that much clear she then reversed her words to make her declaration clearer still. "The good we secure for ourselves is precarious and uncertain until it is secured for all of us and incorporated into *our common life*."

No, Hull House changed Chicago and changed the United States, not because it was a successful institution but because it was an eloquent action by a woman capable of action regardless of the dark ahead. We talk as though the great question before our society was whether the things that need to be done in America to keep this last best hope of earth alive should be done by the federal government or by the states or perhaps by the cities or by industries or by some other kind of organization. But that, of course, is not the question. The question before our society is simply whether or not those things *will* be *done*. And the answer is that they will be done if we ourselves see to it as Jane Addams and her friends saw it — if we accept, as she accepted, responsibility for our lives. That, when all is said and done, is why our time remembers her — that she accepted for herself responsibility for the "common life."

The Great-Grandfather

1949

THERE are two kinds of history — the public history of the printed books, the battle monuments, and the steel engravings and the private history of the letters tied in bundles and the flowers from the rainy graves. The attics of the forty-eight states are filled with the private history of the Republic as every good librarian knows. But because the fragments are scattered, and because the names are obscure, and because the incidents are unimportant in themselves, the record is allowed to dwindle and to disappear.

As far back as I can remember there was an old-fashioned yellow shirt-waist box in the attic of the house in Illinois where I was born. "Papers from Captain Hillard's Sea Chest" my mother had written across the corner. But Captain Hillard, who was her father's father, was a man remarkably unknown to fame, and the box was never opened. All we were sure of was that Moses Hillard had been born in Preston in Connecticut during the Revolution and that he had been a sea captain through the years of the Embargo and the War of 1812. Aside from the family tradition that it was his ship which stood off and on in the "lowland sea" after the Battle of Waterloo waiting to smuggle the defeated emperor through the British blockade in a water butt

with a false bottom, there was nothing to suggest that his papers
had any interest but their age. Sea captains are a dime a dozen
in the public histories of those years.

All this, however, was before the box was opened and the
stock figure of the Yankee sea captain gave place to the private
and particular figure of the man. Moses Hillard with his
Salem ancestors, and his Puritan name, and his hard-scrabble
Connecticut farm, and his year-long Atlantic voyages, and
his hatred of Tom Jefferson and James Madison, and his long
roster of brigs and schooners and ships — the *Neptune*, and
the *Antelope* and the *Favourite* and the *Marcus* and the *Amiable
Matilda* — Moses Hillard turned out to be a legitimate part of
the American record in his own right.

He was something the textbook definition of a sea captain
didn't cover. If he commanded ships at sea he was also able to
survive the starvation years of non-intercourse and the Embargo
by farming a hundred and thirty of the most ungrateful acres on
earth. If he saved his ship's company by the skill of his seaman-
ship when the *Oneida* went down, he made profits for his
owners in the markets of Surinam and La Guaira and Hamburg
and Le Havre and Marseilles by his foresight as a merchant and
his knowledge of the art of exchanging money in a dozen cur-
rencies. If he had fine friends who wrote him charming letters
from Paris and Marseilles and London, and if he dined sometimes
at Justin's in Le Havre at a voyage's end, he was also chairman
of the committee to repair the South Society School in Preston, a Federal Freeman of that town, and the father, by his first
wife, Sally Pride, and his second, Patty Brewster, of nine
children who lived to grow up and respect his authority in his
house.

There is a letter dated at Preston on the fifteenth of January, 1809 — "of a Sunday morning and a Stormy Day that Deprives me of my Usual Sundays tour of going to meeting" — which gives a better picture of the man himself than any amount of talk about him. Captain Hillard made copies — "coppies" he spelled them — of all his letters, writing them out in an obstinate, crooked hand with no particular respect for punctuation and with capitals applied by way of emphasis or by way of decoratiton or just to relieve the monotony of a long dull line. This particular letter was addressed to a friend in New York named Doyle who was apparently familiar with the shipping trade whether he went to sea himself or not.

Of a Sunday morning and a Stormy Day, [writes the Captain], and with a handful of Sore fingers bruised getting wood for this Cold weather and A heart worse bruised by the tyrannical Acts of our Government I sit down to Inform you of my and my family's good health and to Enquire After yours. . . . For my share I can assure you there is but little left for people of my profession to Rejoice in. however to keep off the blue Devils my brothers and myself are busying ourselves in Getting wood out of a Dismal Swamp. We have already 100 loads out heapd up so that of freezing we are in no Danger. if tom Jefferson and his thundering Administration Starve us out we will go to hell with a fire.

My Dear Friend I must beg you to Devote A leisure hour to write me of your and your family's health. Say if you have any boys yet as Our Devils are Raising Such Armies that Every man ought to do his best in the way of Manufacturing boys. Say Doyle what is going forward in New York if there is any news and what you think is Agoing to be the Result of the present measure being Adopted by his Democratic Majesty and his troops. how do the people seem Disposed to act in the State of New York About Continuing to Support Madison and his Administration. will they be true to him till they are Completely Shackled or will they allow themselves to see their Danger Erre it is too late and Quit him.

If I have Raved in my Expressions when you Consider me Compelled to Abandon my own profession and Knock about here in the woods with broken shins and jammed fingers growling like A bear with A Sore head I trust your goodness will Excuse me.

There follow some eager inquiries about the trial of a new ship and how it terminated, a request for a quotation on a bale of good upland cotton to keep the "manufacturers" in his family at work since he can no longer afford to buy raw cotton at retail, and a nautically metaphoric account of the Captain's state of mind at the moment — he is, he says, "beating up Against wind and tide . . . Every now and then Splitting a Sail," but "Although Already on Soundings" he won't anchor because he sees a "Strong Eddy Current not far from the Ship which may Set up Strong I hope ere the Barkee is Ashore." The letter closes with a postscript from his brothers, seamen like himself, who "beg me to inform you that they are both of them on a lee shore under Close Reefed Top Sails Carrying Almost keel out and Damd Squally."

Somehow the public history of those last months of Jefferson's Administration is brought a little more sharply into human focus by his picture of the sailor brothers, cutting wood with clumsy axes in a frozen swamp to keep off the blue devils, while their ships swing uselessly in the Thames at Norwich or New London waiting for Washington to change its mind.

As for the Captain, the portrait he unwittingly paints of himself is as revealing as the background of great events which lies beyond it. If he raves in his expressions it is partly because the state of the world calls for indignation and partly because Moses Hillard was the kind of man to whom all governments are enemies. He had suffered from three of them — the French, the British, and his own — before he was twenty-five, and he claimed the right to know. The French had robbed him and thrown him into prison in a festering tropic town. The British had robbed him and insulted him on his own quarter-deck on the high seas. And Tom Jefferson had kept him at home, hacking away at the winter woods, when he longed to be off for Havre de Grace or Demerara or Surinam.

The story begins before he was twenty. He tells it, without any attempt at drama, in a document which must certainly be one of the most dramatic of the minor chronicles of our history: a document bound in sail cloth, stitched at home or in the forecastle, and entitled "Moses Hillard's Journal." The first entry gives the color of the whole: "July 2nd, 1799, took my departure from my father's house in Preston and Sailed from Norwich for New York, got to New London and Set out from there with a light westerly wind."

The first half of the little book is filled with what was probably Moses Hillard's earliest venture on blue water. In a dutiful boy's hand, which gets worse as the callouses grow harder, young Moses puts down the bare facts of his arrival in New York on the fourth of July — which was apparently no holiday; his finding board at Mrs. Baker's at three dollars and a half a week; his signing on with the ship *Mary*, Pollard master, Coit and Woolsey owners, "on monthly Wages not Determined until they Ship hands what it will be"; the fixing of his wages at "22 dollars for the Month and received 1 Month advance"; the hauling off of the *Mary* into the stream; their departure on the eighteenth of July "and got to Staten Island wind ahead"; their four days of head winds anchored "at the Hook"; their final departure on the twenty-second — "Wind Ahead in the forenoon but went to Sea in the Afternoon"; their arrival off Hamburg on the third of September; the unloading of their cargo of indigo and sugar through September and October; the young seaman's illness — "Monday 21 this Day gave out and had the Doctor on board, he left some things for me to take a puke and several other things"; their departure on the twenty-third October; their landfall at the Jersey Highlands on the tenth of January, 1800, after weathering a gale in which they were "expecting every moment when the Masts would go over the Side"; Moses's discharge and return to Preston — "This day was paid off from the Ship mary and got my chest and bed on board the packet Sally for New London."

At the bottom of that page of the little journal, Moses Hillard has written, in large letters with enormous flourishes, the words, "This Ends the Voyage." He was home again in the small house with the huge chimney which his father had built just off the Norwich road, the dangers were past, the fire was warm, and his mother, Sabra, had undoubtedly made a suitable fuss over his return. The next voyage, however, was a very different matter, and the record shows it. "Journal of Our Intended Voyage from Norwich to Barbadoes or Some Other West India Island" is the tentative title. And the account, instead of ending with a flourish of manly pride, peters out after a few pages of ink, into a scuffed and weathered lead-pencil script which can barely be read.

The vessel this time was the brig *Caroline* of Norwich, Winchester master. The wages were seventeen dollars a month. The departure was May 8, 1800. And the end was disaster. They rounded Montauk Point on the eastern tip of Long Island the ninth of May, arrived at St. Pierre the eleventh of June, sold their cargo there and at St. Lucia, and started back "for America" on June 23 with a fair wind. It was the following day that the blow fell. "Tuesday June 24th," says the Journal, "at 8 A.M. was taken by a French Privateer of 4 guns and 50 men and robbed of most of our cloathes and adventures and scuttled the brig after taking us all on board the privateer." The next day the French took another American ship "and put us all in irons." On Thursday, the twenty-sixth, they were "kept close confined and under water most of the time" and on Friday "after having had several skirmishes arrived in Bassetterre not allowed to leave our irons on any emergency." Finally, on Saturday, June 28, they were "put on shore and turned to prison after being robbed of our money one and all and most of our cloathes thus we are set naked and helpless ashore in a foreign country."

For a month thereafter Moses Hillard and a few of his ship mates lived miserably "toughing it out in the usual way half starved." The fare was "two or three ounces of pork poor stuff and bread in proportion," and the only way to keep alive was to "work out" on French sloops or prizes. Captain Winchester and his mate and most of the other prisoners were sent off on the first of July — to carry the news, no doubt, to the boy's family in Preston — "leaving us to wait for the next cartel thus the luck goes." It proved to be a long wait. The entries in the Journal became fewer and fewer. The lead pencil grows fainter. Not until the end of July did the young sailor get away from his

French prison, and it was months after that before he worked his way home to his father's farm.

The French, however, were only half the problem. There were also, and always, the British. In 1804, when he was master of the schooner *Antelope*, Captain Hillard wrote his owner from latitude forty-one degrees north and longitude forty-two degrees west, sending the letter back by Captain Robinson of the ship *Nancy*, to report that he had been "boarded by the British Ship Leander Sandy Hook bearing WNW dist 219 Miles and treated in A most Rascally Manner Who Plundered us of a Number of Small articles and Left Us for a Parcle of Saucy Yankeys Assuring us he had taken a Number of our Countrymen and Were in hopes of taking More." The *Leander*, moreover, was not the sole offender. She was only the first. On at least two other occasions the Captain was boarded and ill-used by British men-of-war — once in December of 1812 when he brought the "elegant corvette-built ship, Thomas" through the blockade from Archangel on the most momentous voyage of his career, and once in 1808 when a "British cruizer" forced the *Amiable Matilda*, of which he was then master, into Gibraltar Roads, losing him a voyage. "I have Concluded," he wrote his owners on that occasion, sending copies for safety by three different ships, "to Return Direct to New York as the best possible thing that I Can Do for your Interest in this Dreadful Dilemma. I shall Sail with the first Ship of force that goes through the Gut for a Convoy and make the best of my way home."

That decision throws a considerable light on the responsibilities of a ship-master under the early American practice. The captain of a Yankee vessel was not only accountable for his ship, he was accountable also for the venture. A letter of instruction from Joseph Otis, owner of one of Moses Hillard's early vessels, the *Sussex*, begins with a characteristic paragraph:

> The Big *Sussex* under your Command, being now Loaded and ready for Sea, you will proceed with all possible Dispatch for La Guira and there dispose of your Cargo on the best Terms the market will admit and invest the proceeds in such Articles as you may Judge most for our interest and return direct for this Place. . . . In case you are not permitted an Entry at La Guira, You will if You think it advisable try one Other Port on the main, and also St. Thomas if it becomes necessary.

But this kind of general authority could be extended indefinitely. In the case of the *Thoma*s in 1812, for example, Captain Hillard was sent to Archangel by Noah Talcott, owner, with an open credit of four thousand pounds sterling to take command of the ship and "either sell, freight, or load her for my account as you may think best for my interest." Given the location of Archangel, the then state of the world, the presence of The French army at Moscow, and the blockade of the British fleet across the sea routes, to say nothing of the imminence of a war affecting the United States, this "liberty and full power" imposed a heavy responsibility indeed.

What makes such liberties and powers even more remarkable is the fact that they were granted to men who were extraordinarily young by contemporary standards. Moses Hillard was thirty-two when he went to Russia, having been a mate before his twenty-first birthday and a master — of the brig *Neptune*, 123 tons — while he was still twenty-two. His commercial apprenticeship, however, had begun almost as early as his training for the sea. In 1801 when he was mate on the brig *Harriot* of Norwich, a certain Isaac Thompson of New London had entrusted him with a number of boxes of garden seeds, packed after Mr. Thompson's own notions, to be sold in Demerara and the proceeds to be laid out in rum, cotton, and coffee with a "good, light-colored Castor Oil at 3 or 3/6 the bottle" and a "bbl of Cow itch if to be had for four or six dollars." There were other missions of like kind on almost every voyage, and the cumulative effect can hardly have helped but be instructive.

Later on, the special commissions became more substantial, both in character and value, but they were never without their curiosities. There is a frantic request from a lady in Paris for information about her husband, to whom she had been married *"le 4 Fructidor l'an 6 de la republique."* She had had no word of him for eighteen years, but she had now heard he was a merchant in America. *"Vite, Vite, une response et je suis sur son coeur."* There is a commission from a punctilious Britisher, apparently a passenger on one of the Captain's eastbound trips, who had left the ship at Le Havre in such haste he had been "unable to arrange for the payment of the little amounts towards the dinner at Justin's and the losses at Cards which were to be appropriated to the Cost of the Dinner." Strangest and most touching of all, there is a letter from a gentleman in Paris begging the Captain to bring a quantity of the Indian herb pipsissewa to Paris on his next trip to relieve the suffering of a lady dying of cancer.

"You have a plant in the United States said to be a cure for the cancer. I take the liberty of begging you to send some of it by the very first occasion. We hope it may do some good to poor Mrs. Pruny who you know is very ill with that dreadful disorder. I subjoin the name of the plant below. I shall with

many thanks pay any expense your kind attention to procuring
and sending it may incur. . . . Name of the Plant *Pipsissaway*
— an herbe celebrated in America for the Cure of old long standing Ruptures and Cronic affections."

Varied as the business of a sea captain was, however, and difficult as the British and the French and the American governments
made it during the Napoleonic wars, the first and most dangerous antagonist was always the sea. Captain Hillard had his fair
share of wind and weather.

On one voyage in the winter of 1809-10 he brought the brig
Havana Packet of 162 tons into Toningen in Norway "in want
of wood and water" with "no more than two well men on
board." A long run of persistent gales varied, in the North Sea,
by two weeks of unlifting fogs, all but ended the Captain's career within sight — or what should have been sight — of Heligo-
land. From the time the *Havana Packet* left the Grand Banks she
had

> but little else than Constant and Severe Gales of wind generally
> from the westward till passing the Shetland Islands During
> which time we had our head Rails and Quarter boards Washed
> Away by the Sea and our Crew were Very Much Disabled
> from the fatigue of the passage. After Entering the North Sea
> which was on the 30th December had . . . constant thick
> fog for most of the time till 15th January 1810 for the last ten
> Days of Which time was never more than Seventy or Eighty
> Miles from Heligoland nor had an Observation, and on the 15th
> Jany Made the Island of Heligoland at which time the wind was
> blowing a verry hard Gale and Excessive Cold which Gale Drave
> us past the Horn Reef to the Northward the vessel Much loaded
> with Ice and our Crew Mostly frozen and Disabled from the
> Severity of the Weather. found it impossible with Such
> Weather in our Disabled State to Remain Much Longer at Sea.

Seven years later the luck that saved the *Havana Packet* deserted him. He lost his ship. It was a tragic story as Captain Hillard told it in the office of the American Consul for the Island of St. Thomas where he and his wife and a part of the rescued company were brought to shore. It is a moving story still. For one thing, the sufferings of passengers and crew were intense and protracted. For another, the ship was the *Oneida*, one of the queens of the North Atlantic and the particular pride of the Captain's heart. He had taken her over for her owners in March of 1815 a few months after the Treaty of Ghent had ended the War of 1812, and he had put her into shape to sail, in spite of the lack of labor and lumber and everything else, by the sheer violence of his determination to get back to sea. There are five letters among the Captain's papers which tell, with a wonderful wealth of nautical detail, how the *Oneida* was refitted, but the long and the short of it is that he loved her from the moment he saw her in the river off Norwich, where she had been laid up throughout the war, "her top Masts and yards aloft and all of her Standing Rigging hanging overhead in the weather." By the end of the month he was able to bring her over Norwich bar "with as light a draft of water as possible," and a few weeks later she was on her way to France. If the letters the Captain received from his passengers meant what they said she was a comfortable ship as well as a stanch one. And if the story of the proposed escape of Napoleon after Waterloo is authentic, it was the *Oneida* by which the Emperor was to have crossed the Atlantic.

The Captain lost her in one of the great storms of his life at sea, and in circumstances which were unusually painful, for his wife was on board. Whether she had sailed with him before I have no means of knowing, but there is every indication that this particular voyage was to have been a kind of holiday for them both, with Paris and the Captain's many friends, and the shops full of stockings and shawls, as a recompense at the other end. Instead there was disaster and a misery so great that the Captain swore a solemn oath never to go to sea again — an oath which, as one of his passengers reminded him later, "you did not hesitate in the least to break . . . the very first opportunity you found."

Departure from New York was on January 19, 1817, and the weather broke on the twentieth at three in the morning as they passed the east end of Long Island. For the next four days there was a continuing heavy gale of wind from the westward

until the Night of the 24th being then in latitude 41″ 10 North and Longitude 59″ West at which time the wind veered round to South East and blew a Perfect Hurricane. when laying too at 11 P.M. the Ship was struck by a Sea and thrown on her beam ends with the lee Combings of the Hatches in the water which Obliged them to get up their axes in Readiness to cut away the masts when the wind suddenly shifted to N.W. blowing a gale at which time the Ship Righted and it was Discovered that She had opened a Dangerous leak.

As the intense Cold from the time of leaving New York had almost frozen the Crew who were also Exhausted with fatigue, the Passengers were prevailed upon to go to the Pumps. Laid the ship's head to the southward as the only Means of safety. 27th January encountered another Dreadful gale in Lat. 40″ 00 North the leak still increasing. The Ships Upper Works had been so much strained that they became fearful of their separating from the bottom. Commenced heaving overboard the spare spars Cables and every thing that could be got at and stove the water casks but Retained the long boat for the purpose of saving their lives. from Excessive fatigue only two of the Crew were now capable of Doing Duty and the leak still Continuing the Passengers were compelled to work at the Pumps without intermission. 28th and 29th had heavy gales from N.W. with hail and snow. Lay too to be enabled to keep the ship free with the pumps.

30th at 1 A.M. found the leak increasing at Day got off the hatches and hove overboard from fifteen to twenty tons ashes, flour, Beeswax, etc. but at 11 A.M. were Obliged to Close them again in Consequence of its blowing heavy from S.S.W. the leak so great that it was only with the greatest Efforts they were enabled to keep the ship free. 31st Gale continued had the small boat stove over the stern. feby 1st hove the anchors and part of the Cargo overboard the Passengers and Crew now falling at the Pumps in Despair. 2nd searched for the leak but were unable to discover it. 3rd got the small boat on deck and endeavoured to repair it. 4th 5th and 6th Gale Continued her upper works so loose that it was expected every roll that they would separate from her bottom. 7th Pleasant weather at 6 P.M. believed it impossible to keep the ship afloat many hours longer got some water and Provisions in the boat and prepared to leave the wreck.

on the 8th got out the boats and Commenced forming a Raft when suddenly the leak lessened one half took the boats in again in doing which they sustained much Damage. 9th a sail passed to windward but took no Notice of our signals of Distress. 10th the leak again increasing saw a sail and set Signals of Distress which she observed and bore down. she proved to be the Schooner Mars of Newport R.I., George W. Carr Master, from New York bound to Surrinam. they prevailed on Captain Carr to Receive them on board 24 in number with a part of their baggage and a small Quantity of Provisions. Abandoned the wreck in Latd 33″ 20 North and Long 59″ 00 she having 4 feet water in the hold and the Pumps Stopped.

The tenth of February, 1817, was almost certainly the black-

est day of Captain Hillard's life. The brightest may have been
the sixth of January, 1813. It was on this day that the first word
of Napoleon's defeat near Moscow reached the United States,
and the ship by which it came was the *Thomas*, Hillard master,
forty-eight days from London in ballast, and, before that, an
unrecorded number of days from Archangel. Every newspaper
in New York carried a report of her arrival in the lower bay
and an account of her news, but not all of them were ready to
accept the astonishing story as true. Napoleon's myth was
stronger than Napoleon, and the New York *Post* was obliged to
apologize to its readers on the seventh for its skepticism of the
sixth. The effect of all this, however, was to keep the *Thomas*
in the public eye, and one can imagine that Mr. Noah Talcott,
the owner, took a certain satisfaction in that circumstance which
he presumably shared with his skipper. The skipper deserved it.
He had had a dangerous voyage full of "Hair Breadth Scapes"
including a boarding off the Grand Banks by his old friends the
British, who were in search of Commodore Rogers, and a narrow delivery from being burned at sea — perhaps by British
hands, for there is a reference to the fire in a letter from Talcott's
British agents which describes it as "a violation of the protection
afforded by this Government."

The whole story of the Captain's life is tantalizing, told as it is
in bits and pieces. Only the roster of the ships is really complete, and the roster breaks off at about the time of the Captain's
fortieth year though he lived to be fifty-seven. Whether he finally made good his vow to quit the sea, or whether his first
wife's death and his marriage to Patty Brewster, altered his way
of living there is no means now to know. The stones in the Long
Society Burying Ground are laconic. All they really tell is this
— that the Hillards followed the sea. There are four stones

for four brothers — Moses, Chester, Benjamin Franklin, and George Washington. Captain Chester died in Havana at the age of thirty-one. George died at thirty-three in Madeira. Benjamin was lost at sea off the coast of Spain in his nineteenth year. Moses alone lies in the Long Society Burying Ground under the stone that bears his name.

Thirteen Candles
One for Every State

1948

WE THINK of the war of the American Revolution as a war fought in schoolbooks long ago where armies and generals move like myths through a distant landscape of wilderness and winter. Actually it was a war fought by living men whose last survivors my grandfather saw and talked to in 1864.

My grandfather, the Reverend Elias Brewster Hillard, was a Congregational clergyman of Connecticut, upon whose mind the cares and worries of a war-weary congregation weighed with increasing heaviness as the conflict between the States went on, year after year. When he was approached by a firm of Hartford publishers who had discovered the possibilities of the camera and wished to preserve the photographs of the "Last Men of the Revolution," he accepted their proposal that he should find the surviving veterans and talk to them about that other war and about the Republic and about their views of "the present rebellion." The little book which resulted contains photographs of the six survivors who could be reached, together with some account of all of them. Since none, however, was less than a hundred, the eldest being a hundred and five, and since some were very weak, one being actually at the point of death as my grandfather approached his house — "death was dealing with the old man" — not all of them could be asked to talk. Only three were vigorous enough to bring back living moments of that far-off time.

One was Sam Downing, a hundred and two, who lived in the first framed house in the town of Edinburgh in York State which he had built himself seventy years before. To get to Edinburgh in 1864 you took the Central Railroad to Saratoga, rode a stage twenty miles from Saratoga to Luzerne on the Hudson River and then made your way on horseback up the valley of the Sacandaga twenty-five miles more. The second was Lemuel Cook, one hundred and five, who lived in Clarendon in Orleans County near Rochester. The third was Alexander Millener, one hundred and four, who lived nearby at Adam's Basin on the Rochester and Niagara Falls.

Sam Downing was the spryest. The day before my grandfather's visit — that day being "one of the hottest of the season, so much so that coming up by stage from Saratoga, we could scarcely endure the journey" — he had walked two miles and a half "over a very tedious road" to the shoemaker's, got his boots tapped and walked home again. Lemuel Cook, a man of gigantic frame, had retained the full power of a voice "marvellous for its volume and strength" but his talk was broken and fragmentary. "He recalls the past slowly and with difficulty; but when he has fixed his mind upon it, all seems to come up clear." How firmly he was able to fix his mind upon it my grandfather makes evident. "He has voted the Democratic ticket since the organization of the government, supposing that it still represents the same party that it did in Jefferson's time."

But if Sam Downing could walk five miles on the hottest day

of a hot summer, and if Lemuel Cook, with his great voice and his stubborn loyalty to the past could feel his way back through the difficult words to the actual bloody business of soldiering and war, it was little Alexander Millener, the ancient drummer boy, who was the real miracle. Alexander Millener had had nine children, forty-three grandchildren, seventeen great-grandchildren and three great-great-grandchildren but nevertheless "for sixty-two years he and his wife had lived together without a death in the family or a coffin in the house." He had never troubled himself about his health — "he uses tea and coffee and still takes regularly his dram" — could read his Bible without glasses at a hundred and four, played his drum "with excellent time and flourishes" and sang songs "both amorous and warlike . . . half a dozen verses successively, giving correctly both the words and the tune." Only when it came to long connected accounts of the war did Alexander Millener's memory fail him and even there he proved to be able to recall precisely individual events which had happened as much as ninety years before.

Samuel Downing, whom my grandfather found beside his framed house at the head of the narrow valley of the Sacandaga at noon of a summer day "seated between two bee-hives, bending over, leaning upon his cane and looking on the ground, an old man . . ." was ready enough to talk about the bees ("they don't hurt me and I don't hurt them") the weather ("If I had my way about it, I should like it about so. But we can't do that: we have to take it as it comes.") and the war.

"What do you think [General Washington] would say if he was here now?"

"Say! I don't know. But he'd be mad to see me sitting here. I tell 'em if they'll give me a horse I'll go as it is. If the rebels come here I shall sartingly take my gun. I can see best furtherest off."

"You don't believe, then, in letting men stay at their homes and help the enemy."

"Not by a grand sight!" And then, lost in the other war: "The men that caught André were true. He wanted to get away, offered them everything. Washington hated to hang him; he cried they said."

Whether or not the old man understood what lay behind my grandfather's question — the whole misery of the draft in the last months of the Civil War — he understood the nature of the problem of loyalty and the minds of the two met at a point in the history of their country which was not very far away to either of them.

Sam Downing's story of his enlistment in the Continental Army went back to his childhood in Newburyport in the Commonwealth of Massachusetts. There, in the absence of his parents over the Bay, a man had carried him off as an apprentice to learn the trade of spinning-wheel making in the town of Antrim out past Haverhill. "It was the fall of the year. I remember the fruit was on the ground, and I went out and gathered it. I was happy yet." But six years later the happiness had worn off and he ran away to enlist, making his way to Colonel Fifield over in Charlestown who accepted him, small as he was, but wasn't quite ready to go: "He had his haying to do; so I stayed with him and helped him through it and then I started for the war." He remembered guarding wagons from Exeter to Springfield, and the fighting in the Mohawk Valley and General Benedict Arnold and General Gates.

"Arnold was our fighting general, and a bloody fellow he was. He didn't care for nothing; he'd ride right in. It was 'Come on, boys!' twasn't 'Go, boys!' He was as brave a man as ever lived. He was dark skinned, with black hair, of middling height. There wasn't any waste timber in him. He was a sternlooking man but kind to his soldiers. They didn't treat him right: he ought to have had Burgoyne's sword. But he ought to have been true."

"Gates was an old granny looking fellow. When Burgoyne came up to surrender his sword, he said to Gates, 'Are you a general? You look more like a granny than you do like a general.' 'I be a granny,' said Gates, 'and I've delivered you of ten thousand men today.'"

Sam Downing had taken part in the later campaigns around New York. "There's always policy, you know, in war. We made the British think we were coming to take the city. We drew up in line of battle: the British drew up over there." He pointed over the bee-hives. "They looked very handsome. But Washington went south to Yorktown. LaFayette laid down the white sticks, and we threw up entrenchments by them. We were right opposite Washington's headquarters."

Was Washington as fine looking a man as he was reported, my grandfather wanted to know? "Oh!" said the old man, lifting up both hands and pausing. "But you never got a smile out of him. He was a nice man. We loved him. They'd sell their lives for him."

That was the end of the Revolution for Sam Downing but not of the talk beside the bee-hives. There had been other wars before and after. Sam Downing's father and his wife's father had been out in the French War. His grandson had fought in "the present rebellion" from the beginning. They talked of both but in the end the old man came back to the War of Independence.

"When peace was declared we burnt thirteen candles in every hut, one for each State." A man who will think back can see those candles from here in the oiled paper windows under the tremendous trees.

Alexander Millener had seen even more of his country's battles. He had been born at Quebec, the son of an artificer in Wolfe's army who died on the Plains of Abraham ("at the close of the battle, lying down to drink at a spring on the plain . . .") and an English woman whom her son described as "high larnt." British-bred though he was, however, Alexander Millener had served six and a half years in the American Army in the Revolution, five and a half years in the American Navy in and through the War of 1812 — three of them on the frigate *Constitution* — uncounted months in the Indian Wars in the Mohawk Valley. He had seen action at White Plains — "a nasty battle" — the Brandywine, Saratoga, Monmouth, Yorktown, the Indian attack on Fort Stanwix. He had been in the fight between the *Constitution* and the British ships *Cyane* and *Levant*. He had been badly wounded at Monmouth and captured at sea by the French who mistreated him in prison at Guadeloupe, feeding him bread worse than he had eaten in "seven kingdoms."

Only the brightest moments came back clear — Washington first and clearest. He had served for four years in Washington's Life Guard as drummer boy, his mother following along as washerwoman to be near her son. Washington was "a good man, a beautiful man. He was always pleasant, never changed countenance but wore the same in defeat and retreat as in victory." "Lady Washington . . . was a short thick woman; very pleasant and kind." "They took a great notion to me. One day the General sent for me to come up to headquarters. . . . The

Life Guard came out and paraded and the roll was called. There was an Englishman, Bill Dorchester; the General said to him, 'Come, Bill, play up this 'ere Yorkshire tune.' When he got through, the General told me to play. So I took the drum, overhauled her, braced her up, and played a tune. The General put his hand in his pocket and gave me three dollars . . ."

At Valley Forge, "Lady Washington visited the army. She used thorns instead of pins on her clothes. The poor soldiers had bloody feet." And then back to the General. "We were going along one day, slow march, and came to where the boys were jerking stones. 'Halt!' came the command. 'Now, boys,' said the General, 'I will show you how to jerk a stone.' He beat 'em all. He smiled but didn't laugh out." (In my grandfather's copy of his book a letter has been placed between the leaves at this point. It is dated at Boston the 15 January, 1865 and signed by Edward Everett, the orator of Gettysburg. "The Biographies," says Mr. Everett with the restraint appropriate to great men and Bostonians, "appear to contain all that can be expected." The anecdote of General Washington stopping to jerk stones with his men, he continues, is excellent and is "in accordance with the traditions of his Youth which describe him as being able to throw a stone across the Rappahannock below Fredericksburg." Mr. Millener would doubtless have been grateful for this endorsement.)

Of Arnold, Alexander Millener's opinion was much like Sam Downing's. "Arnold was a smart man; they didn't sarve him quite straight." Cornwallis was "a fine looking man; very mild." The drummer boy shook hands with him at Yorktown. "The day after the surrender the Life Guard came up. Cornwallis sat on an old bench. 'Halt!' he ordered; then looked at us —

viewed us." General Lee was a large man. "He had a most enormous nose. One day a man met him and turned his nose away. 'What do you do that for, you damned rascal?' says he."

The Indian fighting was farther away in the old man's mind and more nearly forgotten. Only the attack on Fort Stanwix remained and that in a kind of broken etching of sharp and dreadful lines. "The Indians burnt all before them. Our women came down in their shirt tails. The Indians got one of our young ones, stuck pine splinters into it and set them afire. They came down a good body of 'em. We had a smart engagement with 'em and whipped 'em. One of 'em got up into a tree — a sharp shooter. He killed our men when they went after water. The colonel see where he was, and says, 'Draw up the twenty-four pounder and load it with grape, canister and ball.' They did it. The Indian sat up in a crotch of the tree. They fired and shot the top of the tree off. The Indian gave a leap and a yell and came down. Three brigades got there just in the nick of time. The Massachusetts Grenadiers and the Connecticut troops went forward and the Indians fled."

When the Civil War broke out the old man had wanted to take his drum and go down to Rochester and "beat for volunteers." It would have been a sight to remember — Washington's drummer boy, no bigger than a boy still for all his thatch of white hair, beating his revolutionary drum for volunteers to save the Union because it was "too bad this country, so hardly got, should be destroyed by its own people." They hadn't let him go, but just before my grandfather's visit he had marched to the church on his one hundred and fourth birthday at the head of a procession of Pioneers of Monroe County, where, after they had sung Washington's Funeral Hymn and heard a memorial address, he had stood on a seat where all could see him and thanked them for their kind attention and appealed to them all to be true to their country, adding with a wry, but not wholly irrelevant, emphasis that he had seen worse looking visages than his own hung up by the neck.

Lemuel Cook, with his great frame and his voice marvelous for its volume was the oldest of the survivors, having been born in Litchfield County in Connecticut almost a hundred and five years before. He had served through the entire war, being mustered in at the age of sixteen "at Northampton in the Bay State, Second Regiment, Light Dragoons; Sheldon, Colonel; Stanton, Captain": mustered out at Danbury, Connecticut, at the age of twenty-four. He had been in the bitter fighting in Westchester County and the battle of the Brandywine and he had seen Cornwallis's surrender. But what gives his recollection, in my grandfather's report of it, so moving a character is not the importance of the events the old man relates but the character of the images which return to his mind. Recalling the past painfully as though from a great distance, and speaking with a very imperfect articulation "so that it is with difficulty that his story can be made out," Lemuel Cook nevertheless conveys a sense of actuality which neither of the others gives. His fragmentary recollections, recovered from far back before his fight with the Indian in the public house in Utica, before his marriage with Hannah Curtis in Cheshire, have the authenticity of an arrow head or a uniform button found in a clearing where a wall once was.

"In conversation with him," my grandfather wrote, "he has to be left to the course of his own thoughts, inquiries and suggestions appearing to confuse him." The course of the old man's thoughts took him from his first whiff of gunpowder at Valen-

tine's Hill in Westchester County ("Up came Darrow, good old
soul! . . . said 'Lem, what do you think of gunpowder? Smell
good to you?' ") to the first time he was fired at personally and
in earnest (" 'Lem, they mean you; go on the other side of the
road' ") to his first sight of the French in action ("They stepped
as though on edge. They were a dreadful proud nation") to the
siege and surrender at Yorktown.

"Baron Steuben was muster master. He had us called out to
select men and horses fit for service. When he came to me he
said, 'Young man, how old are you?' I told him. 'Be on the
ground tomorrow morning at nine o'clock,' said he. My colonel
didn't like to have me go. . . . 'You're a fool,' said the rest,
'they're going to storm New York.' No more idea of it than
of going to Flanders. My horse was a bay and pretty. . . . We
marched off towards White Plains. Then 'left wheel' and struck
right north. Got to King's Ferry below Tarrytown. There
were boats, scows. We went right across into the Jerseys. That
night I stood with my back to a tree."

"Then we went on to the head of Elk."

"There the French were. It was dusty; 'peared to me I should
have choked to death. One of 'em handed me his canteen. 'Lem,'
said he, 'take a good horn — we're going to march all night.' I
didn't know what it was so I took a full drink. It liked to have
strangled me."

"Then we were in Virginia. There wasn't much fighting.
Old Rochambeau told 'em, 'I'll land five hundred from the fleet
against your eight hundred.' But they darsn't."

"We were on a kind of side hill. We had plaguey little to eat
and nothing to drink under Heaven. We hove up some brush
to keep the flies off."

"Washington ordered that there should be no laughing at the British; said it was bad enough to have to surrender without being insulted. The army came out with guns clubbed on their backs. They were paraded on a great smooth lot, and there they stacked their arms. Then came the devil — old women, and all. One said, 'I wonder if the damned Yankees will give me any bread.' "

"The horses were starved out. Washington turned out with his horses and helped 'em up the hill. When they see the artillery, they said, 'There, them's the very artillery that belonged to Burgoyne.' "

"Greene come from the southward: the awfullest set you ever see. Some, I should presume, had a pint of lice on 'em. No boots or shoes . . ."

Lem Cook died a few days after my grandfather talked to him and my grandfather died in his turn at the end of the century and I remember the one who remembered the other who remembered General Greene and the crawling lice and the exhausted soldiers. When we think as we sometimes do these days that the Republic is old and tired and defensive we might do worse than consider that three long human lives can reach from here to Yorktown. We might do worse than think of old Sam Downing and his thirteen candles, one for every State.

Acknowledgments

MOST of the essays and addresses in this book appeared originally in other publications, to whose editors and publishers the author wishes to extend grateful acknowledgment for permission to print them here:

PART ONE — *The Idea of Man*

"Who Precisely Do You Think You Are?" Commencement Address at Smith College, 1965; printed in the *Smith Alumnae Quarterly*, Summer, 1965, under the title "Who precisely . . . ?" Portions of this essay not included in the commencement address are from "There Was Something about the Twenties," *Saturday Review*, December 31, 1966.

"Yeats and the Belief in Life" An address in the Distinguished Lecture Series at the University of New Hampshire, January 17, 1957; published by the University of New Hampshire in January, 1958.

"Poetry and Journalism" Gideon D. Seymour Memorial Lecture, October 12, 1958, University of Minnesota; published by the University of Minnesota Press in 1958.

PART TWO — *The State of the Union*

"Changes in the Weather" *The New Republic*, July 2, 1956.

"The Conquest of the United States" *The Atlantic Monthly*, August, 1949, under the title "The Conquest of America."

" 'National Purpose' " *Life*, May 30, 1960, under the title "We Have Purpose, We All Know It."

"The Unimagined America" *The Atlantic Monthly*, June, 1943.

"A View of Oxford, Mississippi" *The Atlantic Monthly*, February, 1963, under the title "Must We Hate?"

"A Decent Respect" *Saturday Review*, June 3, 1965, under the title "What Is 'Realism' Doing to American History?"

PART THREE — *The Second Civil War*

"A Dedication" Dedication of the Carleton Library, Carleton College, Northfield, Minnesota, September 22, 1956; printed in the *Carleton College Bulletin*, November, 1956.

"The Alternative" Lecture on March 21, 1955, at Columbia University; printed in *The Yale Review*, June, 1955.

PART FOUR — *Writers in a Wrong Time*

"Faulkner at Stockholm" Published in the Special William Faulkner Issue of *The Harvard Advocate*, November, 1951, under the title "Faulkner and the Responsibility of the Artist."

"The Muses' Sterner Laws" *The New Republic*, July 13, 1953.

"The Isolation of the American Artist" *The Atlantic Monthly*, January, 1958.

"Why Can't They Say What They Mean?" The Hopwood Lecture, University of Michigan, May 19, 1955. Reprinted by permission of *The Michigan Alumnus Quarterly Review* (now *The Michigan Quarterly Review*), LXI (Summer, 1955), 291–301; copyright © 1955 by The University of Michigan.

PART FIVE — *Teaching and Harvard*

"Why Do We Teach Poetry?" *The Atlantic Monthly*, March, 1956.

"On the Teaching of Writing" *Harper's*, October, 1959.

"Education and the *Work* of Art" Address, titled "Art Education and the Creative Process," delivered in New York, March 20, 1954. Copyright 1954 by the Committee on Art Education, New York (The Museum of Modern Art, New York) and reprinted with its permission.

"The Knowable and the Known" Address at Countway Library, Harvard Medical School. Published in *Biblioteca Medica; Physician for Tomorrow; Dedication of the Countway Library of Medicine, May 26 and 27, 1965*, edited by David McCord and published by the Harvard Medical School.

"What Is English?" *Saturday Review*, December 9, 1961.

"A Retiring View of Harvard" An address to the Department of English at Harvard, published in the *Harvard Alumni Bulletin*, January 12, 1963.

"An Hellenic Center in Washington" An address delivered in Washington. Reprinted in *Addresses Delivered at the Center for Hellenic Studies, 1963*, published by Harvard University Press. Copyright © 1963 by the President and Fellows of Harvard College.

PART SIX — *People*

"Eleanor Roosevelt" *The Nation*, November, 17, 1962, under the title "Eleanor Roosevelt: 1884–1962."

"Mrs. Roosevelt: An Anniversary" *New York Times Magazine*, November 3, 1963, under the title "Tribute to a 'Great American Lady.'"

"F. F." *Saturday Review*, November 27, 1965, under the title "A Talent for Joy."

"Adlai Stevenson" Tribute at Memorial Ceremony, United Nations General Assembly Hall, July 19, 1965; reprinted in *Department of State Bulletin*, August 9, 1965.

"Elmer Davis" *The Nation*, March 6, 1954, under the title "Elmer Davis: Undwindled American."

"Robert Frost and John F. Kennedy" Remarks at the breaking of ground, by John Fitzgerald Kennedy, for the Frost Library at Amherst; printed in *The Atlantic Monthly*, February, 1964, under the title "The Gift Outright."

"Ernest Hemingway" *Life*, July 14, 1961, under the title "His Mirror Was Danger."

"St. John Perse" *Saturday Review*, July 16, 1949, under the title "The Living Spring."

"A Memoir of Muir" Foreword to *The Estate of Poetry*, by Edwin Muir, Harvard University Press, 1962. Copyright © 1962 by the President and Fellows of Harvard College.

"Mark Van Doren" Remarks at a meeting at Columbia University in his honor in 1959.

"Jorge Guillén" *The Atlantic Monthly*, January, 1961.

374 *Acknowledgments*

"Jane Addams in Chicago" Tribute on occasion of the 100th Anniversary observance of the birth of Jane Addams at the Conrad Hilton Hotel in Chicago, November 21, 1960.

"The Great-Grandfather" *Yale Review*, July, 1949, under the title "Yankee Skipper."

"Thirteen Candles: One for Every State" *Life*, May 31, 1948, under the title "Last Soldiers of the Revolution."

"The Conquest of the United States," "The Unimagined America," and "Thirteen Candles" also appeared in *Freedom Is the Right to Choose*, a collection of essays by Archibald MacLeish published by Beacon Press, Boston, 1951.

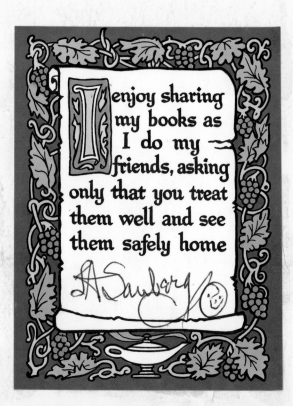

I enjoy sharing my books as I do my friends, asking only that you treat them well and see them safely home